Rookledge's INTERNATIONAL TYPEFINDER

Rookledge's

INTERNATIONAL TYPE-FINDER

THE ESSENTIAL HANDBOOK OF TYPEFACE RECOGNITION AND SELECTION

CHRISTOPHER PERFECT & GORDON ROOKLEDGE

PBC International, Inc., NEW YORK

Published in the U.S. by PBC INTERNATIONAL, Inc.,
One School Street, Glen Cove, NY 11542.

Originally published in London by Sarema Press (Publishers),
an imprint wholly owned by Gavin Martin Limited.

Library of Congress Cataloging-in-Publication Data

Perfect, Christopher.
  Rookledge's International Typefinder.

  Bibliography: p.
  Includes index.
  1. Printing - Specimens. 2. Type and type-founding.
I. Rookledge, Gordon. II. Title. III. Title: Typefinder.
Z250.P42 1986   686.2'24   86-25147
ISBN 0-86636-101-4

Design and artwork by The Perfect Design Company Limited.
Print Production by Gavin Martin Limited and Brian Thompson.
Text Setting by Text Filmsetters Limited, Orpington, Kent.
Printed by The John D. Lucas Printing Company.

PRINTED IN THE UNITED STATES

10 9 8 7 6 5 4 3 2 1

CONTENTS

Acknowledgements

We are indebted to the principal collaborators
who helped formulate the content of this book:
Eiichi Kono MA (RCA) MSTD and Alfred Lubran
FRSA. Without their considerable efforts and skill
its publication would not have been possible.

Our thanks are also due to the staff of
The Perfect Design Company Limited, especially
Fiona Barton and Matthew Kirby, as well as
Leslie Carvalho and Andrew Bennett for their
painstaking skills in the preparation of the
artwork; to the staff of Gavin Martin Limited and
Brian Thompson for print production; to
Mel Hobbs and his staff at Text Filmsetters for
supplying a large percentage of the typeface
specimens and for getting the most out of a
Linotron 202 typesetting machine.

Also to the following companies and individuals
who supplied typeface specimens and
information: Alphabet Limited, Apex
Typesetting Limited, Apex Photosetting
Limited, H. Berthold AG, Character
Photosetting Limited, Diagraphic Typesetters
Limited, Face Ronchetti Limited,
Filmcomposition, Linotype-Paul Limited,
Margaret Calvert, The Monotype Corporation,
Pinnacle Phototype Limited and Stempel Haas.

CHRISTOPHER PERFECT,
GORDON ROOKLEDGE

PREFACE
by Herbert Spencer RDI DrRCA

AS WITH OTHER inspired innovations – such as the safety pin, the paper clip, the zip-fastener, and the ball-point pen – now that *Rookledge's International Typefinder* is here one wonders how it was possible to function for so long without it. Though it may lack the universal significance of some of the other innovations I mentioned, for the graphic designer and typographer this publication is without doubt a real milestone.

Fundamental changes in printing technology and the rapid development of alternative media for distributing ideas and information during the past twenty-five years have released a torrent of new type designs – some good, a few excellent, and, inevitably, many bad.

This book will be used, first, as an invaluable working tool enabling the designer quickly to identify and to select particular typefaces for his immediate purposes. However, for the student this publication will serve another – and, in the long term, perhaps an even more important – function: by highlighting and indicating the essential characteristics of each typeface shown it will *educate* the user to distinguish between good and bad designs, between sound and sloppy solutions, between the imaginative and the merely perverse – in fact, to separate the grain from the chaff. And for that the publisher and editor will deserve the gratitude of all readers as well as of all designers.

This typefinder, then, is a publication of major importance. The task of assembling and arranging the enormous number of specimens it contains must have been a daunting one. It was Gordon Rookledge who recognised the need for such a book and it is due to his enthusiasm, persistence and tenacity that the idea has become a reality. Christopher Perfect has worked with exceptional editorial dedication and design skill to define and evolve the original concept for this book, and, in collaboration with Eiichi Kono, to bring the project to fruition. Both of them, publisher and editor, are to be congratulated on having fashioned not just a tool but a powerful weapon in the fight for better, more effective, typography.

To Jennie, Sarah, Gavin and Emma for all their patience and understanding over the years. (G.R.)

For my wife, Tessa. (C.P.)

INTRODUCTION

THE RECOGNITION AND selection of typefaces is a regular everyday task for the practising graphic designer and typographer. Yet, up until now, no single reference source has been available to assist in these processes. This book has been produced especially to fill this gap, serving as an invaluable working tool for everyone who works with type.

It is the editor's experience that other than expert or highly-experienced typographers, the majority of creative people have difficulty in recognising and identifying individual typefaces. Therefore, the primary purpose of the book is to satisfy this need and simplify this essential task as fully as possible.

A secondary purpose is to help in the process of typeface selection. The graphic designer often has difficulty in obtaining good, comprehensive reference material despite an abundance of typefounders' and typesetters' catalogues. It is the aim of this book to make this job easier and to contribute to the educational experience in the process.

This book is divided into two parts, *Text* and *Decorative* (non-continuous text) typefaces. The classification system used in each part is entirely new and does not follow previous established type classifications. The typefaces selected were all available at the time of compilation of the book and all the major international typefounders' current lists were consulted so as to make the choice as comprehensive as possible. Readers should note that 'bastard' versions of well-known typefaces have not been included but are cross-referenced in the index. The possible number of *Decorative* typefaces is endless so, with limited space, selection has been confined to a cross-section of the more commonly-used designs. (NB. It is not the purpose of this book to act as a complete typeface dictionary or specimen book.)

The listings of *Text* typefaces are all, as far as possible, in the normal weight of type for text setting (i.e. regular roman). It was not the editor's intention to include the many other variations of one typeface family (e.g. light, bold, italic, condensed etc.) as it is the regular weight which is most commonly used and which establishes the 'style' characteristics of a particular typeface. In order to obtain information on the range of different weights and variations of a typeface it is suggested that readers should consult their own typesetters.

Whilst the selection and compilation of the typefaces in this book were carried out with great care some may have been omitted which readers feel should be included. Your suggestions, submitted through the publisher, will be welcome.

CHRISTOPHER PERFECT
GORDON ROOKLEDGE

Part One

TEXT

TYPEFACES

SLOPING E-BAR
(VENETIAN SERIF)

**ANGLED STRESS
OBLIQUE SERIFS**
(OLD STYLE SERIF)

**VERTICAL STRESS
OBLIQUE SERIFS**
(TRANSITIONAL SERIF)

**VERTICAL STRESS
STRAIGHT SERIFS**
(NEW TRANSITIONAL)

**ABRUPT CONTRAST
STRAIGHT SERIFS**
(MODERN SERIF)

SLAB SERIF

WEDGE SERIF
(HYBRID SERIF)

SANS SERIF

TEXT TYPEFACE CATEGORIES

THIS PART OF the book contains typefaces which are commonly used for continuous text setting. The characteristic features of each of the eight typeface categories are described below and are illustrated on the opposite page.

The classification system used in this book is entirely new and is based on the grouping of typefaces according to specific design features. This will sometimes mean that typefaces of a similar historical origin fall into different categories. This book, therefore, does not follow established classifications such as the British Standards Typeface Nomenclature and Classification System (BS 2961). (NB. a comparison to this can be found in the Appendix at the back of the book.)

Each category is further divided into smaller groups according to more specific design features which are explained at the beginning of each section. Typeface specimens are then arranged alphabetically within each group and have an individual specimen number which is cross-referenced to both the index and 'Earmark' Tables starting on p. 97.

NB. There is a small overlap between the *Text* and *Decorative* parts of the book. For instance, some *Decorative* typefaces in special circumstances may be used for continuous text setting and vice-versa.

Categories 1 to 5 are all variations of the roman serif design and begin with:

1. Sloping e-Bar (Venetian Serif). *Nos. 1-34*
Typefaces in this category all have a sloping bar on the lower case e. All roman serif typefaces with this feature, *plus those which have slab or wedge serif characteristics*, will be found here. Generally, these typefaces are of a heavy appearance and have poor contrast between thick and thin strokes. They usually have oblique ascender serifs.

2. Angled Stress/Oblique Serifs (Old Style Serif) *Nos. 35-53*
Typefaces in this group are characterised by an angled stress on the bowls of letters (e.g. the lower case o) and have oblique serifs on the

ascenders of lower case letters. The foot serif on the lower case d is also oblique. There is a stronger contrast between the thick and thin strokes of letters than in Category 1.

3. Vertical Stress/Oblique Serifs (Transitional Serif) *Nos. 54-110*
Typefaces in this category have vertical stress (or nearly so) on the bowls of letters (such as the lower case o) but still have distinct oblique serifs on the ascenders. The serif foot of the lower case d is usually horizontal but sometimes slightly oblique. The contrast between the thick and thin strokes of letters is generally more pronounced than in Category 2. All typefaces have bracketed serifs.

4. Vertical Stress/Straight Serifs (New Transitional Serif) *Nos. 111-150*
All typefaces in this group have a definite vertical stress and serifs are normally all horizontal (straight). However, a small number have slightly oblique serifs. These typefaces generally have little contrast between the thick and thin strokes and the serifs are usually bracketed.

5. Abrupt Contrast/Straight Serifs (Modern Serif) *Nos. 151-187*
These typefaces feature a strong and abrupt contrast between the thick and thin strokes of letters and all serifs are horizontal (straight). The overall stress is clearly vertical. Serifs can be line (unbracketed) or slightly bracketed and typefaces can vary in colour from light to black face.

6. Slab Serif. *Nos. 188-217*
These typefaces are characterised by a generally heavy appearance with thick 'slab' serifs often the same thickness as the main stem of the letters. Serifs can be square (unbracketed) or bracketed. (*NB. Slab serif style typefaces with a sloping bar on the lower case e will be found in Category 1.*)

7. Wedge Serif (Hybrid Serif). *Nos. 218-240*
This category contains typefaces which are not always clearly serif or sans serif (i.e. hybrids).

It includes typefaces both of a general serif-style but with only a thickening at the terminals of letters and sans serif-style typefaces with very small line serifs on the terminals. It includes other groups with wedge-shaped serifs and half serifs. (*NB. Wedge serif-style typefaces with a sloping bar on the lower case e are to be found in Category 1.*)

8. Sans Serif. *Nos. 245-304*
Typefaces with no serifs. Generally, with little or no difference between strokes (i.e. monoline.) These typefaces are primarily divided according to whether the capital G has a spur or not and if it has, whether it is of a wide, medium or narrow design. The category also includes groups of typefaces of a special shape (such as rounded).

The Typefinding Process
1. To identify a typeface, first decide into which of the main categories shown opposite the typeface specimen you wish to identify belongs.

2. By using the thumb index on the edge of the page turn to the appropriate category introduction page.

3. From the 'contents' list given there select the specific group within the category to which your specimen relates.

4. Read off the specimen numbers given for this group and find them in the following listings of typeface specimens.

5. Decide which of the typefaces in the group it equates to with the help of asterisks which show letters with special or 'style' characteristics.

Text Typeface 'Earmark' Tables
These will be found at the end of this part of the book, beginning on p. 97, and offer an alternative but companion method of identifying *Text* typefaces by comparing to 'earmarks' or features on individual letters. The tables are divided into two parts, 'Common' and 'Special Earmarks', and letters are arranged in a continuous sequence from a to z in both capital and lower case forms (plus ampersand and figures.)

Type categories

General characteristics

1. Sloping e-Bar (Venetian Serif) *Nos 1-34*

e.g. **6** Kennerley, **19** Centaur, **30** ITC Souvenir, and **32** Italian Old Style (Monotype).

little contrast — *e-bar sloped* — *angled or vertical stress* — *oblique ascender serif (not always)* — *foot serif often oblique (not always)* — *oblique lower case serif (not always)*

e o l d n

2. Angled Stress/Oblique Serifs (Old Style Serif) *Nos 35-53*

e.g. **35** Bembo, **39** Plantin, **44** Trump Mediaeval and **53** Times New Roman (Monotype).

medium contrast — *e-bar horizontal* — *angled stress* — *oblique ascender serif* — *oblique foot serif* — *oblique lower case serif*

e o l d n

3. Vertical Stress/Oblique Serifs (Transitional Serif) *Nos 54-110*

e.g. **61** Caslon 540, **78** Baskerville 169 (Monotype), **92** Garamond (Stempel) and **105** Romulus.

good contrast — *e-bar horizontal* — *stress vertical (or nearly so)* — *oblique serifs* — *foot serif usually level (not always)* — *oblique lower case serif*

e o l d n

4. Vertical Stress/Straight Serifs (New Transitional Serif) *Nos. 151-187*

e.g. **111** Joanna, **119** Century Schoolbook, **123** Cheltenham, and **138** Melior.

little contrast — *e-bar horizontal* — *vertical stress* — *straight serifs (some slightly oblique)* — *straight serif in lower case (some oblique)*

e o l d n

5. Abrupt Contrast/Straight Serifs (Modern Serif) *Nos 151-187*

e.g. **153** Bauer Bodoni, **161** Walbaum (Linotype), **174** Caledonia and **185** Scotch Roman.

abrupt contrast — *e-bar horizontal* — *vertical stress* — *line or bracketed serifs* — *straight serifs* — *straight serifs*

e o l d n

6. Slab Serif *Nos 188-217*

e.g. **197** Rockwell, **203** Schadow Antiqua, **209** Clarendon (Linotype), and **214** ITC American Typewriter.

little or no contrast — *square slab serifs* — *bracketed serifs* — *rounded serif*

Ig g (single storey) (double storey) Ig g (single storey) (double storey) I

7. Wedge Serif (Hybrid Serif) *Nos 218-240*

e.g. **218** Albertus, **233** Meridien, **236** Copperplate Gothic and **240** Romic.

poor contrast — *wedge-ended serifs* — *wedge-shaped serifs* — *fine line terminals* — *half serif only*

l l l l

8. Sans Serif *Nos 245-304*

e.g. **254** Futura, **259** Gill Sans, **267** Univers 55 and **279** Helvetica.

little or no contrast — *wide medium narrow* — *wide medium narrow* — *special shape (rounded)*

GGG (no spur) GGG (spur) G

1. SLOPING E-BAR
(VENETIAN SERIF)

Specimen nos	Basic characteristics		Secondary characteristics	
1-5	O	steeply inclined axis on bowls of letters		e.g. **5** Windsor
6-12	O	less steeply inclined axis	q	short descenders long serifs	e.g. **7** Lavenham
13	,,		q	short descenders short serifs	e.g. **13** Della Robbia
14-18	,,		q	longer descenders weak contrast	e.g. **17** Schneidler Old Style
19-21	,,		q	longer descenders strong contrast	e.g. **19** Centaur
22-27	o	vertical axis	r	roman serifs	e.g. **25** Lutetia
28-31	,,		r	wedge serifs	e.g. **30** ITC Souvenir
32	o	inclined axis	d	roman and slab serifs (mixed)	e.g. **32** Italian Old Style (Monotype)
33-34	o	vertical or slightly inclined axis	d	slab serifs on ascenders	e.g. **34** Jenson Old Style

NB. *Typefaces in each group are arranged in alphabetical order.*

SLOPING E-BAR
(VENETIAN SERIF)

Bellini
Erasmus
Hollandse Mediaeval
Pastonchi
Windsor
Kennerley
Lavenham
Raleigh
Surrey Old Style
Trajanus

steeply inclined axis

1 Bellini

ABCDEFGHIJKLMNOPQRSTUVWXYZ&

2 Erasmus

ABCDEFGHIJKLMNOPQRSTUVWXYZ&

3 Hollandse Mediaeval

ABCDEFGHIJKLMNOPQRSTUVWXYZ&

4 Pastonchi

ABCDEFGHIJKLMNOPQRSTUVWXYZ&

5 Windsor

ABCDEFGHIJKLMNOPQRSTUVWXYZ&

less steeply inclined axis

short descenders long serifs

6 Kennerley

ABCDEFGHIJKLMNOPQRSTUVWXYZ&

7 Lavenham

ABCDEFGHIJKLMNOPQRSTUVWXYZ&

8 Raleigh

ABCDEFGHIJKLMNOPQRSTUVWXYZ&

9 Surrey Old Style

ABCDEFGHIJKLMNOPQRSTUVWXYZ&

10 Trajanus

ABCDEFGHIJKLMNOPQRSTUVWXYZ&

* These letters show special or 'style' characteristics. (NB. J, Q, & and g will usually vary from one typeface to another).

SLOPING E-BAR
(VENETIAN SERIF)

e

Bellini
Erasmus
Hollandse Mediaeval
Pastonchi
Windsor
Kennerley
Lavenham
Raleigh
Surrey Old Style
Trajanus

Bellini **1**

abcdefghijklmnopqrstuvwxyz1234567890

Erasmus **2**

abcdefghijklmnopqrstuvwxyz1234567890

Hollandse Mediaeval **3**

abcdefghijklmnopqrstuvwxyz1234567890

Pastonchi **4**

abcdefghijklmnopqrstuvwxyz 1234567890

Windsor **5**

abcdefghijklmnopqrstuvwxyz 1234567890

Kennerley **6**

abcdefghijklmnopqrstuvwxyz1234567890

Lavenham **7**

abcdefghijklmnopqrstuvwxyz1234567890

Raleigh **8**

abcdefghijklmnopqrstuvwxyz1234567890

Surrey Old Style **9**

abcdefghijklmnopqrstuvwxyz1234567890

Trajanus **10**

abcdefghijklmnopqrstuvwxyz1234567890

NB. On lower case letters generally look at the x height and length of ascenders and descenders.

SLOPING E-BAR
(VENETIAN SERIF)

Verona
Worcester Round
Della Robbia
Bauer Text
Cloister
Jenson
Schneidler Old Style
Seneca
Centaur
Horley Old Style

11 Verona

ABCDEFGHIJKLMNOPQRSTUVWXYZ&

12 Worcester Round

ABCDEFGHIJKLMNOPQRSTUVWXYZ&

*less steeply inclined axis
short descenders
short serifs*

13 Della Robbia

ABCDEFGHIJKLMNOPQRSTUVWXYZ&

*less steeply inclined axis
longer descenders
weak contrast*

14 Bauer Text

ABCDEFGHIJKLMNOPQRSTUVWXYZ&

15 Cloister

ABCDEFGHIJKLMNOPQRSTUVWXYZ&

16 Jenson

ABCDEFGHIJKLMNOPQRSTUVWXYZ

17 Schneidler Old Style

ABCDEFGHIJKLMNOPQRSTUVWXYZ&

18 Seneca

ABCDEFGHIJKLMNOPQRSTUVWXYZ&

*less steeply inclined axis
longer descenders
strong contrast*

19 Centaur

ABCDEFGHIJKLMNOPQRSTUVWXYZ&

20 Horley Old Style

ABCDEFGHIJKLMNOPQRSTUVWXYZ&

* These letters show special or 'style' characteristics. (NB. J, Q, & and g will usually vary from one typeface to another).

SLOPING E-BAR
(VENETIAN SERIF)

e

Verona
Worcester Round
Della Robbia
Bauer Text
Cloister
Jenson
Schneidler Old Style
Seneca
Centaur
Horley Old Style

Verona **11**

abcdefghijklmnopqrstuvwxyz 1234567890

Worcester Round **12**

abcdefghijklmnopqrstuvwxyz1234567890

Della Robbia **13**

abcdefghijklmnopqrstuvwxyz1234567890

Bauer Text **14**

abcdefghijklmnopqrstuvwxyz1234567890

Cloister **15**

abcdefghijklmnopqrstuvwxyz1234567890

Jenson **16**

abcdefghijklmnopqrstuvwxyz1234567890

Schneidler Old Style **17**

abcdefghijklmnopqrstuvwxyz1234567890

Seneca **18**

abcdefghijklmnopqrstuvwxyz1234567890

Centaur **19**

abcdefghijklmnopqrstuvwxyz1234567890

Horley Old Style **20**

abcdefghijklmnopqrstuvwxyz1234567890

NB. On lower case letters generally look at the x height and length of ascenders and descenders.

SLOPING E-BAR
(VENETIAN SERIF)

Deepdene
Brighton
Clearface Bold 157
(Monotype)
ITC Clearface
Lutetia
Stratford
ITC Tiffany
ITC Benguiat
Seagull
ITC Souvenir

21 Deepdene

vertical axis roman serifs

ABCDEFGHIJKLMNOPQRSTUVWXYZ&

22 Brighton

ABCDEFGHIJKLMNOPQRSTUVWXYZ&

23 Clearface Bold 157 (Monotype)

ABCDEFGHIJKLMNOPQRSTUVWXYZ&

24 ITC Clearface

ABCDEFGHIJKLMNOPQRSTUVWXYZ&

25 Lutetia

ABCDEFGHIJKLMNOPQRSTUVWXYZ&

26 Stratford

ABCDEFGHIJKLMNOPQRSTUVWXYZ&

27 ITC Tiffany

ABCDEFGHIJKLMNOPQRSTUVWXYZ&

vertical axis wedge serifs

28 ITC Benguiat

ABCDEFGHIJKLMNOPQRSTUVWXYZ&

29 Seagull

ABCDEFGHIJKLMNOPQRSTUVWXYZ&

30 ITC Souvenir

ABCDEFGHIJKLMNOPQRSTUVWXYZ&

* These letters show special or 'style' characteristics. (NB. J, Q, & and g will usually vary from one typeface to another).

Deepdene 21

abcdefghijklmnopqrstuvwxyz1234567890

SLOPING E-BAR
(VENETIAN SERIF)

e

Brighton 22

abcdefghijklmnopqrstuvwxyz1234567890

Deepdene
Brighton
Clearface Bold 157
(Monotype)
ITC Clearface
Lutetia
Stratford
ITC Tiffany
ITC Benguiat
Seagull
ITC Souvenir

Clearface Bold 157 (Monotype) 23

abcdefghijklmnopqrstuvwxyz1234567890

ITC Clearface 24

abcdefghijklmnopqrstuvwxyz1234567890

Lutetia 25

abcdefghijklmnopqrstuvwxyz1234567890

Stratford 26

abcdefghijklmnopqrstuvwxyz1234567890

ITC Tiffany 27

abcdefghijklmnopqrstuvwxyz1234567890

ITC Benguiat 28

abcdefghijklmnopqrstuvwxyz1234567890

Seagull 29

abcdefghijklmnopqrstuvwxyz1234567890

ITC Souvenir 30

abcdefghijklmnopqrstuvwxyz1234567890

NB. On lower case letters generally look at the x height and length of ascenders and descenders.

Vendôme
Italian Old Style
(Monotype)
ITC Italia
Jenson Old Style

31 Vendôme

ABCDEFGHIJKLMNOPQRSTUVWXYZ&

*inclined
axis
roman and
slab serifs*

32 Italian Old Style (Monotype)

ABCDEFGHIJKLMNOPQRSTUVWXYZ&

*vertical or
slightly
inclined
axis
slab serifs
on ascenders*

33 ITC Italia

ABCDEFGHIJKLMNOPQRSTUVWXYZ&

34 Jenson Old Style

ABCDEFGHIJKLMNOPQRSTUVWXYZ&

* These letters show special or 'style' characteristics. (NB. J, Q, & and g will usually vary from one typeface to another).

SLOPING E-BAR
(VENETIAN SERIF)

Vendôme
Italian Old Style
(Monotype)
ITC Italia
Jenson Old Style

Vendôme **31**

abcdefghijklmnopqrstuvwxyz1234567890

Italian Old Style (Monotype) **32**

abcdefghijklmnopqrstuvwxyz1234567890

ITC Italia **33**

abcdefghijklmnopqrstuvwxyz1234567890

Jenson Old Style **34**

abcdefghijklmnopqrstuvwxyz1234567890

NB. On lower case letters generally look at the x height and length of ascenders and descenders.

2. ANGLED STRESS/OBLIQUE SERIFS
(OLD STYLE SERIF)

Specimen nos	Basic characteristics	Secondary characteristics	
35-41	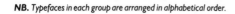 angled stress / definite oblique serifs / (including foot serif)	W crossed centre strokes	e.g. **35** Bembo
42-44	,,	W centre strokes joining at cap height (or nearly so)	e.g. **44** Trump Mediaeval
45-46	,,	W no centre serif	e.g. **45** Berling
47-53	,,	W stepped centre strokes	e.g. **53** Times New Roman

NB. *Typefaces in each group are arranged in alphabetical order.*

capital W with crossed centre strokes

ANGLED STRESS OBLIQUE SERIFS (OLD STYLE SERIF)

od

Bembo
Bernhard Modern
Goudy Old Style
News Plantin
Plantin
Poliphilus
Trajon
Leamington
Missal
Trump Mediaeval

35 Bembo

* * * * * *
ABCDEFGHIJKLMNOPQRSTUVWXYZ&

36 Bernhard Modern

* * * * *
ABCDEFGHIJKLMNOPQRSTUVWXYZ&

37 Goudy Old Style

* * *
ABCDEFGHIJKLMNOPQRSTUVWXYZ&

38 News Plantin

* * * *
ABCDEFGHIJKLMNOPQRSTUVWXYZ&

39 Plantin

* * * *
ABCDEFGHIJKLMNOPQRSTUVWXYZ&

40 Poliphilus

* * * * * *
ABCDEFGHIJKLMNOPQRSTUVWXYZ&

41 Trajon

* * *
ABCDEFGHIJKLMNOPQRSTUVWXYZ&

capital W with centre strokes joining at cap height (or nearly so)

42 Leamington

* * *
ABCDEFGHIJKLMNOPQRSTUVWXYZ&

43 Missal

* *
ABCDEFGHIJKLMNOPQRSTUVWXYZ&

44 Trump Mediaeval

* * * * * *
ABCDEFGHIJKLMNOPQRSTUVWXYZ&

* These letters show special or 'style' characteristics. (NB. J, Q, & and g will usually vary from one typeface to another).

Bembo **35**

abcdefghijklmnopqrstuvwxyz1234567890

Bernhard Modern **36**

abcdefghijklmnopqrstuvwxyz1234567890

Goudy Old Style **37**

abcdefghijklmnopqrstuvwxyz1234567890

News Plantin **38**

abcdefghijklmnopqrstuvwxyz1234567890

Plantin **39**

abcdefghijklmnopqrstuvwxyz1234567890

Poliphilus **40**

abcdefghijklmnopqrstuvwxyz1234567890

Trajon **41**

abcdefghijklmnopqrstuvwxyz1234567890

Leamington **42**

abcdefghijklmnopqrstuvwxyz1234567890

Missal **43**

abcdefghijklmnopqrstuvwxyz1234567890

Trump Mediaeval **44**

abcdefghijklmnopqrstuvwxyz1234567890

**ANGLED STRESS
OBLIQUE SERIFS**
(OLD STYLE SERIF)

od

Bembo
Bernhard Modern
Goudy Old Style
News Plantin
Plantin
Poliphilus
Trajon
Leamington
Missal
Trump Mediaeval

NB. On lower case letters generally look at the x height and length of ascenders and descenders.

ANGLED STRESS OBLIQUE SERIFS (OLD STYLE SERIF)

od

Berling
Nicholas Cochin
Albertina
Emerson
Goudy Catalogue
Life
Minister
Times Roman (Linotype)
Times New Roman (Monotype)

capital W with no centre serif

45 Berling

ABCDEFGHIJKLMNOPQRSTUVWXYZ&

46 Nicholas Cochin

ABCDEFGHIJKLMNOPQRSTUVWXYZ&

capital W with stepped centre strokes

47 Albertina

ABCDEFGHIJKLMNOPQRSTUVWXYZ&

48 Emerson

ABCDEFGHIJKLMNOPQRSTUVWXYZ&

49 Goudy Catalogue

ABCDEFGHIJKLMNOPQRSTUVWXYZ&

50 Life

ABCDEFGHIJKLMNOPQRSTUVWXYZ&

51 Minister

ABCDEFGHIJKLMNOPQRSTUVWXYZ&

52 Times Roman (Linotype)

ABCDEFGHIJKLMNOPQRSTUVWXYZ&

53 Times New Roman (Monotype)

ABCDEFGHIJKLMNOPQRSTUVWXYZ&

* These letters show special or 'style' characteristics. (NB. J, Q, & and g will usually vary from one typeface to another).

Berling **45**

*   *   *
abcdefghijklmnopqrstuvwxyz1234567890

Nicholas Cochin **46**

*   *   *
abcdefghijklmnopqrstuvwxyz1234567890

Albertina **47**

*   *   *   *
abcdefghijklmnopqrstuvwxyz1234567890

Emerson **48**

*   *
abcdefghijklmnopqrstuvwxyz1234567890

Goudy Catalogue **49**

*   *   *
abcdefghijklmnopqrstuvwxyz1234567890

Life **50**

*   *   *
abcdefghijklmnopqrstuvwxyz1234567890

Minister **51**

*   * *   *
abcdefghijklmnopqrstuvwxyz1234567890

Times Roman (Linotype) **52**

*   *   *   * *   *
abcdefghijklmnopqrstuvwxyz1234567890

Times New Roman (Monotype) **53**

*   *   *   * *   *
abcdefghijklmnopqrstuvwxyz1234567890

NB. On lower case letters generally look at the x height and length of ascenders and descenders.

ANGLED STRESS
OBLIQUE SERIFS
(OLD STYLE SERIF)

Berling
Nicholas Cochin
Albertina
Emerson
Goudy Catalogue
Life
Minister
Times Roman
(Linotype)
Times New Roman
(Monotype)

3. VERTICAL STRESS/OBLIQUE SERIFS
(TRANSITIONAL SERIF)

Specimen nos	Basic characteristics	Secondary characteristics	
54-72	**W** centre strokes joining at cap height **M** parallel (or nearly so)		e.g. **59** Caslon Old Face No 2
73-74	,, **M** definitely splayed		e.g. **73** Ehrhardt
75-86	**W** with no centre serif		e.g. **78** Baskerville 169 (Monotype)
87-88	**W** crossed centre strokes **M** with serifs at cap height	**W** centre strokes joining at cap height	e.g. **88** Sabon
89	,, ,,	**W** crossed centre strokes	e.g. **89** Barbou
90-97	,, ,,	**W** centre strokes stepped	e.g. **91** Garamond 156 (Monotype)
98	,, **M** no serifs at cap height		e.g. **98** Weiss
99-107	**W** stepped centre strokes **M** parallel (or nearly so)		e.g. **100** Concorde
108-110	,, **M** definitely splayed		e.g. **108** De Roos

NB. Typefaces in each group are arranged in alphabetical order.

capital W with centre strokes joining at cap height (or nearly so) M parallel (or nearly so)

VERTICAL STRESS
OBLIQUE SERIFS
(TRANSITIONAL SERIF)

od

Fry's Baskerville
Binny Old Style
Bookman
ITC Bookman
Bulmer
Caslon Old Face No 2
Caslon 128 (Monotype)
Caslon 540
Century Old Style
Chiswell Old Face

54 Fry's Baskerville

ABCDEFGHIJKLMNOPQRSTUVWXYZ&

55 Binny Old Style

ABCDEFGHIJKLMNOPQRSTUVWXYZ&

56 Bookman

ABCDEFGHIJKLMNOPQRSTUVWXYZ&

57 ITC Bookman

ABCDEFGHIJKLMNOPQRSTUVWXYZ&

58 Bulmer

ABCDEFGHIJKLMNOPQRSTUVWXYZ&

59 Caslon Old Face No 2

ABCDEFGHIJKLMNOPQRSTUVWXYZ&

60 Caslon 128 (Monotype)

ABCDEFGHIJKLMNOPQRSTUVWXYZ&

61 Caslon 540

ABCDEFGHIJKLMNOPQRSTUVWXYZ&

62 Century Old Style

ABCDEFGHIJKLMNOPQRSTUVWXYZ&

63 Chiswell Old Face

ABCDEFGHIJKLMNOPQRSTUVWXYZ&

* These letters show special or 'style' characteristics. (NB. J, Q, & and g will usually vary from one typeface to another).

Fry's Baskerville **54**

abcdefghijklmnopqrstuvwxyz1234567890

Binny Old Style **55**

abcdefghijklmnopqrstuvwxyz1234567890

Bookman **56**

abcdefghijklmnopqrstuvwxyz1234567890

ITC Bookman **57**

abcdefghijklmnopqrstuvwxyz1234567890

Bulmer **58**

abcdefghijklmnopqrstuvwxyz1234567890

Caslon Old Face No 2 **59**

abcdefghijklmnopqrstuvwxyz1234567890

Caslon 128 (Monotype) **60**

abcdefghijklmnopqrstuvwxyz1234567890

Caslon 540 **61**

abcdefghijklmnopqrstuvwxyz1234567890

Century Old Style **62**

abcdefghijklmnopqrstuvwxyz1234567890

Chiswell Old Face **63**

abcdefghijklmnopqrstuvwxyz 1234567890

**VERTICAL STRESS
OBLIQUE SERIFS
(TRANSITIONAL SERIF)**

od

Fry's Baskerville
Binny Old Style
Bookman
ITC Bookman
Bulmer
Caslon Old Face No 2
Caslon 128 (Monotype)
Caslon 540
Century Old Style
Chiswell Old Face

NB. On lower case letters generally look at the x height and length of ascenders and descenders.

64 Concorde Nova

ABCDEFGHIJKLMNOPQRSTUVWXYZ&

65 Fontana

ABCDEFGHIJKLMNOPQRSTUVWXYZ&

66 Granjon

ABCDEFGHIJKLMNOPQRSTUVWXYZ&

67 Imprint

ABCDEFGHIJKLMNOPQRSTUVWXYZ&

68 Monticello

ABCDEFGHIJKLMNOPQRSTUVWXYZ&

69 Old Style No 2

ABCDEFGHIJKLMNOPQRSTUVWXYZ&

70 Old Style No 7

ABCDEFGHIJKLMNOPQRSTUVWXYZ&

71 Olympian

ABCDEFGHIJKLMNOPQRSTUVWXYZ&

72 Ronaldson

ABCDEFGHIJKLMNOPQRSTUVWXYZ&

capital W
with centre
strokes joining
at cap height
(or nearly so)
M definitely
splayed

73 Ehrhardt

ABCDEFGHIJKLMNOPQRSTUVWXYZ&

VERTICAL STRESS OBLIQUE SERIFS (TRANSITIONAL SERIF)

od

Concorde Nova
Fontana
Granjon
Imprint
Monticello
Old Style No 2
Old Style No 7
Olympian
Ronaldson
Ehrhardt

These letters show special or 'style' characteristics. (NB. J, Q, & and g will usually vary from one typeface to another).

Concorde Nova **64**

abcdefghijklmnopqrstuvwxyz1234567890

Fontana **65**

abcdefghijklmnopqrstuvwxyz1234567890

Granjon **66**

abcdefghijklmnopqrstuvwxyz1234567890

Imprint **67**

abcdefghijklmnopqrstuvwxyz1234567890

Monticello **68**

abcdefghijklmnopqrstuvwxyz1234567890

Old Style No 2 **69**

abcdefghijklmnopqrstuvwxyz1234567890

Old Style No 7 **70**

abcdefghijklmnopqrstuvwxyz1234567890

Olympian **71**

abcdefghijklmnopqrstuvwxyz1234567890

Ronaldson **72**

abcdefghijklmnopqrstuvwxyz1234567890

Ehrhardt **73**

abcdefghijklmnopqrstuvwxyz1234567890

**VERTICAL STRESS
OBLIQUE SERIFS
(TRANSITIONAL SERIF)**

Concorde Nova
Fontana
Granjon
Imprint
Monticello
Old Style No 2
Old Style No 7
Olympian
Ronaldson
Ehrhardt

NB. On lower case letters generally look at the x height and length of ascenders and descenders.

74 Galliard

* * * * * * * * *
ABCDEFGHIJKLMNOPQRSTUVWXYZ&

capital W with no centre serif

75 Aldus

* * * * * * *
ABCDEFGHIJKLMNOPQRSTUVWXYZ&

76 Aster

* * * *
ABCDEFGHIJKLMNOPQRSTUVWXYZ&

VERTICAL STRESS OBLIQUE SERIFS (TRANSITIONAL SERIF)

od

Galliard
Aldus
Aster
Baskerville (Berthold)
Baskerville 169 (Monotype)
Baskerville (Linotype)
Baskerville No. 2
Cartier
Congress
Lectura

77 Baskerville (Berthold)

* * * * *
ABCDEFGHIJKLMNOPQRSTUVWXYZ&

78 Baskerville 169 (Monotype)

* * * * *
ABCDEFGHIJKLMNOPQRSTUVWXYZ&

79 Baskerville (Linotype)

* * * *
ABCDEFGHIJKLMNOPQRSTUVWXYZ&

80 Baskerville No 2

* * * * *
ABCDEFGHIJKLMNOPQRSTUVWXYZ&

81 Cartier

* * * * * * *
ABCDEFGHIJKLMNOPQRSTUVWXYZ&

82 Congress

* * * *
ABCDEFGHIJKLMNOPQRSTUVWXYZ&

83 Lectura

* * * *
ABCDEFGHIJKLMNOPQRSTUVWXYZ&

* These letters show special or 'style' characteristics. (NB. J, Q, & and g will usually vary from one typeface to another).

Galliard **74**

* *   *   *   * *
abcdefghijklmnopqrstuvwxyz1234567890

Aldus **75**

* * *   *   *   *
abcdefghijklmnopqrstuvwxyz1234567890

Aster **76**

*   *   *   *   *
abcdefghijklmnopqrstuvwxyz1234567890

Baskerville (Berthold) **77**

*   *   * * *
abcdefghijklmnopqrstuvwxyz1234567890

Baskerville 169 (Monotype) **78**

*   *   * *   *
abcdefghijklmnopqrstuvwxyz1234567890

Baskerville (Linotype) **79**

*   *   * *   *
abcdefghijklmnopqrstuvwxyz1234567890

Baskerville No 2 **80**

*   * *   *
abcdefghijklmnopqrstuvwxyz1234567890

Cartier **81**

*   * *
abcdefghijklmnopqrstuvwxyz1234567890

Congress **82**

*   *   *   *
abcdefghijklmnopqrstuvwxyz1234567890

Lectura **83**

*   *   *   * *
abcdefghijklmnopqrstuvwxyz1234567890

VERTICAL STRESS
OBLIQUE SERIFS
(TRANSITIONAL SERIF)

Galliard
Aldus
Aster
Baskerville (Berthold)
Baskerville 169 (Monotype)
Baskerville (Linotype)
Baskerville No. 2
Cartier
Congress
Lectura

NB. On lower case letters generally look at the x height and length of ascenders and descenders.

84 Palatino

ABCDEFGHIJKLMNOPQRSTUVWXYZ&

85 Poppl Pontifex

ABCDEFGHIJKLMNOPQRSTUVWXYZ&

86 Times Europa

ABCDEFGHIJKLMNOPQRSTUVWXYZ&

VERTICAL STRESS OBLIQUE SERIFS (TRANSITIONAL SERIF)

Palatino
Poppl Pontifex
Times Europa
Quadriga Antiqua
Sabon
Barbou
Fournier
Garamond 156
(Monotype)
Garamond
(Stempel)
Garamond 3
(Linotype)

capital W with crossed centre strokes

M with serifs at cap height

lower case w with centre strokes joining at cap height

87 Quadriga Antiqua

ABCDEFGHIJKLMNOPQRSTUVWXYZ&

88 Sabon

ABCDEFGHIJKLMNOPQRSTUVWXYZ&

capital W with crossed strokes

M with serifs on tops

lower case w with crossed centre strokes

89 Barbou

ABCDEFGHIJKLMNOPQRSTUVWXYZ&

capital W with crossed centre strokes

M with serifs on tops

lower case w with stepped centre strokes

90 Fournier

ABCDEFGHIJKLMNOPQRSTUVWXYZ&

91 Garamond 156 (Monotype)

ABCDEFGHIJKLMNOPQRSTUVWXYZ&

92 Garamond (Stempel)

ABCDEFGHIJKLMNOPQRSTUVWXYZ&

93 Garamond 3 (Linotype)

ABCDEFGHIJKLMNOPQRSTUVWXYZ&

* These letters show special or 'style' characteristics. (NB. J, Q, & and g will usually vary from one typeface to another).

Palatino **84**

abcdefghijklmnopqrstuvwxyz1234567890

Poppl Pontifex **85**

abcdefghijklmnopqrstuvwxyz1234567890

Times Europa **86**

abcdefghijklmnopqrstuvwxyz1234567890

Quadriga Antiqua **87**

abcdefghijklmnopqrstuvwxyz1234567890

Sabon **88**

abcdefghijklmnopqrstuvwxyz1234567890

Barbou **89**

abcdefghijklmnopqrstuvwxyz 1234567890

Fournier **90**

abcdefghijklmnopqrstuvwxyz1234567890

Garamond 156 (Monotype) **91**

abcdefghijklmnopqrstuvwxyz1234567890

Garamond (Stempel) **92**

abcdefghijklmnopqrstuvwxyz1234567890

Garamond 3 (Linotype) **93**

abcdefghijklmnopqrstuvwxyz1234567890

VERTICAL STRESS OBLIQUE SERIFS (TRANSITIONAL SERIF)

od

Palatino
Poppl Pontifex
Times Europa
Quadriga Antiqua
Sabon
Barbou
Fournier
Garamond 156
(Monotype)
Garamond
(Stempel)
Garamond 3
(Linotype)

NB. On lower case letters generally look at the x height and length of ascenders and descenders.

94 Garamond (Berthold)

ABCDEFGHIJKLMNOPQRSTUVWXYZ&

95 ITC Garamond

ABCDEFGHIJKLMNOPQRSTUVWXYZ&

96 Garamont (Amsterdam)

ABCDEFGHIJKLMNOPQRSTUVWXYZ&

97 Spectrum

ABCDEFGHIJKLMNOPQRSTUVWXYZ&

98 Weiss

ABCDEFGHIJKLMNOPQRSTUVWXYZ&

99 Caslon 3

ABCDEFGHIJKLMNOPQRSTUVWXYZ&

100 Concorde

ABCDEFGHIJKLMNOPQRSTUVWXYZ&

101 ITC Cushing

ABCDEFGHIJKLMNOPQRSTUVWXYZ&

102 Dante

ABCDEFGHIJKLMNOPQRSTUVWXYZ&

103 Gazette

ABCDEFGHIJKLMNOPQRSTUVWXYZ&

**VERTICAL STRESS
OBLIQUE SERIFS
(TRANSITIONAL SERIF)**

od

Garamond
(Berthold)
ITC Garamond
Garamont
(Amsterdam)
Spectrum
Weiss
Caslon 3
Concorde
ITC Cushing
Dante
Gazette

*capital W
with crossed
centre strokes
M with
no serifs at
cap height*

*capital W
with stepped
centre strokes
M parallel
(or nearly so)*

* These letters show special or 'style' characteristics. (NB. J, Q, & and g will usually vary from one typeface to another).

Garamond (Berthold) **94**

abcdefghijklmnopqrstuvwxyz1234567890

ITC Garamond **95**

abcdefghijklmnopqrstuvwxyz1234567890

Garamont (Amsterdam) **96**

abcdefghijklmnopqrstuvwxyz1234567890

Spectrum **97**

abcdefghijklmnopqrstuvwxyz1234567890

Weiss **98**

abcdefghijklmnopqrstuvwxyz1234567890

Caslon 3 **99**

abcdefghijklmnopqrstuvwxyz1234567890

Concorde **100**

abcdefghijklmnopqrstuvwxyz1234567890

ITC Cushing **101**

abcdefghijklmnopqrstuvwxyz1234567890

Dante **102**

abcdefghijklmnopqrstuvwxyz1234567890

Gazette **103**

abcdefghijklmnopqrstuvwxyz1234567890

VERTICAL STRESS
OBLIQUE SERIFS
(TRANSITIONAL SERIF)

Garamond
(Berthold)
ITC Garamond
Garamont
(Amsterdam)
Spectrum
Weiss
Caslon 3
Concorde
ITC Cushing
Dante
Gazette

NB. On lower case letters generally look at the x height and length of ascenders and descenders.

104 ITC Isbell

ABCDEFGHIJKLMNOPQRSTUVWXYZ&

105 Romulus

ABCDEFGHIJKLMNOPQRSTUVWXYZ&

106 Rotation

ABCDEFGHIJKLMNOPQRSTUVWXYZ&

107 Van Dijck

ABCDEFGHIJKLMNOPQRSTUVWXYZ&

108 De Roos

ABCDEFGHIJKLMNOPQRSTUVWXYZ&

109 Janson

ABCDEFGHIJKLMNOPQRSTUVWXYZ&

110 Rundfunk

ABCDEFGHIJKLMNOPQRSTUVWXYZ&

These letters show special or 'style' characteristics. (NB. J, Q, & and g will usually vary from one typeface to another).

**VERTICAL STRESS
OBLIQUE SERIFS
(TRANSITIONAL SERIF)**

ITC Isbell
Romulus
Rotation
Van Dijck
De Roos
Janson
Rundfunk

*capital W
with stepped
centre strokes
M definitely
splayed*

ITC Isbell **104**

* * * * * * *
abcdefghijklmnopqrstuvwxyz1234567890

Romulus **105**

* * * *
abcdefghijklmnopqrstuvwxyz1234567890

Rotation **106**

* * * *
abcdefghijklmnopqrstuvwxyz1234567890

Van Dijck **107**

* * *
abcdefghijklmnopqrstuvwxyz1234567890

De Roos **108**

* * * * * *
abcdefghijklmnopqrstuvwxyz1234567890

Janson **109**

* *
abcdefghijklmnopqrstuvwxyz1234567890

Rundfunk **110**

* * *
abcdefghijklmnopqrstuvwxyz1234567890

**VERTICAL STRESS
OBLIQUE SERIFS
(TRANSITIONAL SERIF)**

ITC Isbell
Romulus
Rotation
Van Dijck
De Roos
Janson
Rundfunk

NB. On lower case letters generally look at the x height and length of ascenders and descenders.

4. VERTICAL STRESS/STRAIGHT SERIFS
(NEW TRANSITIONAL SERIF)

Specimen nos	Basic characteristics		Secondary characteristics	
111-112	r d *horizontal line serifs (or nearly so)*	n *line serifs*		e.g. **111** Joanna
113-117	r d *horizontal bracketed serifs (or nearly so)*	W *centre strokes joining at cap height*	n *light face*	e.g. **117** Primer
118-122	,,	,,	n *black face*	e.g. **121** Ionic 5
123-127	,,	W *crossed centre strokes*		e.g. **123** Cheltenham
128-132	,,	W *stepped centre strokes*		e.g. **130** Columbia
133-140	,,	W *no centre serif*		e.g. **138** Melior
141-146	r d *some definite oblique bracketed serifs*	n *weak contrast*		e.g. **146** Textype
147-150	,,	n *good contrast*		e.g. **147** Cochin

NB. *Typefaces in each group are arranged in alphabetical order.*

horizontal line serifs (or nearly so)

111 Joanna

ABCDEFGHIJKLMNOPQRSTUVWXYZ&

112 Maximus

ABCDEFGHIJKLMNOPQRSTUVWXYZ&

horizontal bracketed serifs (or nearly so)

capital W with centre strokes joining at cap height (or nearly so)

light face

113 Breughel 55

ABCDEFGHIJKLMNOPQRSTUVWXYZ&

114 Century Expanded

ABCDEFGHIJKLMNOPQRSTUVWXYZ&

VERTICAL STRESS STRAIGHT SERIFS (NEW TRANSITIONAL)

Joanna
Maximus
Breughel 55
Century Expanded
Excelsior
Perpetua
Primer
Aurora
Century Schoolbook
Corona

115 Excelsior

ABCDEFGHIJKLMNOPQRSTUVWXYZ&

116 Perpetua

ABCDEFGHIJKLMNOPQRSTUVWXYZ&

117 Primer

ABCDEFGHIJKLMNOPQRSTUVWXYZ&

horizontal bracketed serifs (or nearly so)

capital W with centre strokes joining at cap height (or nearly so)

black face

118 Aurora

ABCDEFGHIJKLMNOPQRSTUVWXYZ

119 Century Schoolbook

ABCDEFGHIJKLMNOPQRSTUVWXYZ&

120 Corona

ABCDEFGHIJKLMNOPQRSTUVWXYZ&

* These letters show special or 'style' characteristics. (NB. J, Q, & and g will usually vary from one typeface to another).

Joanna 111

abcdefghijklmnopqrstuvwxyz1234567890

Maximus 112

abcdefghijklmnopqrstuvwxyz1234567890

Breughel 55 113

abcdefghijklmnopqrstuvwxyz1234567890

Century Expanded 114

abcdefghijklmnopqrstuvwxyz1234567890

Excelsior 115

abcdefghijklmnopqrstuvwxyz1234567890

Perpetua 116

abcdefghijklmnopqrstuvwxyz1234567890

Primer 117

abcdefghijklmnopqrstuvwxyz1234567890

Aurora 118

abcdefghijklmnopqrstuvwxyz1234567890

Century Schoolbook 119

abcdefghijklmnopqrstuvwxyz1234567890

Corona 120

abcdefghijklmnopqrstuvwxyz1234567890

**VERTICAL STRESS
STRAIGHT SERIFS
(NEW TRANSITIONAL)**

od

Joanna
Maximus
Breughel 55
Century Expanded
Excelsior
Perpetua
Primer
Aurora
Century Schoolbook
Corona

NB. On lower case letters generally look at the x height and length of ascenders and descenders.

121 Ionic 5
ABCDEFGHIJKLMNOPQRSTUVWXYZ&

122 Nimrod
ABCDEFGHIJKLMNOPQRSTUVWXYZ&

horizontal bracketed serifs (or nearly so) capital W with crossed centre strokes

123 Cheltenham
ABCDEFGHIJKLMNOPQRSTUVWXYZ&

124 Cheltenham Nova
ABCDEFGHIJKLMNOPQRSTUVWXYZ&

VERTICAL STRESS STRAIGHT SERIFS (NEW TRANSITIONAL)

od

Ionic 5
Nimrod
Cheltenham
Cheltenham Nova
Comenius
Gloucester Old Style
Sorbonne
Bramley
ITC Cheltenham
Columbia

125 Comenius
ABCDEFGHIJKLMNOPQRSTUVWXYZ&

126 Gloucester Old Style
ABCDEFGHIJKLMNOPQRSTUVWXYZ&

127 Sorbonne
ABCDEFGHIJKLMNOPQRSTUVWXYZ&

horizontal bracketed serifs (or nearly so) capital W with stepped centre strokes

128 Bramley
ABCDEFGHIJKLMNOPQRSTUVWXYZ&

129 ITC Cheltenham
ABCDEFGHIJKLMNOPQRSTUVWXYZ&

130 Columbia
ABCDEFGHIJKLMNOPQRSTUVWXYZ&

* These letters show special or 'style' characteristics. (NB. J, Q, & and g will usually vary from one typeface to another).

Ionic 5 121

abcdefghijklmnopqrstuvwxyz1234567890

Nimrod 122

abcdefghijklmnopqrstuvwxyz1234567890

Cheltenham 123

abcdefghijklmnopqrstuvwxyz1234567890

Cheltenham Nova 124

abcdefghijklmnopqrstuvwxyz1234567890

Comenius 125

abcdefghijklmnopqrstuvwxyz1234567890

Gloucester Old Style 126

abcdefghijklmnopqrstuvwxyz1234567890

Sorbonne 127

abcdefghijklmnopqrstuvwxyz1234567890

Bramley 128

abcdefghijklmnopqrstuvwxyz1234567890

ITC Cheltenham 129

abcdefghijklmnopqrstuvwxyz1234567890

Columbia 130

abcdefghijklmnopqrstuvwxyz1234567890

VERTICAL STRESS STRAIGHT SERIFS (NEW TRANSITIONAL)

od

Ionic 5
Nimrod
Cheltenham
Cheltenham Nova
Comenius
Gloucester Old Style
Sorbonne
Bramley
ITC Cheltenham
Columbia

NB. On lower case letters generally look at the x height and length of ascenders and descenders.

131 French Round Face

* * * * * * * * *
ABCDEFGHIJKLMNOPQRSTUVWXYZ&

132 Goudy Modern

* * * *
ABCDEFGHIJKLMNOPQRSTUVWXYZ&

horizontal serifs (or nearly so) no centre serif on capital W

133 Apollo

* * * * * * *
ABCDEFGHIJKLMNOPQRSTUVWXYZ&

134 Athenaeum

* * * * * *
ABCDEFGHIJKLMNOPQRSTUVWXYZ&

135 Diotima

* * * * *
ABCDEFGHIJKLMNOPQRSTUVWXYZ&

French Round Face
Goudy Modern
Apollo
Athenaeum
Diotima
Franklin Antiqua
Impressum
Melior
Orion
Renault

136 Franklin Antiqua

* * *
ABCDEFGHIJKLMNOPQRSTUVWXYZ&

137 Impressum

* * * *
ABCDEFGHIJKLMNOPQRSTUVWXYZ&

138 Melior

* * * * *
ABCDEFGHIJKLMNOPQRSTUVWXYZ&

139 Orion

* * * *
ABCDEFGHIJKLMNOPQRSTUVWXYZ&

140 Renault

* *
ABCDEFGHIJKLMNOPQRSTUVWXYZ&

* These letters show special or 'style' characteristics. (NB. J, Q, & and g will usually vary from one typeface to another).

French Round Face 131

* * * * * * * *
abcdefghijklmnopqrstuvwxyz1234567890

Goudy Modern 132

* * * *
abcdefghijklmnopqrstuvwxyz1234567890

Apollo 133

* * * * * * * *
abcdefghijklmnopqrstuvwxyz1234567890

Athenaeum 134

* *
abcdefghijklmnopqrstuvwxyz1234567890

Diotima 135

* * * * *
abcdefghijklmnopqrstuvwxyz1234567890

Franklin Antiqua 136

* * *
abcdefghijklmnopqrstuvwxyz1234567890

Impressum 137

* * * *
abcdefghijklmnopqrstuvwxyz1234567890

Melior 138

* * * * *
abcdefghijklmnopqrstuvwxyz1234567890

Orion 139

* *
abcdefghijklmnopqrstuvwxyz1234567890

Renault 140

* * *
abcdefghijklmnopqrstuvwxyz1234567890

**VERTICAL STRESS
STRAIGHT SERIFS
(NEW TRANSITIONAL)**

od

French Round Face
Goudy Modern
Apollo
Athenaeum
Diotima
Franklin Antiqua
Impressum
Melior
Orion
Renault

NB. On lower case letters generally look at the x height and length of ascenders and descenders.

some definite
oblique bracketed
serifs
weak contrast

141 Dominante

ABCDEFGHIJKLMNOPQRSTUVWXYZ&

142 Lo-type

ABCDEFGHIJKLMNOPQRSTUVWXYZ&

143 Menhart

ABCDEFGHIJKLMNOPQRSTUVWXYZ&

144 Paragon

ABCDEFGHIJKLMNOPQRSTUVWXYZ

145 Primus Antiqua

ABCDEFGHIJKLMNOPQRSTUVWXYZ&

146 Textype

ABCDEFGHIJKLMNOPQRSTUVWXYZ&

some definite
oblique bracketed
serifs
good contrast

147 Cochin

ABCDEFGHIJKLMNOPQRSTUVWXYZ&

148 Electra

ABCDEFGHIJKLMNOPQRSTUVWXYZ&

149 Iridium

ABCDEFGHIJKLMNOPQRSTUVWXYZ&

150 ITC Zapf International

ABCDEFGHIJKLMNOPQRSTUVWXYZ&

**VERTICAL STRESS
STRAIGHT SERIFS
(NEW TRANSITIONAL)**

Dominante
Lo-Type
Menhart
Paragon
Primus Antiqua
Textype
Cochin
Electra
Iridium
ITC Zapf
International

* These letters show special or 'style' characteristics. (NB. J, Q, & and g will usually vary from one typeface to another).

Dominante 141

* * * *   *
abcdefghijklmnopqrstuvwxyz1234567890

Lo-type 142

*   *   *   *   *
abcdefghijklmnopqrstuvwxyz1234567890

Menhart 143

*   *   *   *   * *
abcdefghijklmnopqrstuvwxyz1234567890

Paragon 144

*   *   *   *
abcdefghijklmnopqrstuvwxyz1234567890

Primus Antiqua 145

*   *   *   * *
abcdefghijklmnopqrstuvwxyz1234567890

Textype 146

* *   *   * *
abcdefghijklmnopqrstuvwxyz1234567890

Cochin 147

* * *   * *
abcdefghijklmnopqrstuvwxyz1234567890

Electra 148

*   *   *   * *   *
abcdefghijklmnopqrstuvwxyz1234567890

Iridium 149

*   *   *   *
abcdefghijklmnopqrstuvwxyz1234567890

ITC Zapf International 150

*   * * *
abcdefghijklmnopqrstuvwxyz1234567890

**VERTICAL STRESS
STRAIGHT SERIFS
(NEW TRANSITIONAL)**

od

Dominante
Lo-Type
Menhart
Paragon
Primus Antiqua
Textype
Cochin
Electra
Iridium
ITC Zapf
International

NB. On lower case letters generally look at the x height and length of ascenders and descenders.

5. ABRUPT CONTRAST/STRAIGHT SERIFS
(MODERN SERIF)

Specimen nos	Basic characteristics	Secondary characteristics	
151-161	N *line serifs*	n *light face*	e.g. **161** Walbaum (Linotype)
162-169	,,	n *black face*	e.g. **162** Bodoni 135 (Monotype)
170-187	N *bracketed serifs*		e.g. **185** Scotch Roman (Monotype)

NB. Typefaces in each group are arranged in alphabetical order.

line serifs
light face

151 Auriga

A B C D E F G H I J K L M N O P Q R S T U V W X Y Z &

152 Basilia

A B C D E F G H I J K L M N O P Q R S T U V W X Y Z &

153 Bauer Bodoni

A B C D E F G H I J K L M N O P Q R S T U V W X Y Z &

154 Bodoni Book (Linotype)

A B C D E F G H I J K L M N O P Q R S T U V W X Y Z &

155 Corvinus

A B C D E F G H I J K L M N O P Q R S T U V W X Y Z &

ABRUPT CONTRAST STRAIGHT SERIFS
(MODERN SERIF)

156 Didot

A B C D E F G H I J K L M N O P Q R S T U V W X Y Z &

157 Egmont

A B C D E F G H I J K L M N O P Q R S T U V W X Y Z &

Auriga
Basilia
Bauer Bodoni
Bodoni Book
(Linotype)
Corvinus
Didot
Egmont
Fairfield
Tiemann
Torino

158 Fairfield

A B C D E F G H I J K L M N O P Q R S T U V W X Y Z &

159 Tiemann

A B C D E F G H I J K L M N O P Q R S T U V W X Y Z &

160 Torino

A B C D E F G H I J K L M N O P Q R S T U V W X Y Z &

* These letters show special or 'style' characteristics. (NB. J, Q, & and g will usually vary from one typeface to another).

Auriga 151

* * * * *
abcdefghijklmnopqrstuvwxyz1234567890

Basilia 152

* * *
abcdefghijklmnopqrstuvwxyz1234567890

Bauer Bodoni 153

* * * * *
abcdefghijklmnopqrstuvwxyz1234567890

Bodoni Book (Linotype) 154

* * *
abcdefghijklmnopqrstuvwxyz1234567890

Corvinus 155

* * * * *
abcdefghijklmnopqrstuvwxyz1234567890

Didot 156

* * * * *
abcdefghijklmnopqrstuvwxyz1234567890

Egmont 157

* * * * * *
abcdefghijklmnopqrstuvwxyz1234567890

Fairfield 158

* * * *
abcdefghijklmnopqrstuvwxyz1234567890

Tiemann 159

* * *
abcdefghijklmnopqrstuvwxyz1234567890

Torino 160

* * * *
abcdefghijklmnopqrstuvwxyz1234567890

ABRUPT CONTRAST STRAIGHT SERIFS (MODERN SERIF)

Auriga
Basilia
Bauer Bodoni
Bodoni Book (Linotype)
Corvinus
Didot
Egmont
Fairfield
Tiemann
Torino

NB. On lower case letters generally look at the x height and length of ascenders and descenders.

161 Walbaum (Linotype)

ABCDEFGHIJKLMNOPQRSTUVWXYZ&

line serifs
black face

162 Bodoni 135 (Monotype)

ABCDEFGHIJKLMNOPQRSTUVWXYZ&

163 Bodoni (Haas)

ABCDEFGHIJKLMNOPQRSTUVWXYZ&

164 Craw Modern

ABCDEFGHIJKLMNOPQRSTUVWXYZ&

165 ITC Fenice

ABCDEFGHIJKLMNOPQRSTUVWXYZ&

**ABRUPT CONTRAST
STRAIGHT SERIFS
(MODERN SERIF)**

Walbaum (Linotype)
Bodoni 135 (Monotype)
Bodoni (Haas)
Craw Modern
ITC Fenice
Modern (Linotype)
Walbaum Book
(Berthold)
Walbaum (Monotype)
ITC Zapf Book
Albion 42

166 Modern (Linotype)

ABCDEFGHIJKLMNOPQRSTUVWXYZ&

167 Walbaum Book (Berthold)

ABCDEFGHIJKLMNOPQRSTUVWXYZ&

168 Walbaum (Monotype)

ABCDEFGHIJKLMNOPQRSTUVWXYZ&

169 ITC Zapf Book

ABCDEFGHIJKLMNOPQRSTUVWXYZ&

bracketed
serifs

170 Albion 42

ABCDEFGHIJKLMNOPQRSTUVWXYZ&

These letters show special or 'style' characteristics. (NB. J, Q, & and g will usually vary from one typeface to another).

Walbaum (Linotype) **161**

abcdefghijklmnopqrstuvwxyz1234567890

Bodoni 135 (Monotype) **162**

abcdefghijklmnopqrstuvwxyz1234567890

Bodoni (Haas) **163**

abcdefghijklmnopqrstuvwxyz1234567890

Craw Modern **164**

abcdefghijklmnopqrstuvwxyz1234567890

ITC Fenice **165**

abcdefghijklmnopqrstuvwxyz1234567890

Modern (Linotype) **166**

abcdefghijklmnopqrstuvwxyz1234567890

Walbaum Book (Berthold) **167**

abcdefghijklmnopqrstuvwxyz1234567890

Walbaum (Monotype) **168**

abcdefghijklmnopqrstuvwxyz1234567890

ITC Zapf Book **169**

abcdefghijklmnopqrstuvwxyz1234567890

Albion 42 **170**

abcdefghijklmnopqrstuvwxyz1234567890

ABRUPT CONTRAST STRAIGHT SERIFS (MODERN SERIF)

Walbaum (Linotype)
Bodoni 135 (Monotype)
Bodoni (Haas)
Craw Modern
ITC Fenice
Modern (Linotype)
Walbaum Book (Berthold)
Walbaum (Monotype)
ITC Zapf Book
Albion 42

NB. On lower case letters generally look at the x height and length of ascenders and descenders.

171 Augustea
ABCDEFGHIJKLMNOPQRSTUVWXYZ&

172 Bell
ABCDEFGHIJKLMNOPQRSTUVWXYZ&

173 Bruce Old Style
ABCDEFGHIJKLMNOPQRSTUVWXYZ&

174 Caledonia
ABCDEFGHIJKLMNOPQRSTUVWXYZ&

175 ITC Century
ABCDEFGHIJKLMNOPQRSTUVWXYZ&

176 Century Nova
ABCDEFGHIJKLMNOPQRSTUVWXYZ&

177 De Vinne
ABCDEFGHIJKLMNOPQRSTUVWXYZ&

178 Madison
ABCDEFGHIJKLMNOPQRSTUVWXYZ&

179 Modern No 20
ABCDEFGHIJKLMNOPQRSTUVWXYZ&

180 Neo Didot
ABCDEFGHIJKLMNOPQRSTUVWXYZ&

ABRUPT CONTRAST STRAIGHT SERIFS (MODERN SERIF)

Augustea
Bell
Bruce Old Style
Caledonia
ITC Century
Century Nova
De Vinne
Madison
Modern No 20
Neo Didot

These letters show special or 'style' characteristics. (NB. J, Q, & and g will usually vary from one typeface to another).

Augustea 171

* * * * * *
abcdefghijklmnopqrstuvwxyz1234567890

Bell 172

* * * * * *
abcdefghijklmnopqrstuvwxyz1234567890

Bruce Old Style 173

* * * * *
abcdefghijklmnopqrstuvwxyz1234567890

Caledonia 174

* * * * *
abcdefghijklmnopqrstuvwxyz1234567890

ITC Century 175

* * * * * * *
abcdefghijklmnopqrstuvwxyz1234567890

Century Nova 176

* * * * * * *
abcdefghijklmnopqrstuvwxyz1234567890

De Vinne 177

* * * *
abcdefghijklmnopqrstuvwxyz1234567890

Madison 178

* * * *
abcdefghijklmnopqrstuvwxyz1234567890

Modern No 20 179

* * * *
abcdefghijklmnopqrstuvwxyz1234567890

Neo Didot 180

* * *
abcdefghijklmnopqrstuvwxyz1234567890

ABRUPT CONTRAST STRAIGHT SERIFS (MODERN SERIF)

od

Augustea
Bell
Bruce Old Style
Caledonia
ITC Century
Century Nova
De Vinne
Madison
Modern No 20
Neo Didot

NB. On lower case letters generally look at the x height and length of ascenders and descenders.

181 Paganini

ABCDEFGHIJKLMNOPQRSTUVWXYZ&

182 Photina

ABCDEFGHIJKLMNOPQRSTUVWXYZ&

183 Pilgrim

ABCDEFGHIJKLMNOPQRSTUVWXYZ&

184 Promotor

ABCDEFGHIJKLMNOPQRSTUVWXYZ&

185 Scotch Roman (Monotype)

ABCDEFGHIJKLMNOPQRSTUVWXYZ&

186 Scotch 2 (Linotype)

ABCDEFGHIJKLMNOPQRSTUVWXYZ&

187 Walbaum Standard (Berthold)

ABCDEFGHIJKLMNOPQRSTUVWXYZ&

* These letters show special or 'style' characteristics. (NB. J, Q, & and g will usually vary from one typeface to another).

ABRUPT CONTRAST STRAIGHT SERIFS (MODERN SERIF)

Paganini
Photina
Pilgrim
Promotor
Scotch Roman
(Monotype)
Scotch 2 (Linotype)
Walbaum Standard
(Berthold)

Paganini **181**

abcdefghijklmnopqrstuvwxyz1234567890

Photina **182**

abcdefghijklmnopqrstuvwxyz1234567890

Pilgrim **183**

abcdefghijklmnopqrstuvwxyz1234567890

Promotor **184**

abcdefghijklmnopqrstuvwxyz1234567890

Scotch Roman (Monotype) **185**

abcdefghijklmnopqrstuvwxyz1234567890

Scotch 2 (Linotype) **186**

abcdefghijklmnopqrstuvwxyz1234567890

Walbaum Standard (Berthold) **187**

abcdefghijklmnopqrstuvwxyz1234567890

NB. On lower case letters generally look at the x height and length of ascenders and descenders.

ABRUPT CONTRAST STRAIGHT SERIFS (MODERN SERIF)

Paganini
Photina
Pilgrim
Promotor
Scotch Roman
(Monotype)
Scotch 2 (Linotype)
Walbaum Standard
(Berthold)

6. SLAB SERIF

Specimen nos	Basic characteristics		Secondary characteristics	
188-200	I	*square slab*	g	*single storey*	e.g. **197** Rockwell
201-203	„		g	*double storey*	e.g. **203** Schadow Antiqua
204-205	I	*bracketed slab*	g	*single storey*	e.g. **205** Egyptian 505
206-213	„		g	*double storey*	e.g. **209** Clarendon (Linotype)
214-217	I	*rounded slab*			e.g. **214** ITC American Typewriter

NB. *Typefaces in each group are arranged in alphabetical order.*

SLAB SERIF

II

square
slab
single
storey g

188 A & S Gallatin

ABCDEFGHIJKLMNOPQRSTUVWXYZ&

189 Beton

ABCDEFGHIJKLMNOPQRSTUVWXYZ&

190 Calvert

ABCDEFGHIJKLMNOPQRSTUVWXYZ&

191 Candida

ABCDEFGHIJKLMNOPQRSTUVWXYZ&

192 City

ABCDEFGHIJKLMNOPQRSTUVWXYZ&

193 Glypha 55

ABCDEFGHIJKLMNOPQRSTUVWXYZ&

194 ITC Lubalin Graph

ABCDEFGHIJKLMNOPQRSTUVWXYZ&

195 ITC Lubalin Graph Extra Light

ABCDEFGHIJKLMNOPQRSTUVWXYZ&

196 Memphis

ABCDEFGHIJKLMNOPQRSTUVWXYZ&

197 Rockwell

ABCDEFGHIJKLMNOPQRSTUVWXYZ&

SLAB SERIF

II

A & S Gallatin
Beton
Calvert
Candida
City
Glypha 55
ITC Lubalin Graph
ITC Lubalin Graph
Extra Light
Memphis
Rockwell

These letters show special or 'style' characteristics. (NB. J, Q, & and g will usually vary from one typeface to another).

A & S Gallatin **188**

*   *   *   *   *

abcdefghijklmnopqrstuvwxyz1234567890

Beton **189**

*   *   *   * *   *

abcdefghijklmnopqrstuvwxyz1234567890

Calvert **190**

*   *   *   *   *

abcdefghijklmnopqrstuvwxyz1234567890

Candida **191**

*   *   *   *   *

abcdefghijklmnopqrstuvwxyz1234567890

City **192**

*   *   *   *   *

abcdefghijklmnopqrstuvwxyz1234567890

Glypha 55 **193**

*   *   *   *

abcdefghijklmnopqrstuvwxyz1234567890

ITC Lubalin Graph **194**

*   *   *   *   *   *

abcdefghijklmnopqrstuvwxyz1234567890

ITC Lubalin Graph Extra Light **195**

*   *   *   *   *   *

abcdefghijklmnopqrstuvwxyz1234567890

Memphis **196**

*   *   *   *   *

abcdefghijklmnopqrstuvwxyz1234567890

Rockwell **197**

*   *   *   *   *

abcdefghijklmnopqrstuvwxyz1234567890

NB. On lower case letters generally look at the x height and length of ascenders and descenders.

198 Serifa 55

ABCDEFGHIJKLMNOPQRSTUVWXYZ&

199 Stymie (ATF)

ABCDEFGHIJKLMNOPQRSTUVWXYZ&

200 ITC Stymie Hairline

ABCDEFGHIJKLMNOPQRSTUVWXYZ&

square slab
double storey g

201 Antique No 5

ABCDEFGHIJKLMNOPQRSTUVWXYZ&

202 Egyptian 173

ABCDEFGHIJKLMNOPQRSTUVWXYZ&

203 Schadow Antiqua

ABCDEFGHIJKLMNOPQRSTUVWXYZ&

bracketed slab
single storey g

204 Aachen

ABCDEFGHIJKLMNOPQRSTUVWXYZ&

205 Egyptian 505

ABCDEFGHIJKLMNOPQRSTUVWXYZ&

bracketed slab
double storey g

206 Antique No 3

ABCDEFGHIJKLMNOPQRSTUVWXYZ&

207 Consort

ABCDEFGHIJKLMNOPQRSTUVWXYZ&

* These letters show special or 'style' characteristics. (NB. J, Q, & and g will usually vary from one typeface to another).

Serifa 55 **198**

abcdefghijklmnopqrstuvwxyz1234567890

Stymie (ATF) **199**

abcdefghijklmnopqrstuvwxyz1234567890

ITC Stymie Hairline **200**

abcdefghijklmnopqrstuvwxyz1234567890

Antique No 5 **201**

abcdefghijklmnopqrstuvwxyz1234567890

Egyptian 173 **202**

abcdefghijklmnopqrstuvwxyz1234567890

Schadow Antiqua **203**

abcdefghijklmnopqrstuvwxyz1234567890

Aachen **204**

abcdefghijklmnopqrstuvwxyz1234567890

Egyptian 505 **205**

abcdefghijklmnopqrstuvwxyz1234567890

Antique No 3 **206**

abcdefghijklmnopqrstuvwxyz1234567890

Consort **207**

abcdefghijklmnopqrstuvwxyz1234567890

SLAB SERIF

II

Serifa 55
Stymie (ATF)
ITC Stymie Hairline
Antique No 5
Egyptian 173
Schadow Antiqua
Aachen
Egyptian 505
Antique No 3
Consort

NB. On lower case letters generally look at the x height and length of ascenders and descenders.

208 Clarendon 12 (Monotype)

ABCDEFGHIJKLMNOPQRSTUVWXYZ&

209 Clarendon (Linotype)

ABCDEFGHIJKLMNOPQRSTUVWXYZ&

210 Egyptienne F 55

ABCDEFGHIJKLMNOPQRSTUVWXYZ&

211 New Clarendon

ABCDEFGHIJKLMNOPQRSTUVWXYZ&

212 Egizio

ABCDEFGHIJKLMNOPQRSTUVWXYZ&

213 Fortune

ABCDEFGHIJKLMNOPQRSTUVWXYZ&

rounded slab **214** ITC American Typewriter

ABCDEFGHIJKLMNOPQRSTUVWXYZ&

215 Clarinda Typewriter

ABCDEFGHIJKLMNOPQRSTUVWXYZ&

216 Linotype Typewriter

ABCDEFGHIJKLMNOPQRSTUVWXYZ&

217 Monotype Typewriter 105

ABCDEFGHIJKLMNOPQRSTUVWXYZ

SLAB SERIF

11

Clarendon 12 (Monotype)
Clarendon (Linotype)
Egyptienne F 55
New Clarendon
Egizio
Fortune
ITC American Typewriter
Clarinda Typewriter
Linotype Typewriter
Monotype Typewriter 105

* These letters show special or 'style' characteristics. (NB. J, Q, & and g will usually vary from one typeface to another).

Clarendon 12 (Monotype) **208**

* * * *
abcdefghijklmnopqrstuvwxyz**1234567890**

Clarendon (Linotype) **209**

* * * *
abcdefghijklmnopqrstuvwxyz1234567890

Egyptienne F 55 **210**

* * * *
abcdefghijklmnopqrstuvwxyz1234567890

New Clarendon **211**

* * * *
abcdefghijklmnopqrstuvwxyz1234567890

Egizio **212**

* * * * *
abcdefghijklmnopqrstuvwxyz1234567890

Fortune **213**

* * * *
abcdefghijklmnopqrstuvwxyz1234567890

ITC American Typewriter **214**

* * * *
abcdefghijklmnopqrstuvwxyz1234567890

Clarinda Typewriter **215**

* *
abcdefghijklmnopqrstuvwxyz1234567890

Linotype Typewriter **216**

* *
abcdefghijklmnopqrstuvwxyz1234567890

Monotype Typewriter 105 **217**

* *
abcdefghijklmnopqrstuvwxyz1234567890

NB. On lower case letters generally look at the x height and length of ascenders and descenders.

7. WEDGE SERIF
(HYBRID SERIF)

Specimen nos		Basic characteristics	
218-229	**I** or **I**	*wedge-ended or small wedge serifs*	e.g. **218** Albertus, **229** Romana
230-235	**I**	*wedge-shaped serifs*	e.g. **233** Meridien
236-238	**I**	*line-ended serifs*	e.g. **236** Copperplate Gothic
239-240	**l**	*half serifs*	e.g. **240** Romic

NB. *Typefaces in each group are arranged in alphabetical order.*

WEDGE SERIF
(HYBRID SERIF)

wedge-ended or small wedge serifs **218** Albertus

ABCDEFGHIJKLMNOPQRSTUVWXYZ&

219 Americana

ABCDEFGHIJKLMNOPQRSTUVWXYZ&

220 Flange

ABCDEFGHIJKLMNOPQRSTUVWXYZ&

221 French Old Style

ABCDEFGHI JKLMNOPQRSTUVWXYZ&

222 ITC Friz Quadrata

ABCDEFGHIJKLMNOPQRSTUVWXYZ&

223 Icone

ABCDEFGHIJKLMNOPQRSTUVWXYZ&

224 ITC Korinna

ABCDEFGHIJKLMNOPQRSTUVWXYZ&

225 ITC Newtext

ABCDEFGHIJKLMNOPQRSTUVWXYZ&

226 ITC Novarese

ABCDEFGHIJKLMNOPQRSTUVWXYZ&

227 Poppl-Laudatio

ABCDEFGHIJKLMNOPQRSTUVWXYZ&

Albertus
Americana
Flange
French Old Style
ITC Friz Quadrata
Icone
ITC Korinna
ITC Newtext
ITC Novarese
Poppl-Laudatio

WEDGE SERIF (HYBRID SERIF)

11

* These letters show special or 'style' characteristics. (NB. J, Q, & and g will usually vary from one typeface to another).

Albertus **218**

abcdefghijklmnopqrstuvwxyz1234567890

Americana **219**

abcdefghijklmnopqrstuvwxyz1234567890

Flange **220**

abcdefghijklmnopqrstuvwxyz1234567890

French Old Style **221**

abcdefghijklmnopqrstuvwxyz1234567890

ITC Friz Quadrata **222**

abcdefghijklmnopqrstuvwxyz1234567890

Icone **223**

abcdefghijklmnopqrstuvwxyz1234567890

ITC Korinna **224**

abcdefghijklmnopqrstuvwxyz1234567890

ITC Newtext **225**

abcdefghijklmnopqrstuvwxyz1234567890

ITC Novarese **226**

abcdefghijklmnopqrstuvwxyz1234567890

Poppl-Laudatio **227**

abcdefghijklmnopqrstuvwxyz1234567890

Albertus
Americana
Flange
French Old Style
ITC Friz Quadrata
Icone
ITC Korinna
ITC Newtext
ITC Novarese
Poppl-Laudatio

WEDGE SERIF
(HYBRID SERIF)

II

NB. On lower case letters generally look at the x height and length of ascenders and descenders.

228 ITC Quorum

ABCDEFGHIJKLMNOPQRSTUVWXYZ&

229 Romana

ABCDEFGHIJKLMNOPQRSTUVWXYZ&

wedge-shaped serifs

230 ITC Barcelona

ABCDEFGHIJKLMNOPQRSTUVWXYZ&

231 Biltmore

ABCDEFGHIJKLMNOPQRSTUVWXYZ&

232 ITC LSC Book

ABCDEFGHIJKLMNOPQRSTUVWXYZ&

233 Meridien

ABCDEFGHIJKLMNOPQRSTUVWXYZ&

ITC Quorum
Romana
ITC Barcelona
Biltmore
ITC LSC Book
Meridien
Octavian
Pegasus
Copperplate Gothic
ITC Serif Gothic

234 Octavian

ABCDEFGHIJKLMNOPQRSTUVWXYZ&

235 Pegasus

ABCDEFGHIJKLMNOPQRSTUVWXYZ&

WEDGE SERIF
(HYBRID SERIF)

line-ended serifs

236 Copperplate Gothic

ABCDEFGHIJKLMNOPQRSTUVWXYZ&

237 ITC Serif Gothic

ABCDEFGHIJKLMNOPQRSTUVWXYZ&

* These letters show special or 'style' characteristics. (NB. J, Q, & and g will usually vary from one typeface to another).

ITC Quorum **228**

* * * * *
abcdefghijklmnopqrstuvwxyz1234567890

Romana **229**

* * * * *
abcdefghijklmnopqrstuvwxyz1234567890

ITC Barcelona **230**

* * * * * *
abcdefghijklmnopqrstuvwxyz1234567890

Biltmore **231**

* * * *
abcdefghijklmnopqrstuvwxyz1234567890

ITC LSC Book **232**

* * * *
abcdefghijklmnopqrstuvwxyz1234567890

Meridien **233**

* * * *
abcdefghijklmnopqrstuvwxyz1234567890

Octavian **234**

* * * *
abcdefghijklmnopqrstuvwxyz1234567890

Pegasus **235**

* * *
abcdefghijklmnopqrstuvwxyz1234567890

Copperplate Gothic **236**

small capitals
*
ABCDEFGHIJKLMNOPQRSTUVWXYZ1234567890

ITC Serif Gothic **237**

* * *
abcdefghijklmnopqrstuvwxyz1234567890

ITC Quorum
Romana
ITC Barcelona
Biltmore
ITC LSC Book
Meridien
Octavian
Pegasus
Copperplate Gothic
ITC Serif Gothic

WEDGE SERIF
(HYBRID SERIF)

11

NB. On lower case letters generally look at the x height and length of ascenders and descenders.

238 Spartan 140 (Monotype)

ABCDEFGHIJKLMNOPQRSTUVWXYZ&

half serifs

239 Parsons

ABCDEFGHIJKLMNOPQRSTUVWXYZ&

240 Romic

ABCDEFGHIJKLMNOPQRSTUVWXYZ&

* These letters show special or 'style' characteristics. (NB. J, Q, & and g will usually vary from one typeface to another).

Spartan 140
(Monotype)
Parsons
Romic

WEDGE SERIF
(HYBRID SERIF)

II

Spartan 140 (Monotype) **238**

1234567890 _{no lower case}

Parsons **239**

abcdefghijklmnopqrstuvwxyz1234567890

Romic **240**

abcdefghijklmnopqrstuvwxyz1234567890

NB. Nos 241-244 have been deleted.

NB. On lower case letters generally look at the x height and length of ascenders and descenders.

Spartan 140
(Monotype)
Parsons
Romic

WEDGE SERIF
(HYBRID SERIF)

11

8. SANS SERIF

Specimen nos	Basic characteristics	Secondary characteristics	
245-248	G wide, no spur	E wide	e.g. **245** Adonis
249-257	G wide, no spur	E narrow	e.g. **254** Futura
258-265	G medium width, no spur	G round base	e.g. **259** Gill Sans
266-267	,,	G flatter base	e.g. **267** Univers 55
268-269	,,	G no bar, stressed strokes	e.g. **268** Optima
270	,,	G no bar, unstressed strokes	e.g. **270** Syntax
271-272	G narrow, no spur (or bar)		e.g. **271** Antique Olive
273	G wide, with spur		e.g. **273** Akzidenz Grotesk
274-283	G medium width, with spur		e.g. **279** Helvetica
284-289	G narrow, with spur		e.g. **287** News Gothic

NB. Typefaces in each group are arranged in alphabetical order.

continued on next page

SANS SERIF

GG

continued from previous page

Specimen nos

290-294	Gg	*(sans serif)* square	e.g. **291** Eurostile
295	Gg	*sloped*	e.g. **295** ITC Eras
296-301	Gg	*rounded*	e.g. **296** ITC Bauhaus
302-304	G	*electronic or machine-read*	e.g. **303** OCR-A

N.B. *Typefaces in each group are arranged in alphabetical order.*

SANS SERIF

Gg

*wide
capital G
no spur
wide
capital E*

245 Adonis

ABCDEFGHIJKLMNOPQRSTUVWXYZ&

246 Doric

ABCDEFGHIJKLMNOPQRSTUVWXYZ&

247 2-Line Block Gothic

ABCDEFGHIJKLMNOPQRSTUVWXYZ&

248 4-Line Block Gothic

ABCDEFGHIJKLMNOPQRSTUVWXYZ &

*wide
capital G
no spur
narrow
capital E*

249 Adsans

ABCDEFGHIJKLMNOPQRSTUVWXYZ&

250 ITC Avant Garde Gothic

ABCDEFGHIJKLMNOPQRSTUVWXYZ&

251 Bernhard Gothic

ABCDEFGHIJKLMNOPQRSTUVWXYZ&

252 20th Century

ABCDEFGHIJKLMNOPQRSTUVWXYZ&

253 Erbar

ABCDEFGHIJKLMNOPQRSTUVWXYZ&

254 Futura

ABCDEFGHIJKLMNOPQRSTUVWXYZ&

Adonis
Doric
2-Line Block Gothic
4-Line Block Gothic
Adsans
ITC Avant Garde Gothic
Bernhard Gothic
20th Century
Erbar
Futura

SANS SERIF

G G

* These letters show special or 'style' characteristics. (N.B. J, Q, & and g will usually vary from one typeface to another).

Adonis 245

* * * *
abcdefghijklmnopqrstuvwxyz1234567890

Doric 246

* * * *
abcdefghijklmnopqrstuvwxyz1234567890

small capitals (no lower case)

2-Line Block Gothic 247

* * *
ABCDEFGHIJKLMNOPQRSTUVWXYZ1234567890

small capitals (no lower case)

4-Line Block Gothic 248

* * *
ABCDEFGHIJKLMNOPQRSTUVWXYZ1234567890

Adsans 249

* * **
abcdefghijklmnopqrstuvwxyz1234567890

ITC Avant Garde Gothic 250

* * * * *
abcdefghijklmnopqrstuvwxyz1234567890

Bernhard Gothic 251

* * * *
abcdefghijklmnopqrstuvwxyz1234567890

20th Century 252

* * * ** * * *
abcdefghijklmnopqrstuvwxyz1234567890

Erbar 253

* * * *
abcdefghijklmnopqrstuvwxyz1234567890

Futura 254

* * * * * *
abcdefghijklmnopqrstuvwxyz1234567890

Adonis
Doric
2-Line Block Gothic
4-Line Block Gothic
Adsans
ITC Avant Garde Gothic
Bernhard Gothic
20th Century
Erbar
Futura

SANS SERIF

G G

NB. On lower case letters generally look at the x height and length of ascenders and descenders.

255 Neuzeit-Grotesk

ABCDEFGHIJKLMNOPQRSTUVWXYZ&

256 Nobel

ABCDEFGHIJKLMNOPQRSTUVWXYZ&

257 Spartan

ABCDEFGHIJKLMNOPQRSTUVWXYZ&

*medium
width
capital G
no spur
round base*

258 Cable (Klingspor)

ABCDEFGHIJKLMNOPQRSTUVWXYZ&

259 Gill Sans

ABCDEFGHIJKLMNOPQRSTUVWXYZ&

260 Granby

ABCDEFGHIJKLMNOPQRSTUVWXYZ&

261 Grotesque 215

ABCDEFGHIJKLMNOPQRSTUVWXYZ&

Neuzeit Grotesk
Nobel
Spartan
Cable (Klingspor)
Gill Sans
Granby
Grotesque 215
ITC Kabel
Metro
Tempo

262 ITC Kabel

ABCDEFGHIJKLMNOPQRSTUVWXYZ&

263 Metro

ABCDEFGHIJKLMNOPQRSTUVWXYZ&

SANS SERIF

G G

264 Tempo

ABCDEFGHIJKLMNOPQRSTUVWXYZ&

* These letters show special or 'style' characteristics. (NB. J, Q, & and g will usually vary from one typeface to another).

Neuzeit-Grotesk **255**

abcdefghijklmnopqrstuvwxyz1234567890

Nobel **256**

abcdefghijklmnopqrstuvwxyz1234567890

Spartan **257**

abcdefghijklmnopqrstuvwxyz1234567890

Cable (Klingspor) **258**

abcdefghijklmnopqrstuvwxyz1234567890

Gill Sans **259**

abcdefghijklmnopqrstuvwxyz1234567890

Granby **260**

abcdefghijklmnopqrstuvwxyz1234567890

Grotesque 215 **261**

abcdefghijklmnopqrstuvwxyz1234567890

ITC Kabel **262**

abcdefghijklmnopqrstuvwxyz1234567890

Metro **263**

abcdefghijklmnopqrstuvwxyz1234567890

Tempo **264**

abcdefghijklmnopqrstuvwxyz1234567890

Neuzeit Grotesk
Nobel
Spartan
Cable (Klingspor)
Gill Sans
Granby
Grotesque 215
ITC Kabel
Metro
Tempo

SANS SERIF

G G

NB. On lower case letters generally look at the x height and length of ascenders and descenders.

265 Venus

* * * * * *
ABCDEFGHIJKLMNOPQRSTUVWXYZ&

medium
with capital G
no spur
flatter base

266 Frutiger

* * *
ABCDEFGHIJKLMNOPQRSTUVWXYZ&

267 Univers 55

* * * * *
ABCDEFGHIJKLMNOPQRSTUVWXYZ&

medium
width
capital G
no spur
no bar
stressed
strokes

268 Optima

* * * * * *
ABCDEFGHIJKLMNOPQRSTUVWXYZ&

269 ITC Souvenir Gothic

* * * * *
ABCDEFGHIJKLMNOPQRSTUVWXYZ&

medium
width
capital G
no spur
no bar
unstressed
strokes

270 Syntax

* * *
ABCDEFGHIJKLMNOPQRSTUVWXYZ&

narrow
capital G
no spur
no bar

271 Antique Olive

* * * *
ABCDEFGHIJKLMNOPQRSTUVWXYZ&

Venus
Frutiger
Univers 55
Optima
ITC Souvenir Gothic
Syntax
Antique Olive
Clearface Gothic
Akzidenz Grotesk
Berthold Imago

SANS SERIF

G G

272 Clearface Gothic

* * * *
ABCDEFGHIJKLMNOPQRSTUVWXYZ&

wide
capital G
with spur

273 Akzidenz Grotesk

* * * * *
ABCDEFGHIJKLMNOPQRSTUVWXYZ&

medium
width
capital G
with spur

274 Berthold Imago

* * *
ABCDEFGHIJKLMNOPQRSTUVWXYZ&

* These letters show special or 'style' characteristics. (NB. J, Q, & and g will usually vary from one typeface to another).

Venus **265**

* * * *
abcdefghijklmnopqrstuvwxyz1234567890

Frutiger **266**

* * * * *
abcdefghijklmnopqrstuvwxyz1234567890

Univers 55 **267**

* * * *
abcdefghijklmnopqrstuvwxyz1234567890

Optima **268**

* * * *
abcdefghijklmnopqrstuvwxyz1234567890

ITC Souvenir Gothic **269**

* *
abcdefghijklmnopqrstuvwxyz**1234567890**

Syntax **270**

* * *
abcdefghijklmnopqrstuvwxyz1234567890

Antique Olive **271**

* * * * *
abcdefghijklmnopqrstuvwxyz1234567890

Clearface Gothic **272**

* * * *
abcdefghijklmnopqrstuvwxyz1234567890

Akzidenz Grotesk **273**

* * * *
abcdefghijklmnopqrstuvwxyz1234567890

Berthold Imago **274**

* * * *
abcdefghijklmnopqrstuvwxyz1234567890

Venus
Frutiger
Univers 55
Optima
ITC Souvenir Gothic
Syntax
Antique Olive
Clearface Gothic
Akzidenz Grotesk
Berthold Imago

SANS SERIF

G G

NB. On lower case letters generally look at the x height and length of ascenders and descenders.

275 Folio

ABCDEFGHIJKLMNOPQRSTUVWXYZ&

276 Franklin Gothic (ATF)

ABCDEFGHIJKLMNOPQRSTUVWXYZ&

277 ITC Franklin Gothic

ABCDEFGHIJKLMNOPQRSTUVWXYZ&

278 Haas Unica

ABCDEFGHIJKLMNOPQRSTUVWXYZ&

279 Helvetica

ABCDEFGHIJKLMNOPQRSTUVWXYZ&

280 Mercator

ABCDEFGHIJKLMNOPQRSTUVWXYZ&

281 Standard

ABCDEFGHIJKLMNOPQRSTUVWXYZ&

282 Transport

ABCDEFGHIJKLMNOPQRSTUVWXYZ&

283 Video

ABCDEFGHIJKLMNOPQRSTUVWXYZ&

284 Bell Centennial

ABCDEFGHIJKLMNOPQRSTUVWXYZ&

Folio
Franklin Gothic (ATF)
ITC Franklin Gothic
Haas Unica
Helvetica
Mercator
Standard
Transport
Video
Bell Centennial

SANS SERIF

G G

*narrow
capital G
with spur*

These letters show special or 'style' characteristics. (NB. J, Q, & and g will usually vary from one typeface to another).

Folio **275**

* * * * *
abcdefghijklmnopqrstuvwxyz1234567890

Franklin Gothic (ATF) **276**

* * * * *   *   *
abcdefghijklmnopqrstuvwxyz**1234567890**

ITC Franklin Gothic **277**

* * * *   *
abcdefghijklmnopqrstuvwxyz1234567890

Haas Unica **278**

* * *   *
abcdefghijklmnopqrstuvwxyz1234567890

Helvetica **279**

* * *   *
abcdefghijklmnopqrstuvwxyz1234567890

Mercator **280**

*   *   *   *   *
abcdefghijklmnopqrstuvwxyz1234567890

Standard **281**

*   *   *   *
abcdefghijklmnopqrstuvwxyz1234567890

Transport **282**

*   *   *   *
abcdefghijklmnopqrstuvwxyz**1234567890**

Video **283**

*   *   *   *
abcdefghijklmnopqrstuvwxyz1234567890

Bell Centennial **284**

*   *   **   *
abcdefghijklmnopqrstuvwxyz1234567890

Folio
Franklin Gothic (ATF)
ITC Franklin Gothic
Haas Unica
Helvetica
Mercator
Standard
Transport
Video
Bell Centennial

SANS SERIF

GG

NB. On lower case letters generally look at the x height and length of ascenders and descenders.

285 Bell Gothic

ABCDEFGHIJKLMNOPQRSTUVWXYZ&

286 Lightline Gothic

ABCDEFGHIJKLMNOPQRSTUVWXYZ&

287 News Gothic

ABCDEFGHIJKLMNOPQRSTUVWXYZ&

288 Record Gothic

ABCDEFGHIJKLMNOPQRSTUVWXYZ&

289 Trade Gothic

ABCDEFGHIJKLMNOPQRSTUVWXYZ&

square-shaped

290 Bank Gothic

ABCDEFGHIJKLMNOPQRSTUVWXYZ&

291 Eurostile

ABCDEFGHIJKLMNOPQRSTUVWXYZ&

292 Eurostile Extended No 2

ABCDEFGHIJKLMNOPQRSTUVWXYZ&

293 Heldustry

ABCDEFGHIJKLMNOPQRSTUVWXYZ&

294 Microgramma

ABCDEFGHIJKLMNOPQRSTUVWXYZ&

* These letters show special or 'style' characteristics. (NB. J, Q, & and g will usually vary from one typeface to another).

Bell Gothic
Lightline Gothic
News Gothic
Record Gothic
Trade Gothic
Bank Gothic
Eurostile
Eurostile Extended No 2
Heldustry
Microgramma

SANS SERIF

G G

Bell Gothic **285**

* * *** *

abcdefghijklmnopqrstuvwxyz1234567890

Lightline Gothic **286**

* * * *

abcdefghijklmnopqrstuvwxyz1234567890

News Gothic **287**

* * * *

abcdefghijklmnopqrstuvwxyz1234567890

Record Gothic **288**

* * * *

abcdefghijklmnopqrstuvwxyz1234567890

Trade Gothic **289**

* * * *

abcdefghijklmnopqrstuvwxyz1234567890

Bank Gothic **290**

small capitals

* * *

ABCDEFGHIJKLMNOPQRSTUVWXYZ 1234567890

Eurostile **291**

* * *

abcdefghijklmnopqrstuvwxyz1234567890

Eurostile Extended No 2 **292**

* * *

abcdefghijklmnopqrstuvwxyz1234567890

Heldustry **293**

* * * *

abcdefghijklmnopqrstuvwxyz1234567890

Microgramma **294**

* *

1234567890 *no lower case*

Bell Gothic
Lightline Gothic
News Gothic
Record Gothic
Trade Gothic
Bank Gothic
Eurostile
Eurostile Extended No 2
Heldustry
Microgramma

SANS SERIF

NB. On lower case letters generally look at the x height and length of ascenders and descenders.

sloped

295 ITC Eras

ABCDEFGHIJKLMNOPQRSTUVWXYZ&

rounded

296 ITC Bauhaus

ABCDEFGHIJKLMNOPQRSTUVWXYZ&

297 ITC Benguiat Gothic

ABCDEFGHIJKLMNOPQRSTUVWXYZ&

298 Berliner Grotesk

ABCDEFGHIJKLMNOPQRSTUVWXYZ&

299 Churchward 70

ABCDEFGHIJKLMNOPQRSTUVWXYZ&

300 ITC Ronda

ABCDEFGHIJKLMNOPQRSTUVWXYZ&

301 VAG Rundschrift

ABCDEFGHIJKLMNOPQRSTUVWXYZ&

electronic or machine read

302 IC – Alphabet

ABCDEFGHIJKLMNOPQRSTUVWXYZ

303 OCR-A

ABCDEFGHIJKLMNOPQRSTUVWXYZ

304 OCR-B

ABCDEFGHIJKLMNOPQRSTUVWXYZ&

ITC Eras
ITC Bauhaus
ITC Benguiat Gothic
Berliner Grotesk
Churchward 70
ITC Ronda
VAG Rundschrift
IC – Alphabet
OCR-A
OCR-B

SANS SERIF

G G

* These letters show special or 'style' characteristics. (NB. J, Q, & and g will usually vary from one typeface to another).

ITC Eras **295**

* * * * * *
abcdefghijklmnopqrstuvwxyz1234567890

ITC Bauhaus **296**

* * * * *
abcdefghijklmnopqrstuvwxyz1234567890

ITC Benguiat Gothic **297**

* * *
abcdefghijklmnopqrstuvwxyz1234567890

Berliner Grotesk **298**

* * * *
abcdefghijklmnopqrstuvwxyz1234567890

Churchward 70 **299**

* * *
abcdefghijklmnopqrstuvwxyzl234567890

ITC Ronda **300**

* * * *
abcdefghijklmnopqrstuvwxyz1234567890

VAG Rundschrift **301**

* * *
abcdefghijklmnopqrstuvwxyz1234567890

IC – Alphabet **302**

*
1234567890 *no lower case*

OCR-A **303**

* *
1234567890 *no lower case*

OCR-B **304**

* * * * * *
abcdefghijklmnopqrstuvwxyz1234567890

ITC Eras
ITC Bauhaus
ITC Benguiat Gothic
Berliner Grotesk
Churchward 70
ITC Ronda
VAG Rundschrift
IC – Alphabet
OCR-A
OCR-B

SANS SERIF

G G

NB. On lower case letters generally look at the x height and length of ascenders and descenders.

TEXT TYPEFACE 'EARMARK' TABLES

THESE TABLES OFFER a method of identifying *Text* typefaces (Specimen Nos 1-304) by means of 'earmarks' or special characteristic features on individual letters. They represent an alternative but companion identification process to the *Text* typeface classification system beginning on page 12.

The tables are divided into two parts — 'Common' and 'Special Earmarks', but there is, however, a small overlap between the two parts.

'Common Earmark' Tables

These show typical, commonplace letter features and give examples of typefaces with each feature. 'Common' letters are identifiable either by their general appearance or by 'marked' features or captions. (see illustration below).

poor contrast

119 Century Schoolbook
137 Impressum
145 Primus Antiqua

153 Bauer Bodoni
156 Didot
161 Walbaum (Linotype)

'Special Earmark' Tables

These show more distinctive and unusual identifying features.

'Special earmarks' are indicated on letters by arrows, lines or captions and *Text* typefaces with each feature are listed by number below each. (see illustration below). Each letter has been 'analysed' in parts or by features generally starting from the top and working downwards to the bottom. It should be noted that the general 'style' of typefaces with the same 'earmark' can vary slightly.

27, 60, 63

35, **38**-41, 61-2, 74, 76, 99, 123-4, 132, 147

Figures are divided throughout into two kinds — 'lining' and 'non-lining'. An example of each is given below:

lining
1234567890

non-lining
1234567890

e.g. Baskerville

In both sets of tables, letters are arranged in a continuous sequence from a to z in both capital and lower case forms (plus ampersand and figures). The 'earmarks' of each letter are then divided (by rules) into groups representing *Text* typeface categories used in the book as follows:

Category Nos. 1-4 (Roman Serif) *(Specimen Nos. 1-150)*
No. 5 (Modern Serif) *(Specimen Nos. 151-187)*
No. 6 (Slab Serif) *(Specimen Nos. 188-217)*
No. 7 (Wedge Serif) *(Specimen Nos. 218-240)*
No. 8 (Sans Serif) *(Specimen Nos. 245-304)*

NB. There are no 'common earmarks' for the Wedge Serif category since it generally comprises of more 'unusual' typefaces.

Looking for 'earmarks'

1. Consult the recommended selection order for 'earmarks' on this page and choose a letter as early in the order as possible.

2. Look in the 'Common Earmark' Tables to see whether or not the specimen letter you have chosen has a 'common earmark'. If it has, then select alternative specimen letters until you find one which has features which do not appear in these tables as 'common features will not generally assist in rapid typeface identification.

3. Find this letter in the following 'Special Earmark' Tables.

4. Look through the listings of illustrated specimen letters which are divided by rules into typeface categories (as listed previously) and match your specimen against the 'earmarks' shown.

5. When you have successfully matched your specimen to one or more of the 'earmarks' then look up in turn the typeface specimens whose numbers are given below each until you identify your particular typeface specimen.

6. If specific typeface identification is not easily obtainable with the specimen letter you have chosen then select alternative letters until a positive 'photofit' picture of the typeface is achieved.

Recommended order for selecting 'earmarks':

Capital letters and ampersand:
Q, &, J, G, W, A, K, C, R, M, E, P, S, T, F, B, N, O, U, X, Y, D, H, Z, L, V, I.

Lower case letters:
g, a, j, y, k, t, f, r, q, w, e, b, s, c, d, p, m, u, x, o, v, h, n, i, l, z.

Figures:
3, 7, 5, 2, 1, 4, 9, 6, 8, 0

'Common Earmarks'

The 'common earmarks' (or typical identifying features) are indicated either by the general appearance of letters or by 'marked' features. The general 'style' of typefaces with the same 'earmark' may vary. Example typefaces with their specimen numbers are listed against each letter.

Throughout these tables 'earmarks' are divided into Text typeface categories by fine horizontal rules as described in the introduction on page 97.

Column 1 — A / B

A
- 19 Centaur
- 52 Times Roman (Linotype)
- 79 Baskerville (Linotype)

A *flat top*
- 56 Bookman
- 70 Old Style No. 7
- 86 Times Europa

A *wide flat top*
- 57 ITC Bookman
- 71 Olympian
- 138 Melior

A
- 35 Bembo
- 39 Plantin
- 76 Aster

A
- 59 Caslon Old Face No. 2
- 73 Ehrhardt
- 94 Garamond (Stempel)

A *poor contrast*
- 119 Century Schoolbook
- 137 Impressum
- 145 Primus Antiqua

A
- 153 Bauer Bodoni
- 156 Didot
- 161 Walbaum (Linotype)

A
- 196 Memphis
- 197 Rockwell
- 199 Stymie (ATF)

A
- 254 Futura
- 258 Cable (Klingspor)
- 264 Tempo

A
- 259 Gill Sans
- 267 Univers 55
- 279 Helvetica

B *equal size bowls*
- 24 ITC Clearface
- 67 Imprint
- 90 Fournier

B *bottom heavy*
- 19 Centaur
- 79 Baskerville (Linotype)
- 88 Sabon

Column 2 — B / C

B *poor contrast*
- 115 Excelsior
- 119 Century Schoolbook
- 121 Ionic 5

B
- 153 Bauer Bodoni
- 156 Didot
- 161 Walbaum (Linotype)

B
- 194 ITC Lubalin Graph
- 197 Rockwell
- 198 Serifa 55

B
- 261 Grotesque 215
- 265 Univers 55
- 279 Helvetica

C
- 5 Windsor
- 56 Bookman
- 69 Old Style No. 2

C
- 49 Goudy Catalogue
- 52 Times Roman (Linotype)
- 67 Imprint

C
- 35 Bembo
- 39 Plantin
- 92 Garamond (Stempel)

C
- 20 Horley Old Style
- 61 Caslon 540
- 79 Baskerville (Linotype)

C *poor contrast*
- 119 Century Schoolbook
- 121 Ionic 5
- 145 Primus Antiqua

C
- 171 Augustea
- 179 Modern No. 20
- 186 Scotch 2 (Linotype)

C
- 196 Memphis
- 197 Rockwell
- 198 Serifa 55

C
- 254 Futura
- 257 Spartan
- 259 Gills Sans

Column 3 — C / D / E

C
- 256 Nobel
- 261 Grotesque 215
- 273 Akzidenz Grotesque

C
- 267 Univers 55
- 275 Folio
- 279 Helvetica

D
- 39 Plantin
- 52 Times Roman (Linotype)
- 69 Old Style No. 2

D *concave*
- 49 Goudy Catalogue
- 91 Garamond (Monotype)
- 100 Concorde

D *poor contrast*
- 114 Century Expanded
- 119 Century Schoolbook
- 121 Ionic 5

D
- 153 Bauer Bodoni
- 156 Didot
- 163 Bodoni (Haas)

D
- 196 Memphis
- 197 Rockwell
- 198 Serifa 55

D
- 267 Univers 55
- 275 Folio
- 279 Helvetica

E
- 5 Windsor
- 61 Caslon 540
- 69 Old Style No. 2

E
- 35 Bembo
- 39 Plantin
- 52 Times Roman (Linotype)

E
- 153 Bauer Bodoni
- 161 Walbaum (Linotype)
- 174 Caledonia

E
- 193 Glypha 55
- 198 Serifa 55
- 199 Stymie (ATF)

Column 4 — E / F / G

E *bracketed slab*
- 207 Consort
- 209 Clarendon (Linotype)
- 212 Egizio

E *narrow*
- 253 Erbar
- 254 Futura
- 257 Spartan

E *wider*
- 267 Univers
- 279 Helvetica
- 281 Standard

F
- 5 Windsor
- 61 Caslon 540
- 69 Old Style No. 2

F
- 35 Bembo
- 39 Plantin
- 52 Times Roman (Linotype)

F
- 153 Bauer Bodoni
- 161 Walbaum (Linotype)
- 174 Caledonia

F
- 193 Glypha 55
- 198 Serifa 55
- 199 Stymie (ATF)

F *bracketed slab*
- 207 Consort
- 209 Clarendon (Linotype)
- 212 Egizio

F *narrow*
- 253 Erbar
- 254 Futura
- 257 Spartan

F *wider*
- 267 Univers 55
- 279 Helvetica
- 281 Standard

G
- 49 Goudy Catalogue
- 70 Old Style No. 7
- 80 Baskerville No. 2

G
- 15 Cloister
- 97 Spectrum
- 105 Romulus

G
52 Times Roman (Linotype)
67 Imprint
90 Garamond (Stempel)

G *poor contrast*
119 Century Schoolbook
121 Ionic 5
142 Textype

G
175 ITC Century
177 De Vinne
186 Scotch 2 (Linotype)

G
196 Memphis
198 Serifa 55
199 Stymie (ATF)

G *bracketed slab*
207 Consort
209 Clarendon (Linotype)
212 Egizio

G *circular (or nearly so) no spur*
253 Erbar
254 Futura
257 Spartan

G *with spur*
275 Folio
279 Helvetica
281 Standard

H
39 Plantin
60 Caslon 128
79 Baskerville (Linotype)

H
153 Bauer Bodoni
158 Fairfield
161 Walbaum (Linotype)

H
197 Rockwell
198 Serifa 55
199 Stymie (ATF)

H
207 Consort
209 Clarendon (Linotype)
212 Egizio

H
267 Univers 55
279 Helvetica
281 Standard

I
35 Bembo
39 Plantin
92 Garamond (Stempel)

I *poor contrast*
118 Aurora
119 Century Schoolbook
121 Ionic 5

I
152 Basilia
153 Bauer Bodoni
168 Walbaum (Monotype)

I
196 Memphis
197 Rockwell
199 Stymie (ATF)

I *bracketed slab*
207 Consort
209 Clarendon (Linotype)
212 Egizio

I
259 Gill Sans
267 Univers 55
279 Helvetica

J *short tail non-lining*
16 Cloister
60 Caslon 128
67 Imprint

J *medium length tail non-lining*
31 Vendôme
52 Times Roman (Linotype)
99 Caslon 3

J *rounded tail non-lining*
25 Lutetia
66 Granjon
148 Electra

J *poor contrast lining*
119 Century Schoolbook
121 Ionic 5
146 Textype

J
168 Walbaum (Linotype)
171 Augustea
177 De Vinne

J
196 Memphis
197 Rockwell
199 Stymie (ATF)

J *short tail*
253 Erbar
266 Frutiger
282 Standard

J *full rounded tail*
267 Univers 55
275 Folio
279 Helvetica

K *single junction*
70 Old Style No. 7
76 Aster
92 Garamond (Stempel)

K *single junction*
35 Bembo
38 Plantin
88 Sabon

K *double junction*
115 Excelsior
119 Century Schoolbook
121 Ionic 5

K
153 Bauer Bodoni
163 Bodoni (Haas)
165 ITC Fenice

K
196 Memphis
198 Serifa 55
199 Stymie (ATF)

K
261 Grotesque 215
279 Helvetica
281 Standard

L
35 Bembo
38 Plantin
61 Caslon 540

L
79 Baskerville (Linotype)
123 Cheltenham
138 Melior

L *poor contrast*
115 Excelsior
119 Century Schoolbook
121 Ionic 5

L
171 Augustea
174 Caledonia
177 De Vinne

L
197 Rockwell
198 Serifa 55
199 Stymie (ATF)

L *narrow*
254 Futura
257 Spartan
264 Tempo

L *wider*
267 Univers 55
279 Helvetica
281 Standard

M
61 Caslon 540
67 Imprint
79 Baskerville (Linotype)

M
35 Bembo
39 Plantin
73 Ehrhardt

M
153 Bauer Bodoni
158 Fairfield
168 Walbaum (Linotype)

M
193 Glypha 55
196 Memphis
197 Rockwell

M
209 Clarendon (Linotype)
212 Egizio
213 Consort

M
275 Folio
279 Helvetica
281 Standard

N *poor contrast*
61 Caslon 540
92 Garamond (Stempel)
105 Romulus

N *poor contrast*
56 Bookman
71 Olympian
138 Melior

N
153 Bauer Bodoni
156 Didot
158 Fairfield

'Common Earmarks'

The 'common earmarks' (or typical identifying features) are indicated either by the general appearance of letters or by 'marked' features. The general 'style' of typefaces with the same 'earmark' may vary. Example typefaces with their specimen numbers are listed against each letter.

TEXT TYPEFACE 'COMMON EARMARK' TABLES

'Common Earmarks'
The 'common earmarks' (or typical identifying features) are indicated either by the general appearance of letters or by 'marked' features. The general 'style' of typefaces with the same 'earmark' may vary. Example typefaces with their specimen numbers are listed against each letter.

N

N
193 Glypha 55
196 Memphis
197 Rockwell

N *-bracketed slab*
209 Clarendon (Linotype)
212 Egizio
213 Fortune

N
275 Folio
279 Helvetica
281 Standard

O

O
19 Centaur
35 Bembo
39 Plantin

O
52 Times Roman (Linotype)
58 Bulmer
79 Baskerville (Linotype)

O
153 Bauer Bodoni
156 Didot
168 Walbaum (Monotype)

O
189 Beton
196 Memphis
199 Stymie (ATF)

O *circular*
254 Futura
258 Cable (Klingspor)
259 Gill Sans

O
267 Univers 55
279 Helvetica
281 Standard

P

P
35 Bembo
38 Plantin
70 Old Style No. 7

P
49 Goudy Catalogue
84 Palatino
92 Garamond (Stempel)

P *poor contrast*
115 Excelsior
119 Century Schoolbook
137 Impressum

P

P
153 Bauer Bodoni
156 Didot
158 Fairfield

P
196 Memphis
197 Rockwell
198 Serifa 55

P
259 Gill Sans
260 Granby
261 Grotesque 215

Q

Q
35 Bembo
52 Times Roman (Linotype)
116 Perpetua

Q *poor contrast*
115 Excelsior
119 Century Schoolbook
121 Ionic 5

Q
152 Basilia
153 Bauer Bodoni
174 Caledonia

Q
189 Beton
193 Glypha 55
198 Serifa 55

Q
209 Clarendon (Linotype)
212 Egizio
213 Consort

Q
278 Haas Unica
279 Helvetica
283 Video

R

R
35 Bembo
37 Goudy Old Style
87 Quadriga Antiqua

R
39 Plantin
70 Old Style No. 7
94 Garamond (Berthold)

R
19 Centaur
31 Vendôme
75 Aldus

R

R *poor contrast*
115 Excelsior
119 Century Schoolbook
145 Primus Antiqua

R
153 Bauer Bodoni
156 Didot
168 Walbaum (Monotype)

R
188 A & S Gallantin
196 Memphis
198 Serifa 55

R
254 Futura
257 Spartan
258 Cable (Klingspor)

R
273 Akzidenz Grotesque
281 Standard
287 News Gothic

R
267 Univers 55
275 Folio
279 Helvetica

S

S
52 Times Roman (Linotype)
73 Ehrhardt
80 Baskerville No. 2

S
70 Old Style No. 7
77 Baskerville (Berthold)
99 Caslon 3

S
39 Plantin
95 ITC Garamond
130 Columbia

S *poor contrast*
115 Excelsior
119 Century Schoolbook
121 Ionic 5

S
153 Bauer Bodoni
156 Didot
174 Caledonia

S
196 Memphis
197 Rockwell
198 Stymie (ATF)

S

S *narrow*
254 Futura
257 Spartan
262 ITC Kabel

S *wider*
267 Univers 55
279 Helvetica
281 Standard

T

T
35 Bembo
69 Old Style No. 2
107 Van Dijck

T
52 Times Roman (Linotype)
76 Aster
80 Baskerville No. 2

T *poor contrast*
118 Aurora
119 Century Schoolbook
121 Ionic 5

T
153 Bauer Bodoni
158 Fairfield
161 Walbaum (Linotype)

T
196 Memphis
197 Rockwell
198 Serifa 55

T
154 Futura
267 Univers 55
279 Helvetica

U

U
39 Plantin
44 Trump Mediaeval
92 Garamond (Stempel)

U *good contrast*
67 Imprint
79 Baskerville (Linotype)
116 Perpetua

U *poor contrast*
118 Aurora
119 Century Schoolbook
121 Ionic 5

U
153 Bauer Bodoni
156 Didot
168 Walbaum (Monotype)

'Common Earmarks'
The 'common earmarks' (or typical identifying features) are indicated either by the general appearance of letters or by 'marked' features. The general 'style' of typefaces with the same 'earmark' may vary. Example typefaces with their specimen numbers are listed against each letter.

U
196 Memphis
197 Rockwell
198 Serifa 55

U
254 Futura
257 Spartan
264 Tempo

U
267 Univers 55
275 Folio
279 Helvetica

V
52 Times Roman (Linotype)
61 Caslon 540
69 Old Style No. 2

V *poor contrast*
118 Aurora
119 Century Schoolbook
121 Ionic 5

V *line serifs*
153 Bauer Bodoni
156 Didot
168 Walbaum (Monotype)

V *bracketed serifs*
171 Augustea
177 De Vinne
186 Scotch 2 (Linotype)

V
196 Memphis
197 Rockwell
198 Serifa 55

V
254 Futura
258 Cable (Klingspor)
259 Gill Sans

V
261 Grotesque 215
267 Univers 55
279 Helvetica

W *crossed centre strokes*
39 Plantin
88 Sabon
92 Garamond (Stempel)

W *stepped centre strokes*
52 Times Roman (Linotype)
61 Caslon 540
107 Van Dijck

W *centre strokes meet at cap height*
67 Imprint
69 Old Style No. 2
74 Galliard

W *no centre serif*
75 Aldus
79 Baskerville (Linotype)
84 Palatino

W
171 Augustea
174 Caledonia
185 Scotch 2 (Linotype)

W
196 Memphis
197 Rockwell
202 Egyptian 173

W
254 Futura
263 Metro
264 Tempo

W
267 Univers 55
277 ITC Franklin Gothic
279 Helvetica

X
35 Bembo
39 Plantin
92 Garamond (Stempel)

X
115 Excelsior
119 Century Schoolbook
121 Ionic 5

X
158 Fairfield
171 Augustea
174 Caledonia

X
196 Memphis
197 Rockwell
199 Stymie (ATF)

X *narrow*
253 Erbar
254 Futura
264 Tempo

X *wider*
267 Univers 55
279 Helvetica
281 Standard

Y
67 Imprint
92 Garamond (Stempel)
116 Perpetua

Y
153 Bauer Bodoni
158 Fairfield
161 Walbaum (Linotype)

Y
196 Memphis
192 Rockwell
198 Serifa 55

Y *high junction*
253 Erbar
254 Futura
264 Tempo

Y *lower junction*
275 Folio
279 Helvetica
281 Standard

Z
60 Caslon 128
70 Old Style No. 7
88 Sabon

Z
52 Times Roman (Linotype)
84 Palatino
105 Romulus

Z
161 Walbaum (Linotype)
171 Augustea
174 Caledonia

Z
196 Memphis
197 Rockwell
198 Serifa 55

Z
254 Futura
257 Spartan
264 Tempo

Z
267 Univers 55
279 Helvetica
287 News Gothic

&
35 Bembo
39 Plantin
80 Baskerville No. 2

&
97 Spectrum
105 Romulus
138 Melior

&
52 Times Roman (Linotype)
76 Aster
107 Van Dijck

&
161 Walbaum (Linotype)
166 Modern (Linotype)
178 Madison

&
193 Glypha 55
197 Rockwell
198 Serifa 55

&
259 Gill Sans
260 Granby
267 Univers 55

&
255 Neuzeit-Grotesk
263 Metro
268 Optima

&
261 Grotesque 215
277 ITC Franklin Gothic
287 News Gothic

a
20 Horley Old Style
70 Old Style No. 7
97 Spectrum

a
52 Times Roman (Linotype)
100 Concorde
131 French Round Face

a
35 Bembo
39 Plantin
75 Aldus

a *poor contrast*
114 Century Expanded
119 Century Schoolbook
121 Ionic 5

a
153 Bauer Bodoni
156 Didot
186 Scotch 2 (Linotype)

'Common Earmarks'
The 'common earmarks' (or typical identifying features) are indicated either by the general appearance of letters or by 'marked' features. The general 'style' of typefaces with the same 'earmark' may vary. Example typefaces with their specimen numbers are listed against each letter.

a
- 196 Memphis
- 197 Rockwell
- 198 Serifa 55

a *double storey*
- 267 Univers 55
- 279 Helvetica
- 281 Standard

a *single storey*
- 254 Futura
- 255 Neuzeit-Grotesk
- 257 Spartan

b
- 39 Plantin
- 52 Times Roman (Linotype)
- 73 Ehrhardt

b
- 69 Old Style No 2
- 77 Baskerville (Berthold)
- 92 Garamond (Stempel)

b *poor contrast*
- 117 Primer
- 119 Century Schoolbook
- 121 Ionic 5

b
- 153 Bauer Bodoni
- 156 Didot
- 158 Fairfield

b
- 196 Memphis
- 197 Rockwell
- 198 Serifa 55

b *low join to stem*
- 253 Erbar
- 254 Futura
- 257 Spartan

b *higher join to stem*
- 267 Univers 55
- 278 Haas Unica
- 279 Helvetica

c
- 39 Plantin
- 52 Times Roman (Linotype)
- 60 Caslon 128

c
- 35 Bembo
- 79 Baskerville (Linotype)
- 90 Fournier

c *poor contrast*
- 114 Century Expanded
- 119 Century Schoolbook
- 146 Textype

c
- 153 Bauer Bodoni
- 156 Didot
- 161 Walbaum (Linotype)

c
- 194 ITC Lubalin Graph
- 196 Memphis
- 197 Rockwell

c
- 254 Futura
- 257 Spartan
- 259 Gill Sans

c
- 261 Grotesque 215
- 267 Univers 55
- 281 Standard

d
- 35 Bembo
- 52 Times Roman (Linotype)
- 61 Caslon 540

d
- 116 Perpetua
- 117 Primer
- 119 Century Schoolbook

d
- 153 Bauer Bodoni
- 168 Walbaum (Monotype)
- 174 Caledonia

d
- 196 Memphis
- 197 Rockwell
- 198 Serifa 55

d *low join to stem*
- 254 Futura
- 256 Nobel
- 257 Spartan

d *higher join to stem*
- 267 Univers 55
- 273 Akzidenz Grotesk
- 279 Helvetica

e
- 6 Kennerley
- 16 Jenson
- 19 Centaur

e *poor contrast*
- 35 Bembo
- 39 Plantin
- 52 Times Roman (Linotype)

e *poor contrast*
- 71 Olympian
- 119 Century Schoolbook
- 136 Franklin Antiqua

e
- 153 Bauer Bodoni
- 156 Didot
- 161 Walbaum (Linotype)

e
- 194 ITC Lubalin Graph
- 196 Memphis
- 197 Rockwell

e
- 261 Grotesque 215
- 267 Univers 55
- 279 Helvetica

f *short hook*
- 39 Plantin
- 70 Old Style No 7
- 109 Janson

f *medium length hook*
- 69 Old Style No 2
- 123 Cheltenham
- 130 Columbia

f *long hook*
- 19 Centaur
- 35 Bembo
- 94 Garamond (Berthold)

f *poor contrast*
- 114 Century Expanded
- 119 Century Schoolbook
- 137 Impressum

f
- 153 Bauer Bodoni
- 161 Walbaum (Linotype)
- 186 Scotch 2 (Linotype)

f
- 194 ITC Lubalin Graph
- 196 Memphis
- 198 Serifa 55

f *low bar*
- 254 Futura
- 256 Nobel
- 257 Spartan

f *higher bar*
- 267 Univers 55
- 279 Helvetica
- 281 Standard

g
- 44 Trump Mediaeval
- 71 Olympian
- 105 Romulus

g
- 35 Bembo
- 39 Plantin
- 93 Garamond 3 (Linotype)

g *poor contrast*
- 119 Century Schoolbook
- 121 Ionic 5
- 137 Impressum

g
- 153 Bauer Bodoni
- 156 Didot
- 174 Caledonia

g
- 194 ITC Lubalin Graph
- 196 Memphis
- 198 Serifa 55

g
- 267 Univers 55
- 279 Helvetica
- 281 Standard

h
- 39 Plantin
- 52 Times Roman (Linotype)
- 67 Imprint

h
- 19 Centaur
- 51 Minister
- 75 Aldus

h *poor contrast*
- 116 Perpetua
- 117 Primer
- 119 Century Schoolbook

h
- 153 Bauer Bodoni
- 168 Walbaum (Monotype)
- 174 Caledonia

h
- 196 Memphis
- 197 Rockwell
- 198 Serifa 55

h
low junction to stem
254 Futura
257 Spartan
258 Cable (Klingspor)

h
higher junction to stem
277 ITC Franklin Gothic
278 Haas Unica
279 Helvetica

i
37 Goudy Old Style
52 Times Roman (Linotype)
69 Old Style No. 2

i
poor contrast
115 Excelsior
119 Century Schoolbook
137 Impressum

i
153 Bauer Bodoni
156 Didot
158 Fairfield

i
193 Glypha 55
198 Serifa
202 Egyptian 202

i
254 Futura
259 Gill Sans
264 Tempo

i
267 Univers 55
279 Helvetica
281 Standard

j
pointed flat short curve
39 Plantin
138 Melior
148 Electra

j
rounded curve with pear
73 Ehrhardt
84 Palatino
105 Romulus

j
wedge ended curve
35 Bembo
52 Times Roman (Linotype)
70 Old Style No 7

j
'ball' terminal
115 Excelsior
119 Century Schoolbook
121 Ionic 5

j
152 Basilia
162 Bodoni 135 (Monotype)
186 Scotch 2 (Linotype)

j
196 Memphis
197 Rockwell
198 Serifa 55

j
rounded curve
253 Erbar
255 Neuzeit-Grotesk
262 ITC Kabel

j
flatter curve
267 Univers 55
279 Helvetica
281 Standard

k
single junction
35 Bembo
52 Times Roman (Linotype)
93 Garamond 3 (Linotype)

k
single junction
39 Plantin
79 Baskerville (Linotype)
116 Perpetua

k
double junction
6 Kennerley
65 Fontana
92 Garamond (Stempel)

k
double junction
71 Olympian
85 Poppl-Pontifex
132 Goudy Modern

k
158 Fairfield
161 Walbaum (Linotype)
168 Walbaum (Monotype)

k
196 Memphis
197 Rockwell
198 Serifa 55

k
single junction
253 Erbar
254 Futura
258 Cable (Klingspor)

k
single junction
267 Univers 55
278 Haas Unica
283 Video

k
double junction
273 Akzidenz Grotesk
279 Helvetica
287 News Gothic

l
35 Bembo
52 Times Roman (Linotype)
93 Garamond 3 (Linotype)

l
concave
19 Centaur
51 Minister
75 Aldus

l
116 Perpetua
117 Primer
119 Century Schoolbook

l
153 Bauer Bodoni
156 Didot
158 Fairfield

l
194 ITC Lubalin Graph
196 Memphis
197 Rockwell

l
254 Futura
267 Univers 55
279 Helvetica

m
52 Times Roman (Linotype)
61 Caslon 540
79 Baskerville (Linotype)

m
concave
49 Goudy Catalogue
68 Monticello
91 Garamond 156 (Monotype)

m
19 Centaur
35 Bembo
72 Ronaldson

m
poor contrast
115 Excelsior
119 Century Schoolbook
121 Ionic 5

m
153 Bauer Bodoni
156 Didot
158 Fairfield

m
196 Memphis
197 Rockwell
198 Serifa 55

m
267 Univers 55
279 Helvetica
281 Standard

n
52 Times Roman (Linotype)
61 Caslon 540
79 Baskerville (Linotype)

n
concave
49 Goudy Catalogue
68 Monticello
91 Garamond 156 (Monotype)

n
115 Excelsior
119 Century Schoolbook
121 Ionic 5

n
poor contrast
19 Centaur
35 Bembo
72 Ronaldson

n
153 Bauer Bodoni
156 Didot
158 Fairfield

n
196 Memphis
197 Rockwell
198 Serifa 55

n
267 Univers 55
279 Helvetica
281 Standard

o
19 Centaur
35 Bembo
52 Times Roman (Linotype)

o
69 Old Style No 2
79 Baskerville (Linotype)
88 Sabon

o
poor contrast
115 Excelsior
119 Century Schoolbook
146 Textype

'Common Earmarks'

The 'common earmarks' (or typical identifying features) are indicated either by the general appearance of letters or by 'marked' features. The general 'style' of typefaces with the same 'earmark' may vary. Example typefaces with their specimen numbers are listed against each letter.

'Common Earmarks'
The 'common earmarks' (or typical identifying features) are indicated either by the general appearance of letters or by 'marked' features. The general 'style' of typefaces with the same 'earmark' may vary. Example typefaces with their specimen numbers are listed against each letter.

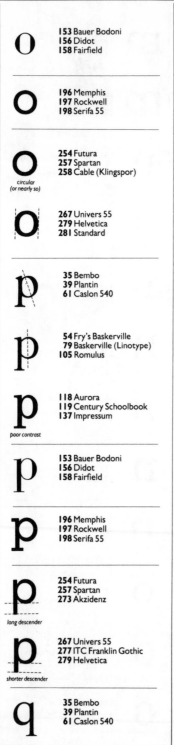

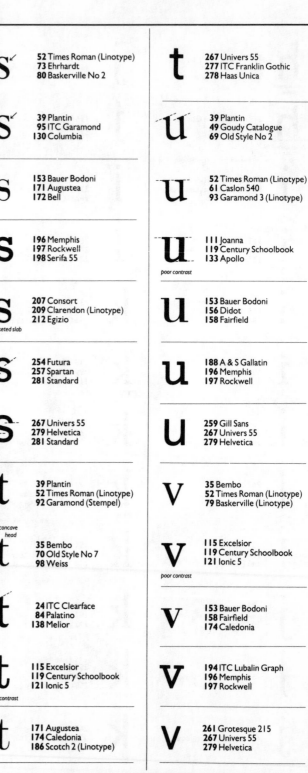

o
153 Bauer Bodoni
156 Didot
158 Fairfield

o
196 Memphis
197 Rockwell
198 Serifa 55

o
254 Futura
257 Spartan
258 Cable (Klingspor)
circular (or nearly so)

o
267 Univers 55
279 Helvetica
281 Standard

p
35 Bembo
39 Plantin
61 Caslon 540

p
54 Fry's Baskerville
79 Baskerville (Linotype)
105 Romulus

p
118 Aurora
119 Century Schoolbook
137 Impressum
poor contrast

p
153 Bauer Bodoni
156 Didot
158 Fairfield

p
196 Memphis
197 Rockwell
198 Serifa 55

p
254 Futura
257 Spartan
273 Akzidenz
long descender

p
267 Univers 55
277 ITC Franklin Gothic
279 Helvetica
shorter descender

q
35 Bembo
39 Plantin
61 Caslon 540

q
114 Century Expanded
119 Century Schoolbook
121 Ionic 5

q
153 Bauer Bodoni
156 Didot
158 Fairfield

q
194 ITC Lubalin Graph
197 Rockwell
199 Stymie (ATF)

q
254 Futura
257 Spartan
273 Akzidenz Grotesk
long descender

q
267 Univers 55
279 Helvetica
277 ITC Franklin Gothic
shorter descender

r
56 Bookman
88 Sabon
92 Garamond (Stempel)

r
52 Times Roman (Linotype)
92 Spectrum
105 Romulus

r
115 Excelsior
119 Century Schoolbook
121 Ionic 5
poor contrast

r
153 Bauer Bodoni
161 Walbaum (Linotype)
177 De Vinne

r
196 Memphis
197 Rockwell
198 Serifa 55

r
254 Futura
257 Spartan
259 Gill Sans

r
258 Cable (Klingspor)
261 Grotesque 215
267 Univers 55

s
52 Times Roman (Linotype)
73 Ehrhardt
80 Baskerville No 2

s
39 Plantin
95 ITC Garamond
130 Columbia

s
153 Bauer Bodoni
171 Augustea
172 Bell

s
196 Memphis
197 Rockwell
198 Serifa 55

s
207 Consort
209 Clarendon (Linotype)
212 Egizio
bracketed slab

s
254 Futura
257 Spartan
281 Standard

s
267 Univers 55
279 Helvetica
281 Standard

t
39 Plantin
52 Times Roman (Linotype)
92 Garamond (Stempel)

t
35 Bembo
70 Old Style No 7
98 Weiss
definite concave head

t
24 ITC Clearface
84 Palatino
138 Melior

t
115 Excelsior
119 Century Schoolbook
121 Ionic 5
poor contrast

t
171 Augustea
174 Caledonia
186 Scotch 2 (Linotype)

t
267 Univers 55
277 ITC Franklin Gothic
278 Haas Unica

u
39 Plantin
49 Goudy Catalogue
69 Old Style No 2

u
52 Times Roman (Linotype)
61 Caslon 540
93 Garamond 3 (Linotype)

u
111 Joanna
119 Century Schoolbook
133 Apollo
poor contrast

u
153 Bauer Bodoni
156 Didot
158 Fairfield

u
188 A & S Gallatin
196 Memphis
197 Rockwell

u
259 Gill Sans
267 Univers 55
279 Helvetica

v
35 Bembo
52 Times Roman (Linotype)
79 Baskerville (Linotype)

v
115 Excelsior
119 Century Schoolbook
121 Ionic 5
poor contrast

v
153 Bauer Bodoni
158 Fairfield
174 Caledonia

v
194 ITC Lubalin Graph
196 Memphis
197 Rockwell

v
261 Grotesque 215
267 Univers 55
279 Helvetica

W centre strokes meet at centre
35 Bembo
39 Plantin
61 Caslon 540

W stepped centre strokes
52 Times Roman (Linotype)
73 Ehrhardt
91 Garamond 156 (Monotype)

W no centre serif
15 Cloister
77 Baskerville (Berthold)
123 Cheltenham

W
188 A & S Gallatin
196 Memphis
197 Rockwell

W
254 Futura
259 Gill Sans
264 Tempo

W
261 Grotesque 215
267 Univers 55
279 Helvetica

X
35 Bembo
78 Baskerville 169 (Monotype)
93 Garamond 3 (Linotype)

X
153 Bauer Bodoni
161 Walbaum (Linotype)
174 Caledonia

x
196 Memphis
197 Rockwell
198 Serifa 55

X
273 Akzidenz Grotesk
281 Standard
287 News Gothic

X narrow

X wider
259 Gill Sans
267 Univers 55
279 Helvetica

y rounded tail with pear
35 Bembo
52 Times Roman (Linotype)
94 Garamond (Berthold)

y short tail
25 Lutetia
59 Caslon Old Face No. 2
79 Baskerville (Linotype)

y rounded tail with ball
114 Century Expanded
119 Century Schoolbook
149 Iridium

y
153 Bauer Bodoni
161 Walbaum (Linotype)
171 Augustea

y
261 Grotesque 215
273 Akzidenz Grotesque
279 Helvetica

z
19 Centaur
69 Old Style No 2
72 Ronaldson

z
52 Times Roman (Linotype)
79 Baskerville (Linotype)
90 Fournier

z
153 Bauer Bodoni
171 Augustea
174 Caledonia

z
193 Glypha 55
196 Memphis
197 Rockwell

z
254 Futura
257 Spartan
259 Gill Sans

z
216 Grotesque 215
267 Univers 55
279 Helvetica

1
52 Times Roman (Linotype)
56 Bookman
73 Ehrhardt

1
35 Bembo
75 Aldus
117 Primer

I non-lining
40 Poliphilus
78 Baskerville 169 (Monotype)
91 Garamond 156 (Monotype)

1
153 Bauer Bodoni
161 Walbaum (Linotype)
181 Paganini

1
194 ITC Lubalin Graph
196 Memphis
197 Rockwell

1
253 Erbar
267 Univers 55
277 Franklin Gothic

1 concave
273 Akzidenz Grotesk
279 Helvetica
281 Standard

2
35 Bembo
52 Times Roman (Linotype)
39 Plantin

2
24 ITC Clearface
119 Century Schoolbook
121 Ionic 5

2 non-lining
19 Centaur
59 Caslon 128
107 Van Dijck

2
153 Bauer Bodoni
175 ITC Century
176 Century Nova

2
196 Memphis
197 Rockwell
198 Serifa 55

2
254 Futura
259 Gill Sans
264 Tempo

2
267 Univers 55
273 Akzidenz Grotesk
281 Standard

3
39 Plantin
52 Times Roman (Linotype)
67 Imprint

3
24 ITC Clearface
119 Century Schoolbook
146 Textype

3 non-lining
69 Old Style No 2
91 Garamond 156 (Monotype)
132 Goudy Modern

3
152 Basilia
153 Bauer Bodoni
156 Didot

3
196 Memphis
197 Rockwell
198 Serifa 55

3
258 Cable (Klingspor)
279 ITC Franklin Gothic
287 News Gothic

3
254 Futura
267 Univers 55
279 Helvetica

4
35 Bembo
39 Plantin
52 Times Roman (Linotype)

4
56 Bookman
64 Concorde Nova
86 Times Europa

4
115 Excelsior
119 Century Schoolbook
121 Ionic 5

4 non-lining
40 Poliphilus
60 Caslon 128
65 Fontana

4
194 ITC Lubalin Graph
197 Rockwell
199 Stymie (ATF)

'Common Earmarks'
The 'common earmarks' (or typical identifying features) are indicated either by the general appearance of letters or by 'marked' features. The general 'style' of typefaces with the same 'earmark' may vary. Example typefaces with their specimen numbers are listed against each letter.

'Common Earmarks'

The 'common earmarks' (or typical identifying features) are indicated either by the general appearance of letters or by 'marked' features. The general 'style' of typefaces with the same 'earmark' may vary. Example typefaces with their specimen numbers are listed against each letter.

4
261 Grotesque 215
267 Univers 55
279 Helvetica

5
39 Plantin
52 Times Roman (Linotype)
67 Imprint

5
75 Aldus
94 Garamond (Berthold)
105 Romulus

5
79 Baskerville (Linotype)
114 Century Expanded
119 Century Schoolbook

5 *non-lining*
19 Centaur
48 Emerson
89 Barbou

5
156 Didot
171 Augustea
186 Scotch 2 (Linotype)

5
188 A & S Gallantin
197 Rockwell
199 Stymie (ATF)

5
254 Futura
257 Spartan
260 Granby

5
267 Univers 55
279 Helvetica
281 Standard

6
35 Bembo
39 Plantin
52 Times Roman (Linotype)

6 *poor contrast*
57 ITC Bookman
119 Century Schoolbook
121 Ionic 5

6 *non-lining*
25 Lutetia
65 Fontana
107 Van Dijck

6
171 Augustea
174 Caledonia
186 Scotch 2 (Linotype)

6
196 Memphis
197 Rockwell
198 Serifa 55

6
254 Futura
258 Cable (Klingspor)
259 Gill Sans

6
267 Univers 55
279 Helvetica
281 Standard

7 *full serif*
35 Bembo
39 Plantin
52 Times Roman (Linotype)

7 *half serif*
61 Caslon 540
67 Imprint
79 Baskerville (Linotype)

7 *half serif*
118 Aurora
119 Century Schoolbook
145 Primus Antiqua

7 *non-lining*
4 Pastonchi
91 Garamond 156 (Monotype)
97 Spectrum

7
171 Augustea
175 ITC Century
177 De Vinne

7
188 A & S Gallatin
197 Rockwell
199 Stymie (ATF)

7 *curve*
207 Consort
209 Clarendon (Linotype)
212 Egizio

7
255 Neuzeit-Grotesk
257 Spartan
260 Granby

7
275 Folio
277 ITC Franklin Gothic
279 Helvetica

8 *diagonal crossover*
16 Jenson
35 Bembo
39 Plantin

8 *bowls touching (no crossover)*
80 Baskerville No 2
119 Century Schoolbook
138 Melior

8 *non-lining*
25 Lutetia
40 Poliphilus
60 Caslon 128

8
174 Caledonia
177 De Vinne
186 Scotch 2 (Linotype)

8
196 Memphis
197 Rockwell
198 Serifa 55

8 *narrow*
254 Futura
257 Spartan
259 Gill Sans

8 *wider*
267 Univers 55
279 Helvetica
281 Standard

9
35 Bembo
39 Plantin
52 Times Roman (Linotype)

9
57 ITC Bookman
119 Century Schoolbook
121 Ionic 5

9 *non-lining*
25 Lutetia
65 Fontana
107 Van Dijck

9
171 Augustea
174 Caledonia
186 Scotch 2 (Linotype)

9
196 Memphis
197 Rockwell
198 Serifa 55

9
254 Futura
258 Cable (Klingspor)
259 Gill Sans

9
267 Univers 55
279 Helvetica
281 Standard

0
35 Bembo
52 Times Roman (Linotype)
77 Baskerville (Berthold)

0 *poor contrast*
56 Bookman
119 Century Schoolbook
121 Ionic 5

0 *non-lining*
69 Old Style No 2
72 Ronaldson
78 Baskerville 169 (Monotype)

0
153 Bauer Bodoni
161 Walbaum (Linotype)
174 Caledonia

0
193 Glypha 55
197 Rockwell
188 A & S Gallatin

0 *narrow*
254 Futura
257 Spartan
262 ITC Kabel

0 *wider*
277 ITC Franklin Gothic
279 Helvetica
281 Standard

For foot serif 'earmarks' of A refer to those of H as they are generally the same. Other 'earmarks' are as follows:

(general)

A wide
99, **112**, 123-4, 127

A narrow
29, 43, **64**, 93

A bowing
1, 12, **30**, 42

(top)

A
27, 60, 63

A sheared
35, **38**-41, 61-2, 74, 76, 99, 123-4, 132, 147

A
36, 46, 126-7, 129

A
32, 44, 56-7, **71**, 73, 85, 101-2, 106, 121, 125, 128, 136, 138, 141, 145-6

A
28, 82

51

33

A
23-4, 27, 59, 66, **72**, 92, 94, 150

110

143

107

A sheared
8, **128**

A16 *A*
1-3, 9, 12, 29, 42, 140, 142

(bar)

A high
6, 14, 20, 47, **65**, 81, 95, 97, 128

A low
12, 29, 36, 78, 98-9, 123-4, **126**-7, 129, 142

74

28

142

A wide
164, **184**

A narrow
160, 176

155

A high bar
182

A low bar
170, **176**-7, 183

189, 194-5

---

half serifs A27
190, 192

A long serifs
201, 207

220, **225**, 227-8, 236, 238

230

231

A no serif
223-4, 229, 232, 234-**5**

226

218-9, **233**, 257

A slightly rounded
239-40

221

'nick' on bar **240**

A wide
246, 249, 290, 292

A narrow
284-**9**

A bowing
269

272

296, **299**

A high bar
256, **258**, 262, 295

A low bar
246, 249, 253, 284-5, 290, 292, 294, 298, 300-1, 303

297

296

270

(general)

B wide
7, 56-7, **131**

B narrow
4, 8, **47**

(top)

B11 *B* concave
2, 3, 12, **14**, 17, 48-9, 102

B12
26, 40, 42, 108

B13 *B* squashed
125, 136, 138, 140, 150

B concave back
113

(bar)

B4 *B* low bar
36, 73, 89

B high bar
3, **5**, 14, 42

B
2

12-3, 22, **104**

9, **28**, 30, 128

29

73, 147

(serifs)

B long
27, **46**, 56-7, 59, 72, 86, 92, 115, 146

B short
5, 7, 13, 22, 28-30, **82**, 98, 123-4, 126-7, 129

no bottom serif **134**

B wide
164, **184**

B narrow
155, **176**

NB. Bold figures indicate the specimen illustrated above.

'Special Earmarks'
The 'special earmarks' (or distinctive identifying features) are indicated on each letter. The general 'style' of typefaces with the same 'earmark' may vary. The figures refer to specimen numbers.

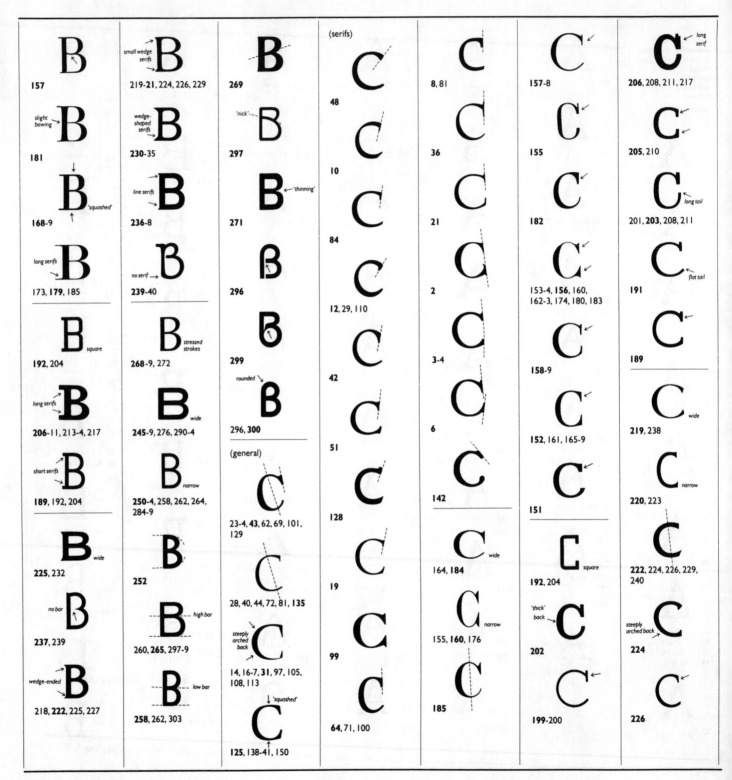

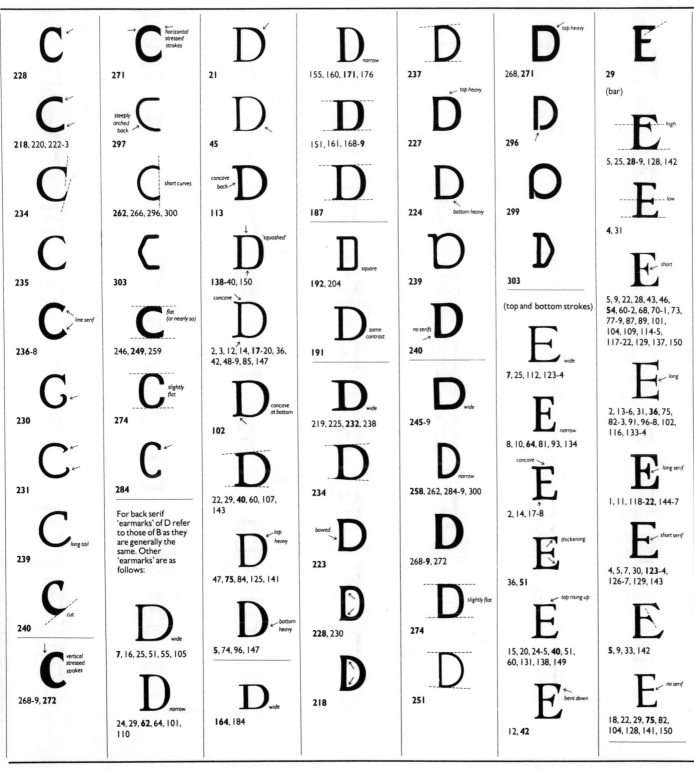

C

228

218, 220, 222-3

234

235

236-8 — line serif

230 — long tail

231

239 — long tail

240 — cut

268-9, **272** — vertical stressed strokes

C

271 — horizontal stressed strokes

297 — steeply arched back

262, 266, 296, 300 — short curves

303

246, **249**, 259 — flat (or nearly so)

274 — slightly flat

284

For back serif 'earmarks' of D refer to those of B as they are generally the same. Other 'earmarks' are as follows:

D

7, 16, 25, 51, 55, 105 — wide

24, 29, **62**, 64, 101, 110 — narrow

D

21

45

113 — concave back

138-40, 150 — 'squashed'

2, 3, 12, 14, **17**-20, 36, 42, 48-9, 85, 147 — concave

102 — concave at bottom

22, 29, **40**, 60, 107, 143

47, **75**, 84, 125, 141 — top heavy / bottom heavy

5, 74, 96, 147

D

155, 160, **171**, 176 — narrow

151, 161, 168-**9**

187

192, 204 — square

191 — some contrast

219, 225, **232**, 238 — wide

234

223 — bowed

228, 230

218 — wide

164, 184 — wide

D

237

227 — top heavy

224 — bottom heavy

239

240 — no serifs

245-9 — wide

258, 262, 284-9, 300 — narrow

268-**9**, 272

274 — slightly flat

251

D

268, **271** — top heavy

296

299

303

(top and bottom strokes)

7, 25, 112, 123-4 — wide

8, 10, **64**, 81, 93, 134 — narrow

2, 14, 17-8 — concave

36, **51** — thickening

15, 20, 24-5, **40**, 51, 60, 131, 138, 149 — top rising up

12, **42** — bent down

E

29 (bar)

5, 25, **28**-9, 128, 142 — high / low

4, 31

5, 9, 22, 28, 43, 46, **54**, 60-2, 68, 70-1, 73, 77-9, 87, 89, 101, 104, 109, 114-5, 117-22, 129, 137, 150 — short

2, 13-6, 31, **36**, 75, 82-3, 91, 96-8, 102, 116, 133-4 — long

1, 11, 118-**22**, 144-7 — long serif

4, 5, 7, 30, **123**-4, 126-7, 129, 143 — short serif

5, 9, 33, 142 — top rising up

18, 22, 29, **75**, 82, 104, 128, 141, 150 — no serif

'Special Earmarks'
*The 'special earmarks'
(or distinctive identifying
features) are indicated on
each letter. The general
'style' of typefaces with the
same 'earmark' may vary.
The figures refer to
specimen numbers.*

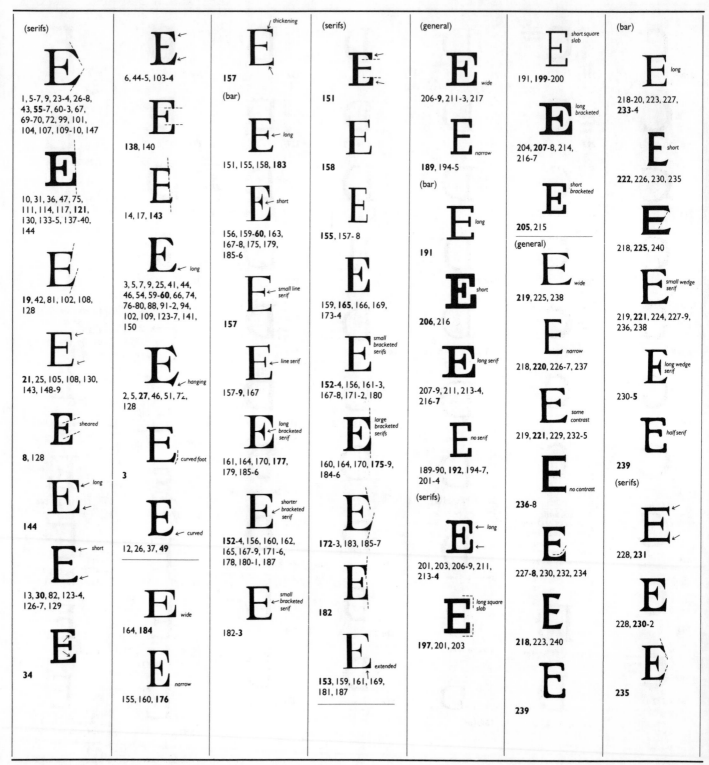

(serifs)

1, 5-7, 9, 23-4, 26-8,
43, **55**-7, 60-3, 67,
69-70, 72, 99, 101,
104, 107, 109-10, 147

10, 31, 36, 47, 75,
111, 114, 117, **121**,
130, 133-5, 137-40,
144

19, 42, 81, 102, 108,
128

21, 25, 105, 108, 130,
143, 148-9

sheared

8, 128

long

144

short

13, **30**, 82, 123-4,
126-7, 129

34

6, 44-5, **103-4**

(bar)

138, 140

14, 17, **143**

3, 5, 7, 9, 25, 41, 44,
46, 54, 59-**60**, 66, 74,
76-80, 88, 91-2, 94,
102, 109, 123-7, 141,
150

hanging

2, 5, **27**, 46, 51, 72,
128

curved foot

3

curved

12, 26, 37, **49**

wide

164, **184**

narrow

155, 160, **176**

---

thickening

157

(bar)

long

151, 155, 158, **183**

short

156, 159-**60**, 163,
167-8, 175, 179,
185-6

small line serif

157

line serif

157-**9**, 167

long bracketed serif

161, 164, 170, **177**,
179, 185-6

shorter bracketed serif

152-4, 156, 160, 162,
165, 167-9, 171-6,
178, 180-1, 187

small bracketed serif

182-3

(serifs)

151

158

155, 157- 8

small bracketed serifs

159, **165**, 166, 169,
173-4

large bracketed serifs

152-4, 156, 161-3,
167-8, 171-2, 180

160, 164, 170, **175**-9,
184-6

172-3, 183, 185-7

182

extended

153, 159, 161, 169,
181, 187

(general)

wide

206-**9**, 211-3, 217

narrow

189, 194-5

(bar)

long

191

short

206, 216

long serif

207-9, 211, 213-4,
216-**7**

no serif

189-90, **192**, 194-7,
201-4

(serifs)

long

201, 203, 206-9, 211,
213-4

long square slab

197, 201, 203

---

short square slab

191, **199**-200

long bracketed

204, **207**-8, 214,
216-7

short bracketed

205, 215

(general)

wide

219, 225, 238

narrow

218, **220**, 226-7, 237

some contrast

219, **221**, 229, 232-5

no contrast

236-8

227-**8**, 230, 232, 234

218, 223, 240

239

(bar)

long

218-20, 223, 227,
233-4

short

222, 226, 230, 235

218, **225**, 240

small wedge serif

219, **221**, 224, 227-9,
236, 238

long wedge serif

230-**5**

half serif

239

(serifs)

228, **231**

228, **230**-2

235

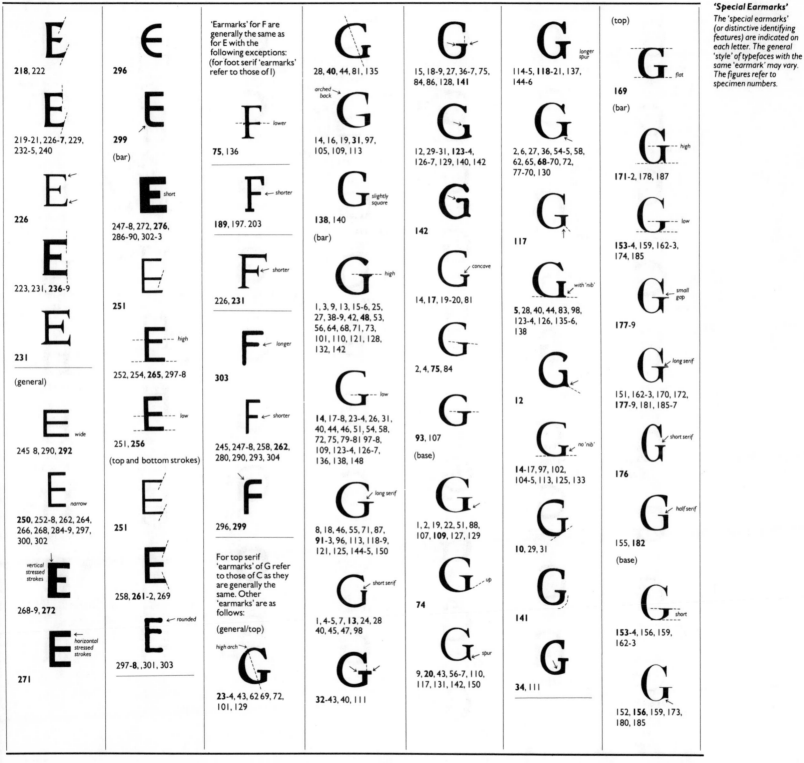

'Special Earmarks'
The 'special earmarks'
(or distinctive identifying
features) are indicated on
each letter. The general
'style' of typefaces with the
same 'earmark' may vary.
The figures refer to
specimen numbers.

218, 222

296

219-21, 226-**7**, 229,
232-5, 240

299
(bar)

226

247-8, 272, **276**,
286-90, 302-3

223, 231, **236-9**

251

231

252, 254, **265**, 297-8
high

(general)

251
low

245 8, 290, **292**

251, **256**
(top and bottom strokes)

vertical stressed strokes

258, **261**-2, 269

268-9, **272**

horizontal stressed strokes

297-8, ,301, 303

271

'Earmarks' for F are
generally the same as
for E with the
following exceptions:
(for foot serif 'earmarks'
refer to those of I)

F lower

75, 136

F shorter

189, 197. 203

F shorter

226, **231**

F longer

303

F shorter

245, 247-8, 258, **262**,
280, 290, 293, 304

F

296, **299**

For top serif
'earmarks' of G refer
to those of C as they
are generally the
same. Other
'earmarks' are as
follows:

(general/top)

G high arch

23-4, 43, 62 69, 72,
101, 129

G

28, **40**, 44, 81, 135

G arched back

14, 16, 19, **31**, 97,
105, 109, 113

G slightly square

138, 140

(bar)

G high

1, 3, 9, 13, 15-6, 25,
27, 38-9, 42, **48**, 53,
56, 64, 68, 71, 73,
101, 110, 121, 128,
132, 142

G low

14, 17-8, 23-4, 26, 31,
40, 44, 46, 51, 54. 58,
72, 75, 79-81 97-8,
109, 123-4, 126-7,
136, 138, 148

G long serif

8, 18, 46, 55, 71, 87,
91-3, 96, 113, 118-9,
121, 125, 144-5, 150

G short serif

1, 4-5, 7, **13**, 24, 28
40, 45, 47, 98

G

32-43, 40, 111

G

15, 18-9, 27, 36-7, 75,
84, 86, 128, **141**

G

12, 29-31, **123**-4,
126-7, 129, 140, 142

142

G concave

14, **17**, 19-20, 81

2, 4, **75**, 84

G

93, 107

(base)

G

1, 2, 19, 22, 51, 88,
107, **109**, 127, 129

G up

74

G spur

9, **20**, 43, 56-7, 110,
117, 131, 142, 150

G longer spur

114-5, **118**-21, 137,
144-6

G high

2, 6, 27, 36, 54-5, 58,
62, 65, **68**-70, 72,
77-70, 130

117

G with 'nib'

5, 28, 40, 44, 83, 98,
123-4, 126, 135-6,
138

12

G no 'nib'

14-17, 97, 102,
104-5, 113, 125, 133

G

10, 29, 31

G short

141

34, 111

(top)

G flat

169

(bar)

G high

171-2, 178, 187

G low

153-4, 159, 162-3,
174, 185

G small gap

177-9

G long serif

151, 162-3, 170, 172,
177-9, 181, 185-7

G short serif

155, **182**

(base)

G half serif

153-4, 156, 159,
162-3

G short

152, **156**, 159, 173,
180, 185

NB. Bold figures indicate the specimen illustrated above.

'Special Earmarks'
The 'special earmarks' (or distinctive identifying features) are indicated on each letter. The general 'style' of typefaces with the same 'earmark' may vary. The figures refer to specimen numbers.

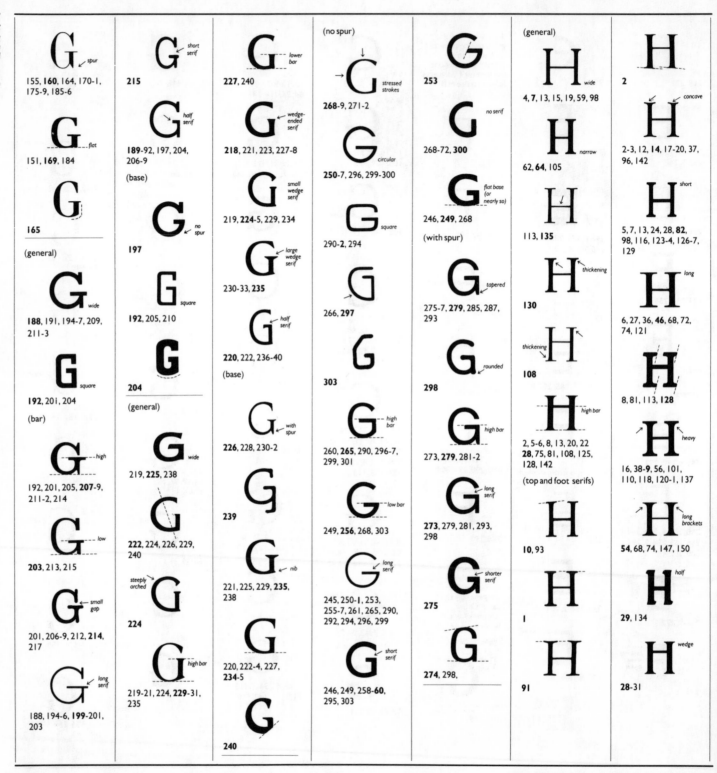

G *spur*
155, **160**, 164, 170-1, 175-9, 185-6

G *flat*
151, **169**, 184

G
165

(general)

G *wide*
188, 191, 194-7, 209, 211-3

G *square*
192, 201, 204

(bar)

G *high*
192, 201, 205, **207-9**, 211-2, 214

G *low*
203, 213, 215

G *small gap*
201, 206-9, 212, **214**, 217

G *long serif*
188, 194-6, **199**-201, 203

G *short serif*
215

G *half serif*
189-92, 197, 204, 206-9

(base)

G *no spur*
197

G *square*
192, 205, 210

G
204

(general)

G *wide*
219, **225**, 238

G
222, 224, 226, 229, 240

G *steeply arched*
224

G *high bar*
219-21, 224, **229**-31, 235

G *lower bar*
227, 240

G *wedge-ended serif*
218, 221, 223, 227-8

G *small wedge serif*
219, **224**-5, 229, 234

G *large wedge serif*
230-33, **235**

G *half serif*
220, 222, 236-40

(base)

G *with spur*
226, 228, 230-2

G
239

G *nib*
221, 225, 229, **235**, 238

G
240

(no spur)

G *stressed strokes*
268-9, 271-2

G *circular*
268-72, **300**

G *square*
250-7, 296, 299-300

G
290-**2**, 294

G
303

G *high bar*
260, **265**, 290, 296-7, 299, 301

G *low bar*
249, **256**, 268, 303

G *long serif*
245, 250-**1**, 253, 255-7, 261, 265, 290, 292, 294, 296, 299

G *short serif*
246, 249, 258-**60**, 295, 303

G
253

G *no serif*
268-72, **300**

G *flat base (or nearly so)*
246, **249**, 268

(with spur)

G *tapered*
275-7, **279**, 285, 287, 293

G *rounded*
298

G *high bar*
273, **279**, 281-2

G *long serif*
273, 279, 281, 293, 298

G *shorter serif*
275

G
274, 298,

(general)

H *wide*
4, **7**, 13, 15, 19, 59, 98

H *narrow*
62, **64**, 105

H
113, **135**

H *thickening*
130

H *thickening*
108

H *high bar*
2, 5-6, 8, 13, 20, 22, **28**, 75, 81, 108, 125, 128, 142

(top and foot serifs)

H
10, 93

H
1

H
91

(general)

H
2

H *concave*
2-3, 12, **14**, 17-20, 37, 96, 142

H *short*
5, 7, 13, 24, 28, **82**, 98, 116, 123-4, 126-7, 129

H *long*
6, 27, 36, **46**, 68, 72, 74, 121

H
8, 81, 113, **128**

H *heavy*
16, 38-**9**, 56, 101, 110, 118, 120-1, 137

H *long brackets*
54, 68, 74, 147, 150

H *half*
29, 134

H *wedge*
28-31

NB. Bold figures indicate the specimen illustrated above.

'Special Earmarks'
The 'special earmarks' (or distinctive identifying features) are indicated on each letter. The general 'style' of typefaces with the same 'earmark' may vary. The figures refer to specimen numbers.

Column 1 (H)

H — *slab*
32-34

(general)

H — *wide*
161, 164, 179, **184**

H — *narrow*
155, 160, 176

→ H ← *slight bowing effect*
181

H — (arrows)
157

H — *high bar*
178

(top and foot serifs)

H — *line*
151-69 (e.g. **153**)

H — *bracketed*
H27
170-87 (e.g. **185**)

H — *very long*
173, **177**, 179, 185-6

H — *short*
155, 157, 165

Column 2 (H)

H — *heavy*
170, 172, 177, **185**-6

(general)

H — *wide*
207, **213**

H — *narrow*
192, **201**, 217

(top and foot serifs)

H — *square slab*
188-203 (e.g. **197**)

H — *bracketed slab*
204-17 (e.g. **211**)

H — *rounded slab*
214-7

H — *half serif*
192

H — *serifs thinner than stem*
191, 201-3

H — *very long*
201, **207**-8, 214

H — *thick and stubby*
204

Column 3 (H)

H — *long*
193, 198, 201, **206**-13

H — *short*
189, 192, 204, 215

(general)

H — *wide*
219, 225, **238**, 240

H — *narrow*
220

H — *high bar*
224, 229-30, **239**

H — *nick*
240

(top and foot serifs)

H — *half*
H46
223, 239-40

H — *wedge-ended*
218, 221-2, **225**, 227-8

H — *small wedge*
219-20, 224, 226, 229

H — *large wedge*
230-5

Column 4 (H)

H — *line-ended*
236-8

→ H ↓ *stressed strokes*
268-9, 272

H — *wide*
245, 247-9, **290**-4

H — *narrow*
250, 253, 264, 272, 284-9, 302-4

H — *low bar*
251, 284-9, 290, 292

H — *high bar*
265, **297**-8

H — (thick)
297-8, **301**, 303

Top and foot serifs of I are generally the same as H but are repeated with other 'earmarks' as follows:

I
10, 93

I
2- 3, 40

Column 5 (I)

↓ *uneven* (arrows)
49, 130

↓ *concave*
2, 12, **14**, 17-20, 37, 96, 142

I — *short*
5, 7, 13, 24, 28, **82**, 98, 116, 123-4, 126-7, 129

I — *long*
250, 253, 264, 272, 284-9, 302-4

I — *sheared*
8, 81, 113, **128**

I — *thick bracket*
16, 38-**9**, 56, 101, 110, 118, 120-1, 137

I — *long bracket*
54, 68, 79, 147, 150

I — *slightly thickened*
108

I — *half*
29, 134

Column 6 (I)

↓ *slight bowing effect* (arrow)
181

I — *line*
151-69 (e.g. **153**)

I — *bracketed*
170-87 (e.g. **185**)

I — *long*
173, **177**, 179, 185-6

I — *short*
155, 157, 165

I — *thick bracket*
170, 172, 177, **185**-6

I
157

I — *square slab serif*
188-203

I — *bracketed slab serif*
204-217 (e.g. **211**)

I — *rounded serif*
214-7

Column 7 (I)

I — *serif thinner than stem*
191, 210-3

I — *thick and stubby*
204

I — *short*
189, 192. 204, 215

I — *long*
193, 198, 201, **206**-13

I — *half*
223, **239**-40

I — *wedge-ended*
218, 221-2, **225**, 227-8

I — *small wedge*
219-20, 224, 226, 229

I — *large wedge*
230-5

I — *line-ended*
236-8

I — (thick)
297-8, **301**, 303

NB. Bold figures indicate the specimen illustrated above.

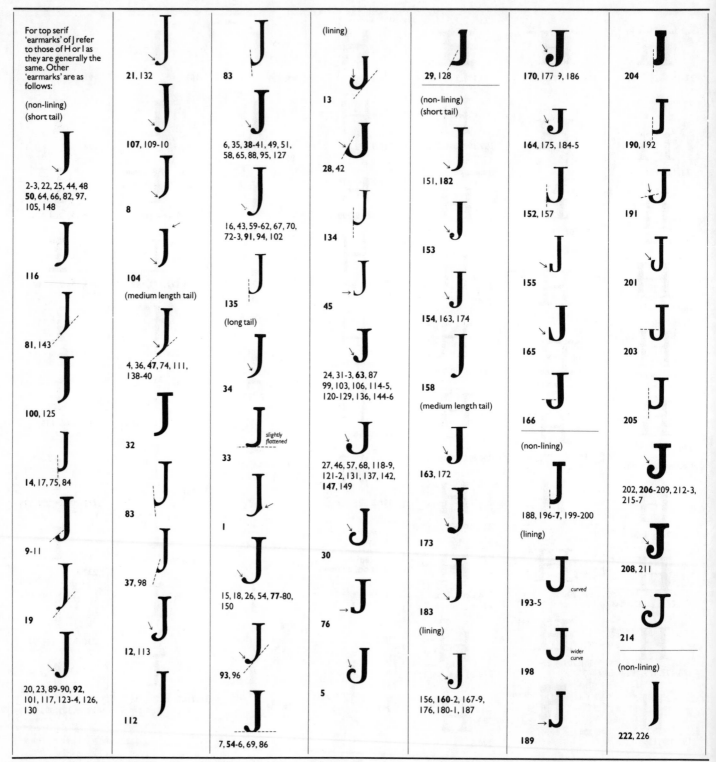

'Special Earmarks'
The 'special earmarks' (or distinctive identifying features) are indicated on each letter. The general 'style' of typefaces with the same 'earmark' may vary. The figures refer to specimen numbers.

For top serif 'earmarks' of J refer to those of H or I as they are generally the same. Other 'earmarks' are as follows:

(non-lining)
(short tail)

2-3, 22, 25, 44, 48 **50**, 64, 66, 82, 97, 105, 148

116

81, 143

100, 125

14, 17, 75, 84

9-11

19

20, 23, 89-90, **92**, 101, 117, 123-4, 126, 130

21, 132

107, 109-10

8

104

(medium length tail)

4, 36, **47**, 74, 111, 138-40

32

83

37, 98

12, 113

112

83

6, 35, **38**-41, 49, 51, 58, 65, 88, 95, 127

16, 43, 59-62, 67, 70, 72-3, **91**, 94, 102

135

(long tail)

34

slightly flattened

33

1

15, 18, 26, 54, **77**-80, 150

93, 96

7, **54**-6, 69, 86

(lining)

13

28, 42

134

45

24, 31-3, **63**, 87 99, 103, 106, 114-5, 120-129, 136, 144-6

27, 46, 57, 68, 118-9, 121-2, 131, 137, 142, **147**, 149

30

76

5

29, 128

(non-lining)
(short tail)

151, **182**

153

154, 163, 174

158

(medium length tail)

163, 172

173

183

(lining)

156, **160**-2, 167-9, 176, 180-1, 187

170, 177 9, 186

164, 175, 184-5

152, 157

155

165

166

(non-lining)

188, 196-**7**, 199-200

(lining)

193-5 *curved*

198 *wider curve*

189

204

190, 192

191

201

203

205

202, **206**-209, 212-3, 215-7

208, 211

214

(non-lining)

222, 226

NB. Bold figures indicate the specimen illustrated above.

'Special Earmarks'
The 'special earmarks' (or distinctive identifying features) are indicated on each letter. The general 'style' of typefaces with the same 'earmark' may vary. The figures refer to specimen numbers.

J
220

229, **235**

221

218, **232**, 240

(lining)

219, **224**, 227, 236, 238

223, **225**, 228, 233

234

237

230

240
(non-lining)

wide tail
246, **249**

short tail
259, 267
(lining)

275

wide tail
245, 247-8

short tail
250-1, 284, 286, 303
279-80, 283, 284, 286, 303

short tail
252, **254**, 257-8, 262, 285, 287-9, 299

short tail
253, **256**, ,264, 266, 270, 272-4, 276-8, 281-2, 296, 300

269

271

square
290-4, 303

rounded
297, **301**

255

302

298

For top and foot serif 'earmarks' of K refer those of H as they are generally the same. Other 'earmarks' are as follows:

(single junction)

K 14, 17, 50, 74, 91, 100, 104-5, 130

K *just touching*
23, **38**, 58, 84, 86, 88, 106, 116, 133, 148

K *horizontal bar*
18, 35, 44, 64, **67**, 87, 90, 107, 109, **136**, 149-50

K *full serif*
4, 16, 25, 31-2, 34, 40, 47, **52**-3, 59-60, 73, 76, 83, 86-7, 90, 93, 95-8, 101, 105-7, 109, 111, 123-4, 126-7, 129-30, 149

K *half serif*
6, 37-9, 41, 61, 75, 81, 88, 104, 108, 116, 125, 135, 138-9, 141, 148, 150

K *half serifs*
10, **84**

K *half serifs*
19

K *sheared*
29

K *hybrid serif*
45, 143

K *blob / half serif*
142

K *tapering*
2-3, 14-5, 17-8, 33, **74**

K *bowing*
11, 91

K *bowing*
8, 19, **68**, 102

K *bowing*
13, **35**, 113, 123-4

K
36, 134
(double junction)

K *full serif*
5, 9, 30, 51, **54**-6, 62-3, 65-6, 69-70, 77-80, 89, 92, 114-5, 117-22, 131, 137, 144-7

K *half serif*
7, 12, 20-1, 26, 46, 48-9, 71-2, 82, 85, **94**, 99, 112, 132, 140

K *tapering*
110

K *half serifs*
128

K
43

K *bowing*
46

K *narrow top*
77, 92

K *full serif*
5, 23-4, 57, 103

K
27

K *bowing*
28

K *bowing*
30
(single junction)

K
183

K *just touching*
162-3, 181-2,

K *horizontal bar*
156, 158, 161, 167-8, 187

K
155

K *full serif*
152-4, 159, **174**, 181-4

K *narrow*
167-8, 187
(double junction)

K *full serif*
160, 164, **166**, 170-1, 173, 175-80, 185-6

K *half serif*
151, 165, 169,

K *curved foot*
157

K
172

'Special Earmarks'
The 'special earmarks' (or distinctive identifying features) are indicated on each letter. The general 'style' of typefaces with the same 'earmark' may vary. The figures refer to specimen numbers.

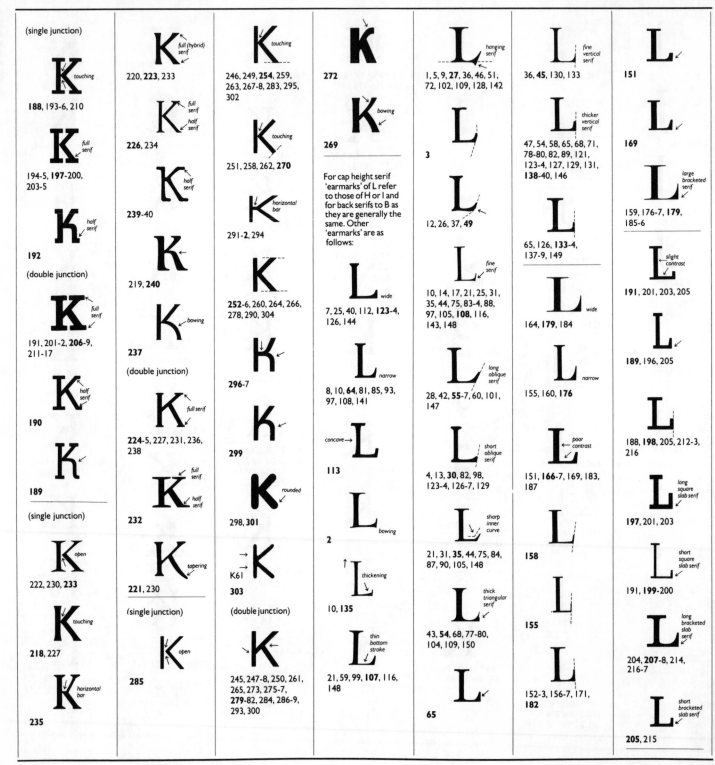

(single junction)

K *touching*
188, 193-6, 210

K *full serif*
194-5, **197**-200, 203-5

K *half serif*
192

(double junction)

K *full serif*
191, 201-2, **206**-9, 211-17

K *half serif*
190

K
189

(single junction)

K *open*
222, 230, **233**

K *touching*
218, 227

K *horizontal bar*
235

K *full (hybrid) serif*
220, **223**, 233

K *full serif* *half serif*
226, 234

K *half serif*
239-40

K
219, **240**

K *bowing*
237

(double junction)

K *full serif*
224-5, 227, 231, 236, 238

K *full serif* *half serif*
232

(single junction)

K *tapering*
221, 230

(single junction)

K *open*
285

K *touching*
246, 249, **254**, 259, 263, 267-8, 283, 295, 302

K *touching*
251, 258, 262, **270**

K *horizontal bar*
291-**2**, 294

K
252-6, 260, 264, 266, 278, 290, 304

K
296-7

K
299

K *rounded*
298, **301**

K61 K
303

(double junction)

K
245, 247-8, 250, 261, 265, 273, 275-7, **279**-82, 284, 286-9, 293, 300

K
272

K *bowing*
269

For cap height serif 'earmarks' of L refer to those of H or I and for back serifs to B as they are generally the same. Other 'earmarks' are as follows:

L *wide*
7, 25, 40, 112, **123**-4, 126, 144

L *narrow*
8, 10, **64**, 81, 85, 93, 97, 108, 141

L *concave→*
113

L *bowing*
2

L *thickening*
10, **135**

L *thin bottom stroke*
21, 59, 99, **107**, 116, 148

L *hanging serif*
1, 5, 9, **27**, 36, 46, 51, 72, 102, 109, 128, 142

L
3

L
12, 26, 37, **49**

L *fine serif*
10, 14, 17, 21, 25, 31, 35, 44, 75, 83-4, 88, 97, 105, **108**, 116, 143, 148

L *long oblique serif*
28, 42, **55**-7, 60, 101, 147

L *short oblique serif*
4, 13, **30**, 82, 98, 123-4, 126-7, 129

L *sharp inner curve*
21, 31, **35**, 44, 75, 84, 87, 90, 105, 148

L *thick triangular serif*
43, **54**, 68, 77-80, 104, 109, 150

L
65

L *fine vertical serif*
36, **45**, 130, 133

L *thicker vertical serif*
47, 54, 58, 65, 68, 71, 78-80, 82, 89, 121, 123-4, 127, 129, 131, **138**-40, 146

L
65, 126, **133**-4, 137-9, 149

L *wide*
164, **179**, 184

L *narrow*
155, 160, **176**

L *poor contrast*
151, **166**-7, 169, 183, 187

L
158

L
155

L
152-3, 156-7, 171, **182**

L
151

L
169

L *large bracketed serif*
159, 176-7, **179**, 185-6

L *slight contrast*
191, 201, 203, 205

L
189, 196, 205

L
188, **198**, 205, 212-3, 216

L *long square slab serif*
197, 201, 203

L *short square slab serif*
191, **199**-200

L *long bracketed slab serif*
204, **207**-8, 214, 216-7

L *short bracketed slab serif*
205, 215

NB. *Bold figures indicate the specimen illustrated above.*

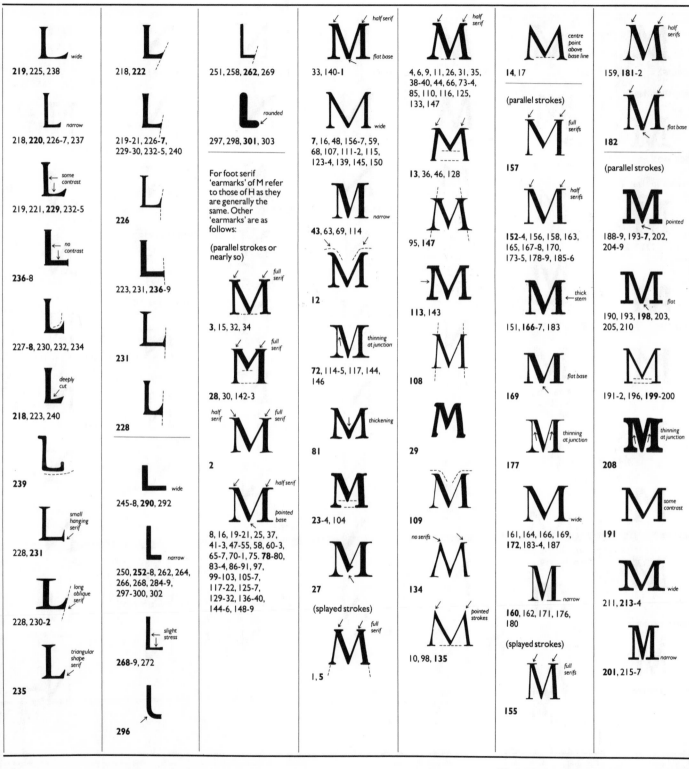

L wide
219, 225, 238

L narrow
218, **220**, 226-7, 237

L some contrast
219, 221, **229**, 232-5

L no contrast
236-8

L
227-**8**, 230, 232, 234

L deeply cut
218, 223, 240

L
239

L small hanging serif
228, **231**

L long oblique serif
228, 230-**2**

L triangular shape serif
235

L
218, **222**

L
219-21, 226-**7**, 229-30, 232-5, 240

L
226

L
223, 231, **236**-9

L
231

L
228

L wide
245-8, **290**, 292

L narrow
250, **252**-8, 262, 264, 266, 268, 284-9, 297-300, 302

L slight stress
268-9, 272

L
296

L
251, 258, **262**, 269

L rounded
297, 298, **301**, 303

For foot serif 'earmarks' of M refer to those of H as they are generally the same. Other 'earmarks' are as follows:

(parallel strokes or nearly so)

M full serif
3, 15, 32, 34

M full serif
28, 30, 142-3

M half serif / full serif
2

M half serif / pointed base
8, 16, 19-21, 25, 37, 41-3, 47-55, 58, 60-3, 65-7, 70-1, 75. **78**-80, 83-4, 86-91, 97, 99-103, 105-7, 117-22, 125-7, 129-32, 136-40, 144-6, 148-9

M half serif / flat base
33, 140-**1**

M wide
7, 16, 48, 156-7, 59, 68, 107, 111-2, 115, 123-4, 139, 145, 150

M narrow
43, 63, 69, 114

M
12

M thinning at junction
72, 114-5, 117, 144, 146

M thickening
81

M
23-4, 104

(splayed strokes)

M full serif
1, **5**

M half serif
4, 6, 9, 11, 26, 31, 35, 38-40, 44, 66, 73-4, 85, 110, 116, 125, 133, 147

M
13, 36, 46, 128

M
95, **147**

M
113, 143

M
108

M
29

M pointed strokes
10, 98, **135**

no serifs **M**
134

M
109

M centre point above base line
14, 17

(parallel strokes)

M full serifs
157

M half serifs
152-4, 156, 158, 163, 165, 167-8, 170, 173-5, 178-9, 185-6

M thick stem
151, **166**-7, 183

M flat base
169

M thinning at junction
177

M wide
161, 164, 166, 169, **172**, 183-4, 187

M narrow
160, 162, 171, 176, 180

(splayed strokes)

M full serifs
155

M half serifs
159, **181**-2

M flat base
182

(parallel strokes)

M pointed
188-9, 193-**7**, 202, 204-9

M flat
190, 193, **198**, 203, 205, 210

M
191-2, 196, **199**-200

M thinning at junction
208

M some contrast
191

M wide
211, **213**-4

M narrow
201, 215-7

'Special Earmarks'

The 'special earmarks' (or distinctive identifying features) are indicated on each letter. The general 'style' of typefaces with the same 'earmark' may vary. The figures refer to specimen numbers.

NB. Bold figures indicate the specimen illustrated above.

'Special Earmarks'
The 'special earmarks' (or distinctive identifying features) are indicated on each letter. The general 'style' of typefaces with the same 'earmark' may vary. The figures refer to specimen numbers.

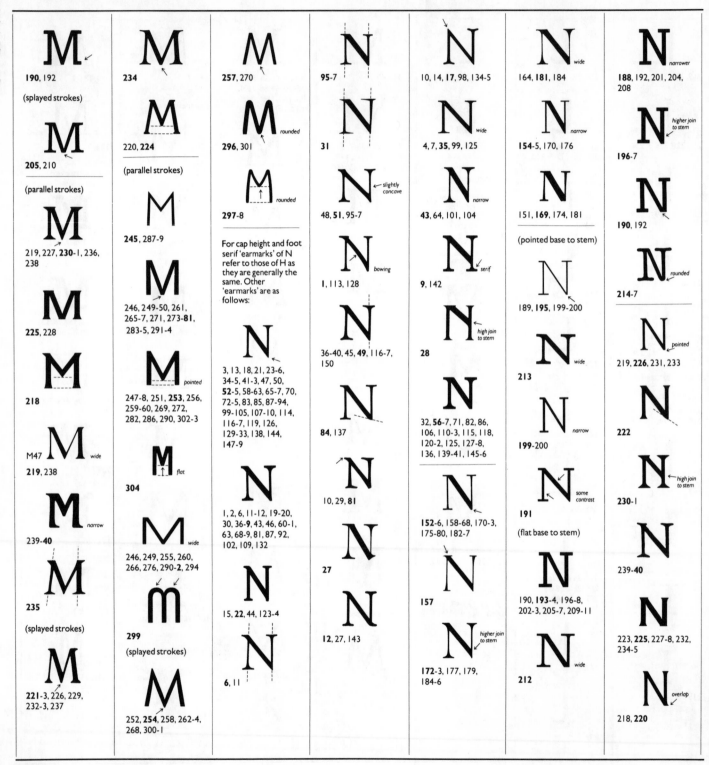

M ↙
190, 192

(splayed strokes)

M
205, 210

(parallel strokes)

M
219, 227, **230**-1, 236, 238

M
225, 228

M
218

M wide
M47
219, 238

M narrow
239-**40**

M
235

(splayed strokes)

M
221-3, 226, 229, 232-3, 237

M
234

M
220, **224**

(parallel strokes)

M
245, 287-9

M
246, 249-50, 261, 265-7, 271, 273-**81**, 283-5, 291-4

M pointed
247-8, 251, **253**, 256, 259-60, 269, 272, 282, 286, 290, 302-3

M flat
304

M wide
246, 249, 255, 260, 266, 276, 290-**2**, 294

m̃
299

(splayed strokes)

M
252, **254**, 258, 262-4, 268, 300-1

M
257, 270

M rounded
296, 301

M rounded
297-8

For cap height and foot serif 'earmarks' of N refer to those of H as they are generally the same. Other 'earmarks' are as follows:

N
3, 13, 18, 21, 23-6, 34-5, 41-3, 47, 50, **52**-5, 58-63, 65-7, 70, 72-5, 83, 85, 87-94, 99-105, 107-10, 114, 116-7, 119, 126, 129-33, 138, 144, 147-9

N
1, 2, 6, 11-12, 19-20, 30, 36-**9**, 43, 46, 60-1, 63, 68-9, 81, 87, 92, 102, 109, 132

N
15, **22**, 44, 123-4

N
6, 11

N
95-7

N
31

N slightly concave
48, **51**, 95-7

N bowing
1, 113, 128

N
36-40, 45, **49**, 116-7, 150

N
84, 137

N
10, 29, **81**

N
27

N
12, 27, 143

N
10, 14, **17**, 98, 134-5

N wide
4, 7, **35**, 99, 125

N narrow
43, 64, 101, 104

N serif
9, 142

N high join to stem
28

N
32, **56**-7, 71, 82, 86, 106, 110-3, 115, 118, 120-2, 125, 127-8, 136, 139-41, 145-6

N
152-6, 158-68, 170-3, 175-80, 182-7

N higher join to stem
172-3, 177, 179, 184-6

N wide
164, **181**, 184

N narrow
154-5, 170, 176

N
151, **169**, 174, 181

(pointed base to stem)

N
189, **195**, 199-200

N wide
213

N narrow
199-200

N some contrast
191

(flat base to stem)

N
190, **193**-4, 196-8, 202-3, 205-7, 209-11

N wide
212

N narrower
188, 192, 201, 204, 208

N higher join to stem
196-7

N
190, 192

N rounded
214-7

N pointed
219, **226**, 231, 233

N
222

N high join to stem
230-1

N
239-40

N
223, **225**, 227-8, 232, 234-5

N overlap
218, **220**

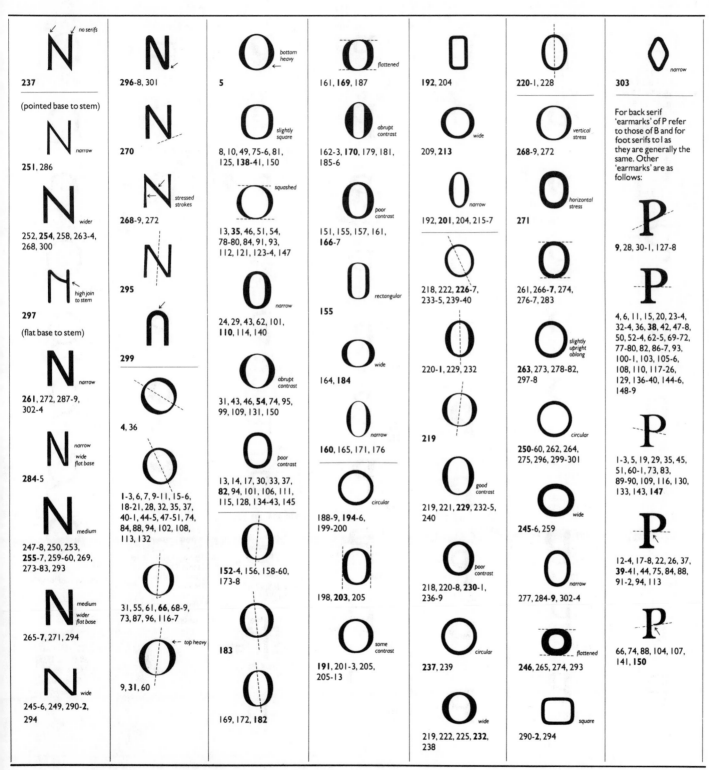

237

(pointed base to stem)

251, 286

252, **254**, 258, 263-4, 268, 300

297

(flat base to stem)

261, 272, 287-9, 302-4

284-5

247-8, 250, 253, **255**-7, 259-60, 269, 273-83, 293

265-**7**, 271, 294

245-6, 249, 290-**2**, 294

296-8, 301

270

268-9, 272

295

299

4, 36

1-3, 6, 7, 9-11, 15-6, 18-21, 28, 32, 35, 37, 40-1, 44-5, 47-51, 74, 84, 88, 94, 102, 108, 113, 132

31, 55, 61, **66**, 68-9, 73, 87, 96, 116-7

9, **31**, 60

5

8, 10, 49, 75-6, 81, 125, **138**-41, 150

13, **35**, 46, 51, 54, 78-80, 84, 91, 93, 112, 121, 123-4, 147

24, 29, 43, 62, 101, **110**, 114, 140

31, 43, 46, **54**, 74, 95, 99, 109, 131, 150

13, 14, 17, 30, 33, 37, **82**, 94, 101, 106, 111, 115, 128, 134-43, 145

152-4, 156, 158-60, 173-8

183

169, 172, **182**

161, **169**, 187

162-3, **170**, 179, 181, 185-6

151, 155, 157, 161, **166**-7

155

164, **184**

160, 165, 171, 176

188-9, **194**-6, 199-200

198, **203**, 205

191, 201-3, 205, 205-13

192, 204

209, **213**

192, **201**, 204, 215-7

218, 222, **226**-7, 233-5, 239-40

219

220-1, 229, 232

219, 221, **229**, 232-5, 240

218, 220-8, **230**-1, 236-9

237, 239

219, 222, 225, **232**, 238

220-1, 228

268-9, 272

271

261, 266-**7**, 274, 276-7, 283

263, 273, 278-82, 297-8

250-60, 262, 264, 275, 296, 299-301

245-6, 259

277, 284-**9**, 302-4

246, 265, 274, 293

290-**2**, 294

303

For back serif 'earmarks' of P refer to those of B and for foot serifs to I as they are generally the same. Other 'earmarks' are as follows:

9, 28, 30-1, 127-8

4, 6, 11, 15, 20, 23-4, 32-4, 36, **38**, 42, 47-8, 50, 52-4, 62-5, 69-72, 77-80, 82, 86-7, 93, 100-1, 103, 105-6, 108, 110, 117-26, 129, 136-40, 144-6, 148-9

1-3, 5, 19, 29, 35, 45, 51, 60-1, 73, 83, 89-90, 109, 116, 130, 133, 143, **147**

12-4, 17-8, 22, 26, 37, **39**-41, 44, 75, 84, 88, 91-2, 94, 113

66, 74, 88, 104, 107, 141, **150**

'Special Earmarks'
The 'special earmarks' (or distinctive identifying features) are indicated on each letter. The general 'style' of typefaces with the same 'earmark' may vary. The figures refer to specimen numbers.

NB. *Bold figures indicate the specimen illustrated above.*

'Special Earmarks'
The 'special earmarks'
(or distinctive identifying
features) are indicated on
each letter. The general
'style' of typefaces with the
same 'earmark' may vary.
The figures refer to
specimen numbers.

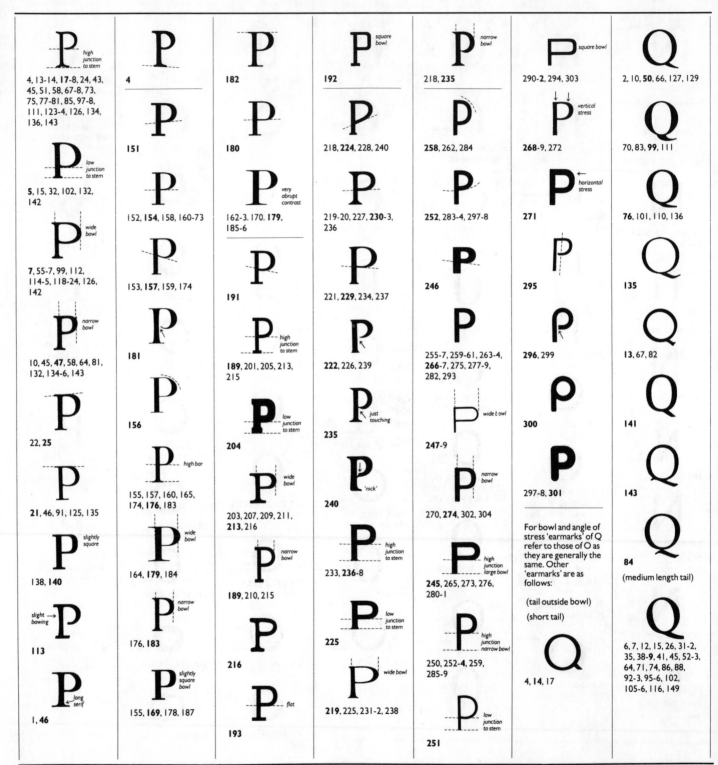

P *high junction to stem*
4, 13-14, **17**-8, 24, 43, 45, 51, 58, 67-8, 73, 75, 77-81, 85, 97-8, 111, 123-4, 126, 134, 136, 143

P *low junction to stem*
5, 15, 32, 102, 132, 142

P *wide bowl*
7, 55-7, 99, 112, 114-5, 118-24, 126, 142

P *narrow bowl*
10, 45, **47**, 58, 64, 81, 132, 134-6, 143

P
22, **25**

P
21, 46, 91, 125, 135

P *slightly square*
138, **140**

P *slight bowing*
113

P *long serif*
1, 46

P
4

P
151

P
152, **154**, 158, 160-73

P
153, **157**, 159, 174

P
181

P
156

P *high bar*
155, 157, 160, 165, 174, **176**, 183

P *wide bowl*
164, **179**, 184

P *narrow bowl*
176, **183**

P *slightly square bowl*
155, **169**, 178, 187

P
182

P
180

P *very abrupt contrast*
162-3. 170. **179**, 185-6

P
191

P *high junction to stem*
189, 201, 205, 213, 215

P *low junction to stem*
204

P *wide bowl*
203, 207, 209, 211, **213**, 216

P *narrow bowl*
189, 210, 215

P
216

P *flat*
193

P *square bowl*
192

P
218, **224**, 228, 240

P
219-20, 227, **230**-3, 236

P
221, **229**, 234, 237

P
222, 226, 239

P *just touching*
235

P *'nick'*
240

P *high junction to stem*
233, **236**-8

P *low junction to stem*
225

P *wide bowl*
219, 225, 231-2, 238

P *narrow bowl*
218, **235**

P
258, 262, 284

P
252, 283-4, 297-8

P
246

P
222, 226, 239

P
255-7, 259-61, 263-4, **266**-7, 275, 277-9, 282, 293

P *wide bowl*
247-9

P *narrow bowl*
270, **274**, 302, 304

P *high junction large bowl*
245, 265, 273, 276, 280-1

P *high junction narrow bowl*
250, 252-**4**, 259, 285-9

P *low junction to stem*
251

P *square bowl*
290-**2**, 294, 303

P *vertical stress*
268-9, 272

P *horizontal stress*
271

P
295

P
296, 299

P
300

P
297-8, **301**

For bowl and angle of stress 'earmarks' of Q refer to those of O as they are generally the same. Other 'earmarks' are as follows:

(tail outside bowl)

(short tail)

Q
4, **14**, 17

Q
2, 10, **50**, 66, 127, 129

Q
70, 83, **99**, 111

Q
76, 101, 110, 136

Q
135

Q
13, 67, 82

Q
141

Q
143

Q *(medium length tail)*
84

Q
6, 7, 12, 15, 26, 31-2, 35, 38-9, 41, 45, 52-3, 64, 71, 74, 86, 88, 92-3, 95-6, 102, 105-6, 116, 149

NB. *Bold figures indicate the specimen illustrated above.*

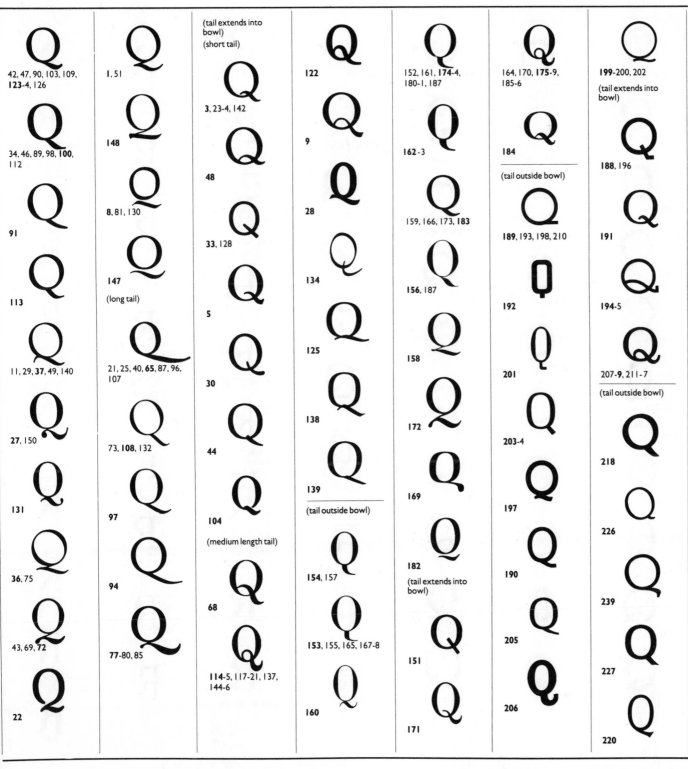

'Special Earmarks'
The 'special earmarks' (or distinctive identifying features) are indicated on each letter. The general 'style' of typefaces with the same 'earmark' may vary. The figures refer to specimen numbers.

42, 47, 90, 103, 109, **123**-4, 126

34, 46, 89, 98, **100**, 112

91

113

11, 29, **37**, 49, 140

27, 150

131

36, 75

43, 69, **72**

22

1, 51

148

8, 81, 130

147

(long tail)

21, 25, 40, **65**, 87, 96, 107

73, **108**, 132

97

94

77-80, 85

(tail extends into bowl)
(short tail)

3, 23-4, 142

48

33, 128

5

30

44

104

(medium length tail)

68

114-5, 117-21, 137, 144-6

122

9

28

134

125

138

139

(tail outside bowl)

154, 157

153, 155, 165, 167-8

160

152, 161, **174**-4, 180-1, 187

162-3

159, 166, 173, **183**

156, 187

158

172

169

182

(tail extends into bowl)

151

171

164, 170, **175**-9, 185-6

184

(tail outside bowl)

189, 193, 198, 210

192

201

203-4

197

190

205

206

199-200, 202

(tail extends into bowl)

188, 196

191

194-5

207-**9**, 211-7

(tail outside bowl)

218

226

239

227

220

NB. *Bold figures indicate the specimen illustrated above.*

'Special Earmarks'
The 'special earmarks' (or distinctive identifying features) are indicated on each letter. The general 'style' of typefaces with the same 'earmark' may vary. The figures refer to specimen numbers.

222, **233**-4

232

223

235

219, 240

225, **228**

(tail extends into bowl)

231, 237

221, 229

224

236, 238

(tail outside bowl)

264, 273, 281

246, 249, 276-7, **288**-9

253, 267

274, 280

266, 302

(tail extends into bowl)

295

251

259, **272**

296

268

263

(tail extends into bowl)

255, 278-9, 282-3

256, 265

245

252, 257, 271

298

250

269, 262, 284, 301

254, 304

261, 269

285-6, 289, 297

300

299

290

291-4

303

(bowl)

9, 28-30, 104, 127

1-3, **5**, 83

open
13, 22, 36, **75**, 84, 104

wide bowl
5, 55-7, **69**, 112, 121, 123-4, 131, 142

narrow bowl
4, 29, 81, 134

(junctions)

high
13, **46**, 56, 123-4, 150

low
1, **5**, 35

138, 140

close to stem
31, 36, 38-9, 65, 79, **135**

junctions wide apart
5, 9, 16, 25, 28-30, 32, **35**, 112, 114-5, 118-21, 123-4, 131, 137, 144-6

27

thinning
42, **68**, 89-90, 100, 149

(second stem)

2, 3, 12, 19-20, 25-6, 31, **37**, 45, 48, 87, 108, 148

1, 40, **74**, 89-90, 105, 107, 131

6, 11, 36, 46, 48-9, 58, 97, 114-5, 117-22, 137, 144-6

1, **15**-6

142

41, 47, 66, 70, 79

tapered
4, 18, 33-4, 44, **51**, 110

42, 75

4

bowed
13, 111

half serif
21-4, 27, 29, 38-9, 42-3, 50, 52-7, **59**-69, 71-3, 75-83, 85-6, 88, 91-6, 99, 106, 109, 111-2, 116, 122-30, 132-6, 138-41, 147, 151

full serif
5, 13, 28, **30**, 98

14, **17**, 19, 31-2, 34, 51, 75

extended foot
7, 8, 11, 16-7, 19, 46, **74**, 107, 132

(bowl)

157

165

square bowl
155, 169

narrow bowl
167-8

NB. Bold figures indicate the specimen illustrated above.

(second stem)

151, 173

straight stem
half serif

157

152-155, 158, 161,
172, 174, 180, 182-3,
184, 187

153-4, 156, 159-60,
62-4, 171, 175-6, 181

(bowl)

wide bowl

170, **177**-9, 85-6

194-5

narrow
bowl

203

(second stem)

straight

197

curved
stem

188, **190**, 192-5, 198,
204

199-200

189, 202-3, **205**,
215-7

201, 106-**9**, 211-14

bowing

216

(bowl)

218

open

222, **226**, 230, 237,
239

'nick'

240

wide

219, 221, 225, **229**,
231-2, 238

half serif

218, **235**

(junctions)

high
junction
to stem

220

low
junction
to stem

221, **234**

close
to stem

218, **223**

wide
apart

219, 225, 238

(second stem)

218, 222-**4**, 226-7

open

250-1, 295-6

tapered

221, 229

tapered
& curved

236

half serif

224, 226, 231-**3**,
239-40

(junctions)

high

234-5

237

full serif

220, **236**, 238

(bowl)

258, 262

263-4, 269

297

open

250-**1**, 295-6

wide bowl

250, **271**, 280

narrow
bowl

253, 259, 262, 264,
284, 302

(junctions)

bowing

265, 276, 297, 303

---

low

251, 298

2nd junction
close
to stem

252-8, 262, 264, 268,
271-2, 298-301

wide apart

245-8, 261, **267**,
273-5, 278-9, 291-4

(second stem)

245, 247-8, 250,
252-7, 260, 265,
268-9, 272-3, 276-**7**
280-90, 295, 300,
302, 304

251. 258. **270**, 299

301, 304

246, 249, 259, 266-7,
274-5, 278-**9**, 291-4
296

298

bowing

269, **297**

(general)

vertical
stress

268-9, 272

horizontal
stress

271

296, 299-**300**

For 'earmarks' for
capital S refer to
those of lower case s
as they are generally
the same. Exceptions
are as follows:

(top and bottom
serifs)

4

12

13

19

23-4, 142

34

49

90

59-60, 63, **67**, 99

61, 148

123-4, 126, 129

134

143

(top serif only)

29

15, 40

86-7

'Special Earmarks'
The 'special earmarks'
(or distinctive identifying
features) are indicated on
each letter. The general
'style' of typefaces with the
same 'earmark' may vary.
The figures refer to
specimen numbers.

NB. Bold figures indicate the specimen illustrated above.

'Special Earmarks'
The 'special earmarks' (or distinctive identifying features) are indicated on each letter. The general 'style' of typefaces with the same 'earmark' may vary. The figures refer to specimen numbers.

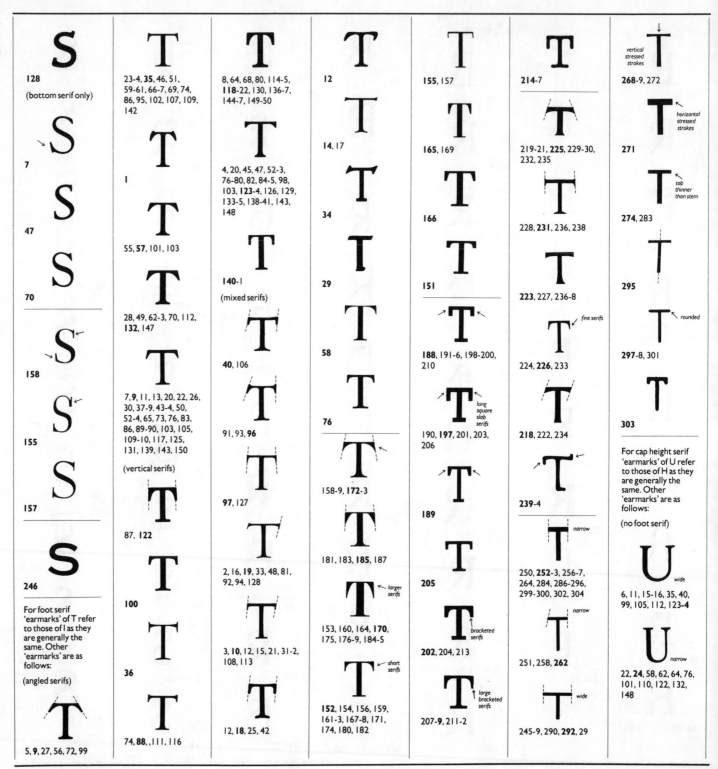

128 (bottom serif only)

7

47

70

158

155

157

246

For foot serif 'earmarks' of T refer to those of I as they are generally the same. Other 'earmarks' are as follows:

(angled serifs)

5, **9**, 27, 56, 72, 99

23-4, **35**, 46, 51, 59-61, 66-7, 69, 74, 86, 95, 102, 107, 109, 142

I

55, **57**, 101, 103

28, 49, 62-3, 70, 112, **132**, 147

7, **9**, 11, 13, 20, 22, 26, 30, 37-9, 43-4, 50, 52-4, 65, 73, 76, 83, 86, 89-90, 103, 105, 109-10, 117, 125, 131, 139, 143, 150

(vertical serifs)

87, **122**

100

36

74, **88**, , 111, 116

8, 64, 68, 80, 114-5, **118**-22, 130, 136-7, 144-7, 149-50

4, 20, 45, 47, 52-3, 76-80, 82, 84-5, 98, 103, **123**-4, 126, 129, 133-5, 138-41, 143, 148

140-1 (mixed serifs)

40, 106

91, 93, **96**

97, 127

2, 16, **19**, 33, 48, 81, 92, 94, 128

3, **10**, 12, 15, 21, 31-2, 108, 113

12, **18**, 25, 42

12

14, 17

34

29

58

76

158-9, **172**-3

181, 183, **185**, 187

153, 160, 164, **170**, 175, 176-9, 184-5 (larger serifs)

152, 154, 156, 159, 161-3, 167-8, 171, 174, 180, 182 (short serifs)

155, 157

165, 169

166

151

188, 191-6, 198-200, 210

190, **197**, 201, 203, 206

189

205

202, 204, 213 (bracketed serifs)

207-9, 211-2 (large bracketed serifs)

214-7

219-21, **225**, 229-30, 232, 235

228, **231**, 236, 238

223, 227, 236-8

224, **226**, 233 (fine serifs)

218, 222, 234 (long square slab serifs)

239-4

250, **252**-3, 256-7, 264, 284, 286-296, 299-300, 302, 304 (narrow)

251, 258, **262** (narrow)

245-9, 290, **292**, 29 (wide)

268-9, 272 (vertical stressed strokes)

271 (horizontal stressed strokes) (top thinner than stem)

274, 283

295 (rounded)

297-8, 301

303

For cap height serif 'earmarks' of U refer to those of H as they are generally the same. Other 'earmarks' are as follows:

(no foot serif)

6, 11, 15-16, 35, 40, 99, 105, 112, 123-**4** (wide)

22, **24**, 58, 62, 64, 76, 101, 110, 122, 132, 148 (narrow)

NB. *Bold figures indicate the specimen illustrated above.*

'Special Earmarks'
The 'special earmarks' (or distinctive identifying features) are indicated on each letter. The general 'style' of typefaces with the same 'earmark' may vary. The figures refer to specimen numbers.

Column 1

U — *long serifs*
27, **46**, 56, 65, 71, 74, 101, 114, 121

U — *short serifs*
7, 13, 30, 37, 45, 82, 98, 108, 123-4, 126-7, 129-30, 148

U — *good contrast*
21, 27, 31, 43, 54, **58**, 60, 95, 99, 131

U — *poor contrast*
4, 8, 13-14, 17-18, 22, **26**, 28, 30-4, 44, 56-7, 71, 106, 110, 113, 115, 127-8, 133, 137, 141, 145-6

U — *no contrast*
13, 32-4, 82

U
68, 71, 73

U — *slightly flattened base*
11, 19, **40**, 57, 105, 132, 138, 140

U — *thicker stem*
111

U — *thickening*
2

Column 2

U — *thickening*
113, 134-5, 150

U — *sheared*
8, **128**

U
147

U
59-**60**, 102, 104, 107-8

U
14, **17**, 19, 31, 87

U
5, 9, 28, 46

U — *bowing*
28, **30**, 134
(with foot serif)

U — *full*
1, 25

U — *half*
48, 81, 116

U
3

Column 3

U
10, 98

U — *high join to stem*
143

U — *wide*
161, 164, **184**

U — *narrow*
154, **160**, 165, 170-1, 176, 182

U — *long serifs*
177-9

U — *short serifs*
155, 157, **180**

U — *poor contrast*
151, 183

U — *abrupt contrast*
162-3, **170**, 179, 185-6

U — *thickening*
157

U — *flattened base*
161, 167-8, **182**, 187

Column 4

U
158

U — *thicker second stem*
183

U — *slight bowing*
181

U
155

U — *wide*
213

U — *narrow*
192, **194**-5, 201, 203-4, 215, 217

U — *poor contrast*
201, 206-9, 211, 213-4, 217

U — *some contrast*
189, **203**-4, 215

U — *poor contrast*
188

Column 5

U — *very*
189, 191, 201-3, **207**-13

U — *half serif*
216

U
192

U
204

U
218, 220, 223, 225, **227-8**

U
219, **221**, 224, 226, 229

U — *wide*
219, 225, 238

U — *narrow*
220, 226, 228, 237, 239

U — *some contrast*
219, 221, 229, 232-**3**, 235

Column 6

U — *long serifs*
230, **232**

U — *thicker second stem*
231

U
223

U — *slightly flattened base*
219

U
240

U
218

U
222

U
224

u
239

U — *wide*
245-8, 290-2, 294

Column 7

U — *narrow*
250, 252-3, 262, 272, 284-9, 296, 299-300, 302, 304

U — *slightly flattened base*
245, **265**, 274, 283, 291, 293

U
290, **292**, 294, 303

U
269, **297**

U — *thicker stem*
276-**7**

U — *vertical stress*
268-9, 272

U — *horizontal stress*
271

u
295

U
298, **301**

u
258, 298

NB. Bold figures indicate the specimen illustrated above.

'Special Earmarks'

The 'special earmarks' (or distinctive identifying features) are indicated on each letter. The general 'style' of typefaces with the same 'earmark' may vary. The figures refer to specimen numbers.

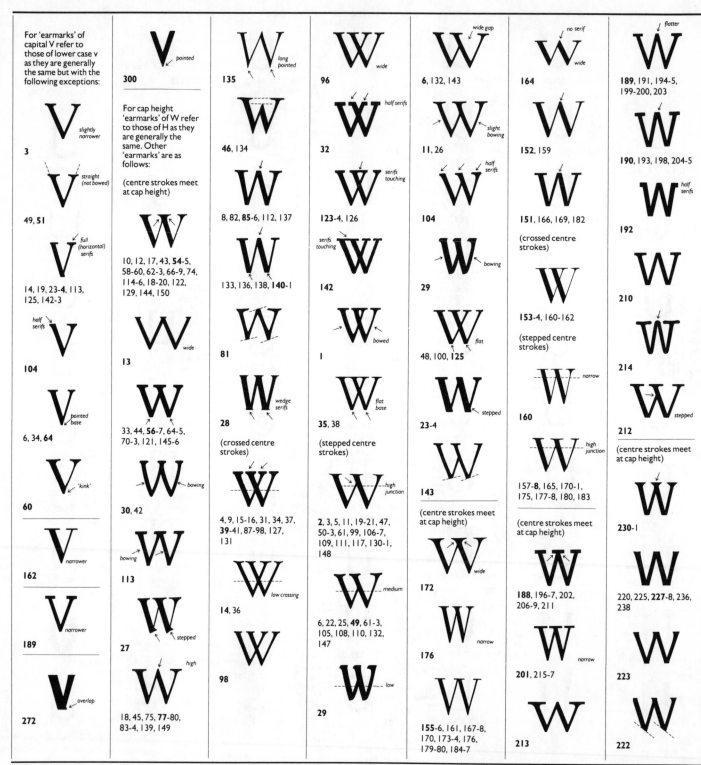

For 'earmarks' of capital V refer to those of lower case v as they are generally the same but with the following exceptions:

300 — pointed

For cap height 'earmarks' of W refer to those of H as they are generally the same. Other 'earmarks' are as follows:

(centre strokes meet at cap height)

V slightly narrower — **3**

V straight (not bowed) — **49, 51**

V full (horizontal) serifs — **14, 19, 23-4, 113, 125, 142-3**

V half serifs — **104**

V pointed base — **6, 34, 64**

V 'kink' — **60**

V narrower — **162**

V narrower — **189**

V overlap — **272**

W — **10, 12, 17, 43, 54-5, 58-60, 62-3, 66-9, 74, 114-6, 18-20, 122, 129, 144, 150**

W wide — **13**

W — **33, 44, 56-7, 64-5, 70-3, 121, 145-6**

W bowing — **30, 42**

W bowing — **113**

W stepped — **27**

W high — **18, 45, 75, 77-80, 83-4, 139, 149**

W long pointed — **135**

W — **46, 134**

W — **8, 82, 85-6, 112, 137**

W — **133, 136, 138, 140-1**

W — **81**

W wedge serifs — **28**

(crossed centre strokes) — **4, 9, 15-16, 31, 34, 37, 39-41, 87-98, 127, 131**

W low crossing — **14, 36**

W — **98**

W wide — **96**

W half serifs — **32**

W serifs touching — **123-4, 126**

W serifs touching — **142**

W bowed — **I**

W flat base — **35, 38**

(stepped centre strokes)

W high junction — **2, 3, 5, 11, 19-21, 47, 50-3, 61, 99, 106-7, 109, 111, 117, 130-1, 148**

W medium — **6, 22, 25, 49, 61-3, 105, 108, 110, 132, 147**

W low — **29**

W wide gap — **6, 132, 143**

W slight bowing — **11, 26**

W half serifs — **104**

W bowing — **29**

W flat — **48, 100, 125**

W stepped — **23-4**

W high junction — **143**

(centre strokes meet at cap height)

W wide — **172**

W narrow — **176**

W — **155-6, 161, 167-8, 170, 173-4, 176, 179-80, 184-7**

W no serif — **164**

W slight bowing — **152, 159**

W — **151, 166, 169, 182**

(crossed centre strokes) — **153-4, 160-162**

(stepped centre strokes)

W narrow — **160**

W high junction — **157-8, 165, 170-1, 175, 177-8, 180, 183**

(centre strokes meet at cap height)

W — **188, 196-7, 202, 206-9, 211**

W narrow — **201, 215-7**

W — **213**

W flatter — **189, 191, 194-5, 199-200, 203**

W — **190, 193, 198, 204-5**

W half serifs — **192**

W — **210**

W — **214**

W stepped — **212**

(centre strokes meet at cap height)

W — **230-1**

W — **220, 225, 227-8, 236, 238**

W — **223**

W — **222**

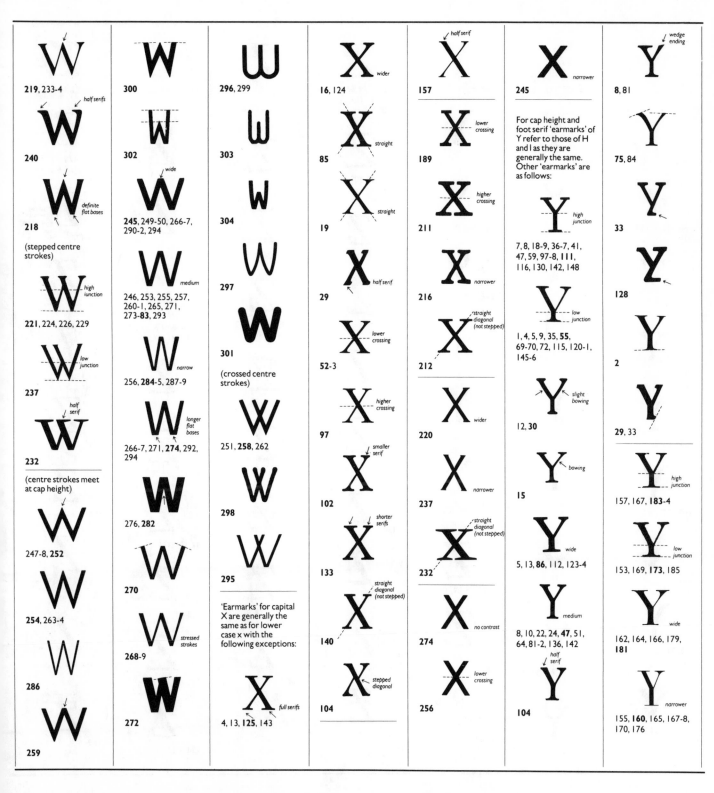

Column 1 (W)
- 219, 233-4
- *half serifs* — 240
- *definite flat bases* — 218
- (stepped centre strokes)
- *high junction* — 221, 224, 226, 229
- *low junction* — 237
- *half serif* — 232
- (centre strokes meet at cap height)
- 247-8, **252**
- **254**, 263-4
- 286
- 259

Column 2 (W)
- 300
- 302
- *wide* — **245**, 249-50, 266-7, 290-2, 294
- *medium* — 246, 253, 255, 257, 260-1, 265, 271, 273-**83**, 293
- *narrow* — 256, **284**-5, 287-9
- *longer flat bases* — 266-7, 271, **274**, 292, 294
- 276, **282**
- 270
- *stressed strokes* — 268-9
- 272

Column 3 (W)
- 296, 299
- 303
- 304
- 297
- 301
- (crossed centre strokes)
- 251, **258**, 262
- 298
- 295
- 'Earmarks' for capital X are generally the same as for lower case x with the following exceptions:
- *full serifs* — 4, 13, **125**, 143

Column 4 (X)
- *wider* — 16, 124
- *straight* — 85
- *straight* — 19
- *half serif* — 29
- *lower crossing* — 52-3
- *higher crossing* — 97
- *smaller serif* — 102
- *shorter serifs* — 133
- *straight diagonal (not stepped)* — 140
- *stepped diagonal* — 104

Column 5 (X)
- *half serif* — 157
- *lower crossing* — 189
- *higher crossing* — 211
- *narrower* — 216
- *straight diagonal (not stepped)* — 212
- *wider* — 220
- *narrower* — 237
- *straight diagonal (not stepped)* — 232
- *no contrast* — 274
- *lower crossing* — 256

Column 6 (X / Y)
- *narrower* — 245
- For cap height and foot serif 'earmarks' of Y refer to those of H and I as they are generally the same. Other 'earmarks' are as follows:
- *high junction* — 7, 8, 18-9, 36-7, 41, 47, 59, 97-8, **111**, 116, 130, 142, 148
- *low junction* — 1, 4, 5, 9, 35, **55**, 69-70, 72, 115, 120-1, 145-6
- *slight bowing* — 12, **30**
- *bowing* — 15
- *wide* — 5, 13, **86**, 112, 123-4
- *medium* — 8, 10, 22, 24, **47**, 51, 64, 81-2, 136, 142
- *half serif* — 104

Column 7 (Y)
- *wedge ending* — 8, 81
- 75, 84
- 33
- 128
- 2
- 29, 33
- *high junction* — 157, 167, **183**-4
- *low junction* — 153, 169, **173**, 185
- *wide* — 162, 164, 166, 179, **181**
- *narrower* — 155, **160**, 165, 167-8, 170, 176

'Special Earmarks'
The 'special earmarks' (or distinctive identifying features) are indicated on each letter. The general 'style' of typefaces with the same 'earmark' may vary. The figures refer to specimen numbers.

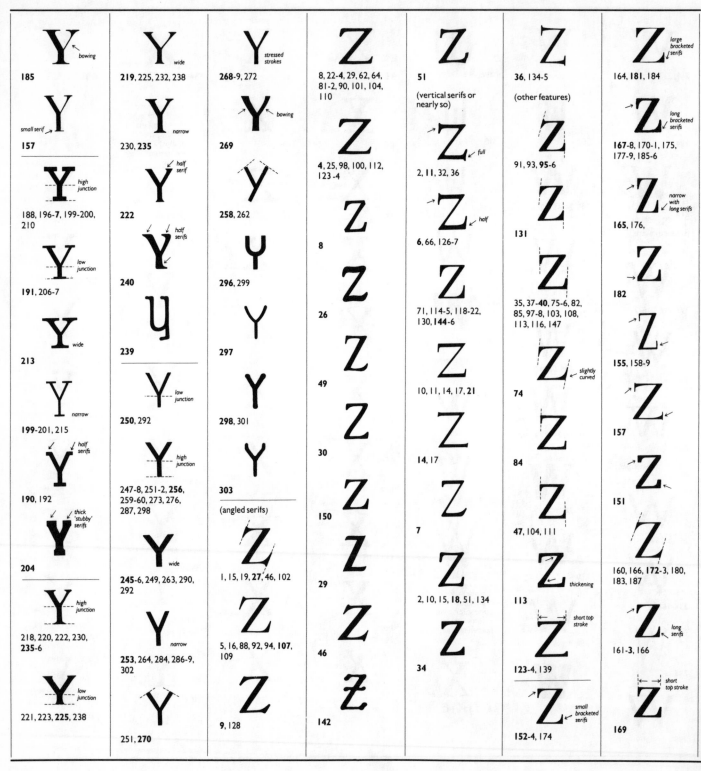

185 — bowing

157 — small serif

188, 196-7, 199-200, 210 — high junction

191, 206-7 — low junction

213 — wide

199-201, 215 — narrow

190, 192 — half serifs

204 — thick 'stubby' serifs

218, 220, 222, 230, 235-6 — high junction

221, 223, 225, 238 — low junction

219, 225, 232, 238 — wide

230, 235 — narrow

222 — half serif

240 — half serifs

239

250, 292 — low junction

247-8, 251-2, 256, 259-60, 273, 276, 287, 298 — high junction

245-6, 249, 263, 290, 292 — wide

253, 264, 284, 286-9, 302 — narrow

251, 270

268-9, 272 — stressed strokes

269 — bowing

258, 262

296, 299

297

298, 301

303
(angled serifs)

1, 15, 19, 27, 46, 102

5, 16, 88, 92, 94, 107, 109

9, 128

8, 22-4, 29, 62, 64, 81-2, 90, 101, 104, 110

4, 25, 98, 100, 112, 123-4

8

26

49

30

150

7

29

46

142

51
(vertical serifs or nearly so)

2, 11, 32, 36 — full

6, 66, 126-7 — half

71, 114-5, 118-22, 130, 144-6

10, 11, 14, 17, 21

14, 17

2, 10, 15, 18, 51, 134

34

36, 134-5
(other features)

91, 93, 95-6

131

74 — slightly curved

84

47, 104, 111

113 — thickening

123-4, 139 — short top stroke

152-4, 174 — small bracketed serifs

164, 181, 184 — large bracketed serifs

167-8, 170-1, 175, 177-9, 185-6 — long bracketed serifs

165, 176, — narrow with long serifs

182

155, 158-9

157

151

160, 166, 172-3, 180, 183, 187

161-3, 166 — long serifs

169 — short top stroke

Z (serifs)	Z	Z / &	&	&	&	&
slightly extended bottom — **187**	**230, 233**	curved — **269, 297**	**50**, 52-3, 76, 101, 107, 112, 114, 119-22, 129, 131	**125**	6, **150**	156, 164, 167, 170, **173**, 186
189, 210	no contrast — **236-8**	**296, 299**	68	5 (open bowls)	2, **108**	161, 166, 170-1, **175**-80, 185, 187
191, **207-9**	full serif — **231**	(closed bowls) 96	58, 62, 69, **79**	**21**, **23-4**, 49, 51, 132	3	153, **160**
short serifs — **194-5**	wide top stroke — **232**	1, 12, 19-20, 27, 42, 45-6, 57, 71, 89-90, **97-8**, 105, 126, 133, 138, 147, 149	56	22, **37**, 140	4	169
longer serifs — **201**, 203, 207-8, 214	**239**	64, 100	142	29, **32**	134	158, 172
218, 220, 225	245, **251**-9, 262-4, 300, 302	113	10, **74-5**, 116, 139, 147	9	135	open — 157
223, 227	253	127	141	104, 110	13	**189**, 193, 196, 198
228	248, 270	44	14, 17-8, ,33, 77	8, **81**	143	197
wedge serifs — **219**, 221, 226, 229, 232, 234-5, 240	stressed strokes — 268	1	82	128	151-2, **159**, 165, 174, 184-4	191
224	**298**, 301, 303	123-4, 126	2	36, 130	154, **162-3**, 165, 181-2	190

129

'Special Earmarks'
The 'special earmarks' (or distinctive identifying features) are indicated on each letter. The general 'style' of typefaces with the same 'earmark' may vary. The figures refer to specimen numbers.

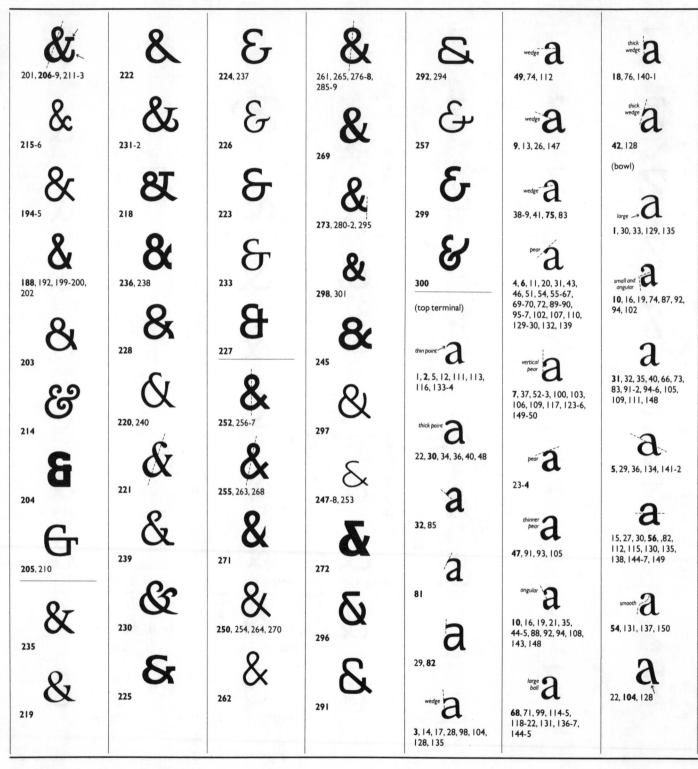

Column 1 (&)
- 201, **206**-9, 211-3
- 215-6
- 194-5
- **188**, 192, 199-200, 202
- 203
- 214
- 204
- **205**, 210
- 235
- 219

Column 2 (&)
- 222
- 231-2
- 218
- 236, 238
- 228
- 220, 240
- 221
- 239
- 230
- 225

Column 3 (&)
- 224, 237
- 226
- 223
- 233
- 227
- **252**, 256-7
- 255, 263, 268
- 271
- 250, 254, 264, 270
- 262

Column 4 (&)
- 261, 265, 276-8, 285-9
- 269
- 273, 280-2, 295
- 298, 301
- 245
- 297
- 247-8, 253
- 272
- 296
- 291

Column 5 (&)
- 292, 294
- 257
- 299
- 300
- (top terminal)
- *thin point* 1, **2**, 5, 12, 111, 113, 116, 133-4
- *thick point* 22, **30**, 34, 36, 40, 48
- 32, 85
- 81
- 29, **82**
- *wedge* **3**, 14, 17, 28, 98, 104, 128, 135

Column 6 (a)
- *wedge* **49**, 74, 112
- *wedge* **9**, 13, 26, 147
- *wedge* 38-9, 41, **75**, 83
- *pear* 4, **6**, 11, 20, 31, 43, 46, 51, 54, 55-67, 69-70, 72, 89-90, 95-7, 102, 107, 110, 129-30, 132, 139
- *vertical pear* **7**, 37, 52-3, 100, 103, 106, 109, 117, 123-6, 149-50
- *pear* 23-4
- *thinner pear* 47, 91, 93, 105
- *angular* **10**, 16, 19, 21, 35, 44-5, 88, 92, 94, 108, 143, 148
- *large ball* **68**, 71, 99, 114-5, 118-22, 131, 136-7, 144-5

Column 7 (a)
- *thick wedge* **18**, 76, 140-1
- *thick wedge* **42**, 128
- (bowl)
- *large* 1, 30, 33, 129, 135
- *small and angular* **10**, 16, 19, 74, 87, 92, 94, 102
- **31**, 32, 35, 40, 66, 73, 83, 91-2, 94-6, 105, 109, 111, 148
- 5, 29, 36, 134, 141-2
- 15, 27, 30, **56**, ,82, 112, 115, 130, 135, 138, 144-7, 149
- *smooth* 54, 131, 137, 150
- 22, **104**, 128

NB. *Bold figures indicate the specimen illustrated above.*

'Special Earmarks'
*The 'special earmarks'
(or distinctive identifying
features) are indicated on
each letter. The general
'style' of typefaces with the
same 'earmark' may vary.
The figures refer to
specimen numbers.*

(back)

5, 13, 104, 123-4, 129

23-4, 29-30

40, **44**, 47, 73, 87, 91-6

wide opening — 8, **14**, 17, 23-4, 48, 77-81, 98, 135, 143

(foot serif)

thin — 1, 75, 84, 125, 131, 134-5

thicker — 81, 113, **133**, 136, 138, 140-3, 150

short and thick — **8**, 12, 22, 29-30, 56, 71, 82, 104, 112, 126, 128

pointed — 28

---

short — **2-3**, 10, 15, 37, 45, 47, 66, 76, 98, 102, 108, 142, 148

short and heavy — 44

longer — 19, 42, 97, 108, 147

14, 17-8, 21, 37, 46, 111, 129

short and rounded — **4**, 7, 15, 23-4, 26, 32-3, 38-9, 41, 48, 50-2, 60-4, 66-8, 74, 78, 89-90, 100, 106, 115, 118-9, 120, 124, 128, 130, 139, 144, 146

long and rounded — 5, **6**, 9, 11, 13, 16, 20, 25, 27, 31, 34-6, 43, 53-4, 65, 69-70, 72, 77-80, 83, 85, 91-2, 99, 101, 103, 107, 109-10, 114, 117, 121, 127, 132, 149

35-6, **40**, 42, 49, 55, 58-9, 73, 76, 83, 87-8, 93-7, 105, 115-6

86, 122

---

long curled up — 70, 78, 114, **137**

(top terminal)

151, 182

157, **165**

155, 166

ball — **160**, 162-4, 170-1, 175-81, 184-6

pear — 152-4, **156**, 167-9, 172-4

thin pear — 158-9, 161, **172**, 187

pointed — 183

(bowl)

155, **157**, 159

153, 161-3, 187

smooth — **156**, 160, 164, 169, 178-81

(foot serif)

angled and flat — 151-2, 155, 165, **183**

161, 167-8, 171, 180, 182, 187

158

curled up — 160, 164, 170, 173, 175-9, **185-6**

(double storey)

188-9, 191, 197, 203

190, 204, 206-9, 211

192, **198**, 201-2, 205, 210, 215

212-4, 216-7

189, 204-5

188, 191

188-**93**, 197-8, 203-5

201, 206-9, 211-5, 217

(single storey)

194-6

199-200

(double storey)

wide — 219, 225

218, 222, 225, 235, 240

227, 231

223-4, 226, 228, 234

pear — 229, 232

curl — 230

curl — 231

pointed — 233

smooth — 222, **226**, 228, 230

239

(single storey)

237

(double storey)

square — 291-2, 297

245-6, **249**, 251, 253, 256, 261, 264-5, 270, 282, 285-9

259, 262, 266, 268-9, 271-2, 295

267, 273-81, 283, 291-3, 304

284

251, **253**, 262, 264

smooth — 245, **261**, 265, 268, 271, 275, 279, 295

large top — 271

small top — 270

259, **270**

NB. *Bold figures indicate the specimen illustrated above.*

'Special Earmarks'
The 'special earmarks' (or distinctive identifying features) are indicated on each letter. The general 'style' of typefaces with the same 'earmark' may vary. The figures refer to specimen numbers.

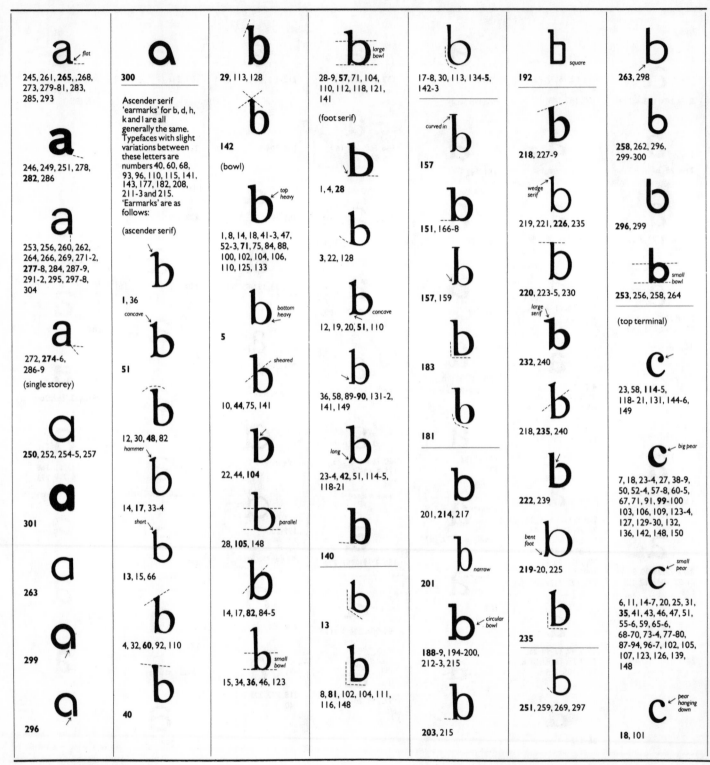

a *flat*
245, 261, **265**, ,268, 273, 279-81, 283, 285, 293

a
246, 249, 251, 278, **282**, 286

a
253, 256, 260, 262, 264, 266, 269, 271-2, **277**-8, 284, 287-9, 291-2, 295, 297-8, 304

a
272, **274**-6, 286-9

(single storey)

a
250, 252, 254-5, 257

a
301

a
263

a
299

a
296

a
300

Ascender serif 'earmarks' for b, d, h, k and l are all generally the same. Typefaces with slight variations between these letters are numbers 40, 60, 68, 93, 96, 110, 115, 141, 143, 177, 182, 208, 211-3 and 215. 'Earmarks' are as follows:

(ascender serif)

b
1, 36

b *concave*
51

b
12, 30, **48**, 82

b *hammer*
14, **17**, 33-4

b *short*
13, 15, 66

b
4, 32, **60**, 92, 110

b
40

b
29, 113, 128

b
142

(bowl)

b *top heavy*
1, 8, 14, 18, 41-3, 47, 52-3, **71**, 75, 84, 88, 100, 102, 104, 106, 110, 125, 133

b *bottom heavy*
5

b *sheared*
10, **44**, 75, 141

b
22, 44, **104**

b *parallel*
28, **105**, 148

b
14, 17, **82**, 84-5

b *small bowl*
15, 34, **36**, 46, 123

b *large bowl*
28-9, **57**, 71, 104, 110, 112, 118, 121, 141

(foot serif)

b
1, 4, **28**

b
3, 22, 128

b *concave*
12, 19, 20, **51**, 110

b
36, 58, 89-**90**, 131-2, 141, 149

b *long*
23-4, **42**, 51, 114-5, 118-21

b
201, **214**, 217

b
140

b
13

b
8, **81**, 102, 104, 111, 116, 148

b
17-8, 30, 113, 134-**5**, 142-3

b *curved in*
157

b
151, 166-8

b
157, 159

b
183

b
181

b
201

b *narrow*
188-9, 194-200, 212-3, 215

b *circular bowl*
203, 215

b *square*
192

b
218, 227-9

b *wedge serif*
219, 221, **226**, 235

b
220, 223-5, 230

b *large serif*
232, 240

b
218, **235**, 240

b
222, 239

b *bent foot*
219-20, 225

b
235

b
251, 259, 269, 297

b
263, 298

b
258, 262, 296, 299-300

b
296, 299

b *small bowl*
253, 256, 258, 264

(top terminal)

c
23, 58, 114-5, 118-21, 131, 144-6, 149

c *big pear*
7, 18, 23-4, 27, 38-9, 50, 52-4, 57-8, 60-5, 67, 71, 91, **99**-100, 103, 106, 109, 123-4, 127, 129-30, 132, 136, 142, 148, 150

c *small pear*
6, 11, 14-7, 20, 25, 31, **35**, 41, 43, 46, 47, 51, 55-6, 59, 65-6, 68-70, 73-4, 77-80, 87-94, 96-7, 102, 105, 107, 123, 126, 139, 148

c *pear hanging down*
18, 101

NB. *Bold figures indicate the specimen illustrated above.*

'Special Earmarks'
The 'special earmarks' (or distinctive identifying features) are indicated on each letter. The general 'style' of typefaces with the same 'earmark' may vary. The figures refer to specimen numbers.

Column 1 (c)

1, 22, 28

2, 3, 5, 10, 12-3, **26**, 29, 42, 49, 128, 143

117

4, 16, **19**, 32, 34, 48, 83, 108

81, 147

rounded wedge
86, **125**

33, **37**, 45, 82, 95, 98, 134-5

hook
75, 84-5, 104, 112-3, 133, 138, 140-1

square pear
44, **76**, 138, 140-1

Column 2 (c)

identical serifs
28, **138**, 140-2

44
(general)

narrow
8, 18, 23-4, 29, **64**, 75, 93, 104, 134

2, 4, 6, 21, **43**, 45, 70, 72, 83

23, 26, 31, 35, 41, 87 **93**, 102, 113

ball
153-4, 160, 162-4, 170-1, 175- 81, 184-6

pear
152, 156, 167-9, 174, 187

thin pear
158-9, 161, 172-3

serif
157, 183

Column 3 (c)

spiked serif
165-6

square
151, 182

155

narrow
155, 165, **176**

188, 191, **196**-7, 199

half serif
189

narrow opening
205, 210

ball
206-9, 211-7

Column 4 (c)

218, 220, 222-3, 225-8

219, 233-4

narrow
221, **229**

flat top
235

hook
224, 231, 240

curl
230-1

250, 265, 267, 273-5, 278-280, 283, 291-3, 304

246, 249, 252, **254**, 257-60, 263-4, 266, 269, 271, 295-6

245, 247-8, 251, 253, **255**-6, 261-2, 270, 276-7, 282, 285-9, 299-300

Column 5 (c)

281

slight contrast
268

top heavy
271

slight contrast
272

bottom heavy
284

small serifs
297

298

For ascender serif and bowl 'earmarks' of d refer to those of b as they are generally the same. Other 'earmarks' are as follows:

(foot serif)

flat
1, 28, 111, 116

Column 6 (d)

4, 8-10, 12, 22, 27, 33, 56-7, **62**, 64, 75, 78, 80-2, 84, 87, 89-90, 104, 110, 112-5, 118-149

6, 7, 11, 14-9, 21, 26, 31-2, 34-5, **37**-44, 47, 49, 52-5, 58-61, 63, 65-72, 74, 76, 83, 85-6, 88, 91-7, 99-103, 105-7, 146, 148

2, 3, 5, 13, **20**, 23-5, 45-6, 48, 50-1, 73, 77, 79, 98, 108-9, 117, 150

30

36

42

rounded
157, 159

171-2, 182-3

angular

Column 7 (d)

wide bowl
169

208-213

218-30

231-5, 240

tapered
246

269

272

top heavy
271

251, 259, 297

299-**300**

NB. *Bold figures indicate the specimen illustrated above.*

'Special Earmarks'
The 'special earmarks' (or distinctive identifying features) are indicated on each letter. The general 'style' of typefaces with the same 'earmark' may vary. The figures refer to specimen numbers.

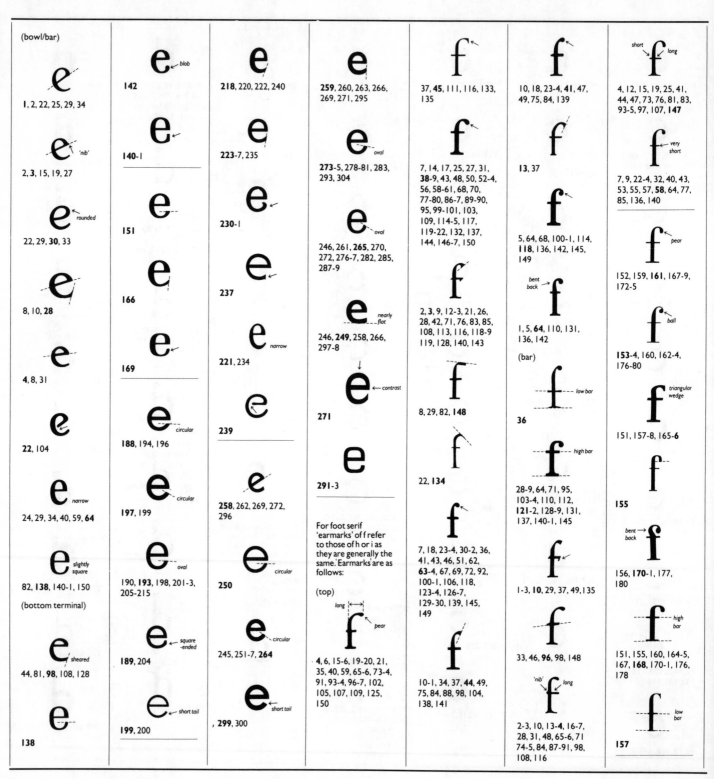

(bowl/bar)

1, 2, 22, 25, 29, 34

2, **3**, 15, 19, 27 — 'nib'

22, 29, **30**, 33 — rounded

8, 10, **28**

4, 8, 31

22, 104

24, 29, 34, 40, 59, **64** — narrow

82, **138**, 140-1, 150 — slightly square

(bottom terminal)

44, 81, **98**, 108, 128 — sheared

138

---

142 — blob

140-1

151

166

169

188, 194, 196 — circular

197, 199 — circular

190, **193**, 198, 201-3, 205-215 — oval

189, 204 — square-ended

199, 200 — short tail

218, 220, 222, 240

223-7, 235

230-1

237

221, 234 — narrow

239

258, 262, 269, 272, 296

250 — circular

245, 251-7, **264** — circular

, **299**, 300 — short tail

259, 260, 263, 266, 269, 271, 295

273-5, 278-81, 283, 293, 304 — oval

246, 261, **265**, 270, 272, 276-7, 282, 285, 287-9 — oval

246, **249**, 258, 266, 297-8 — nearly flat

271 — contrast

291-3

For foot serif 'earmarks' of f refer to those of h or i as they are generally the same. Earmarks are as follows:

(top)

4, 6, 15-6, 19-20, 21, 35, 40, 59, 65-6, 73-4, 91, 93-4, 96-7, 102, 105, 107, 109, 125, 150 — long, pear

---

37, **45**, 111, 116, 133, 135

7, 14, 17, 25, 27, 31, **38**-9, 43, 48, 50, 52-4, 56, 58-61, 68, 70, 77-80, 86-7, 89-90, 95, 99-101, 103, 109, 114-5, 117, 119-22, 132, 137, 144, 146-7, 150

2, **3**, 9, 12-3, 21, 26, 28, 42, 71, 76, 83, 85, 108, 113, 116, 118-9, 119, 128, 140, 143

8, 29, 82, **148**

22, **134**

7, 18, 23-4, 30-2, 36, 41, 43, 46, 51, 62, **63**-4, 67, 69, 72, 92, 100-1, 106, 118, 123-4, 126-7, 129-30, 139, 145, 149

10-1, 34, 37, **44**, 49, 75, 84, 88, 98, 104, 138, 141

10, 18, 23-4, **41**, 47, 49, 75, 84, 139

13, 37

5, 64, 68, 100-1, 114, **118**, 136, 142, 145, 149

1, 5, **64**, 110, 131, 136, 142 — bent back

(bar)

36 — low bar

28-9, 64, 71, 95, 103-4, 110, 112, **121**-2, 128-9, 131, 137, 140-1, 145 — high bar

1-3, **10**, 29, 37, 49, 135

33, 46, **96**, 98, 148

2-3, **10**, 13-4, 16-7, 28, 31, 48, 65-6, 71, 74-5, 84, 87-91, 98, 108, 116 — 'nib' long

---

4, 12, 15, 19, 25, 41, 44, 47, 73, 76, 81, 83, 93-5, 97, 107, **147** — short, long

7, 9, 22-4, 32, 40, 43, 53, 55, 57, **58**, 64, 77, 85, 136, 140 — very short

152, 159, **161**, 167-9, 172-5 — pear

153-4, 160, 162-4, 176-80 — ball

151, 157-8, 165-**6** — triangular wedge

155

156, **170**-1, 177, 180 — bent back

151, 155, 160, 164-5, 167, **168**, 170-1, 176, 178 — high bar

157 — low bar

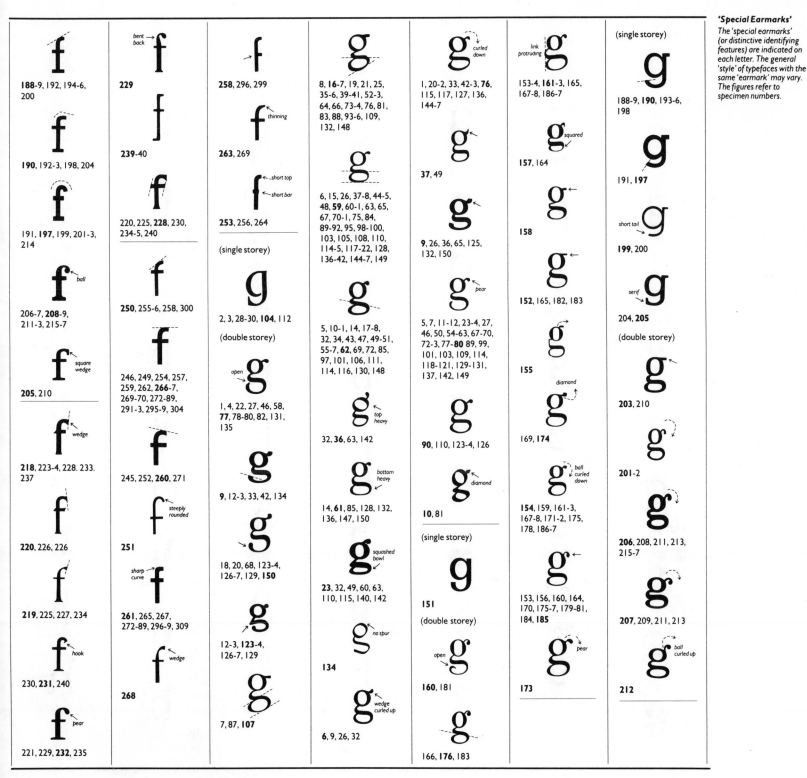

NB. *Bold figures indicate the specimen illustrated above.*

'Special Earmarks'
The 'special earmarks' (or distinctive identifying features) are indicated on each letter. The general 'style' of typefaces with the same 'earmark' may vary. The figures refer to specimen numbers.

'Special Earmarks'
The 'special earmarks' (or distinctive identifying features) are indicated on each letter. The general 'style' of typefaces with the same 'earmark' may vary. The figures refer to specimen numbers.

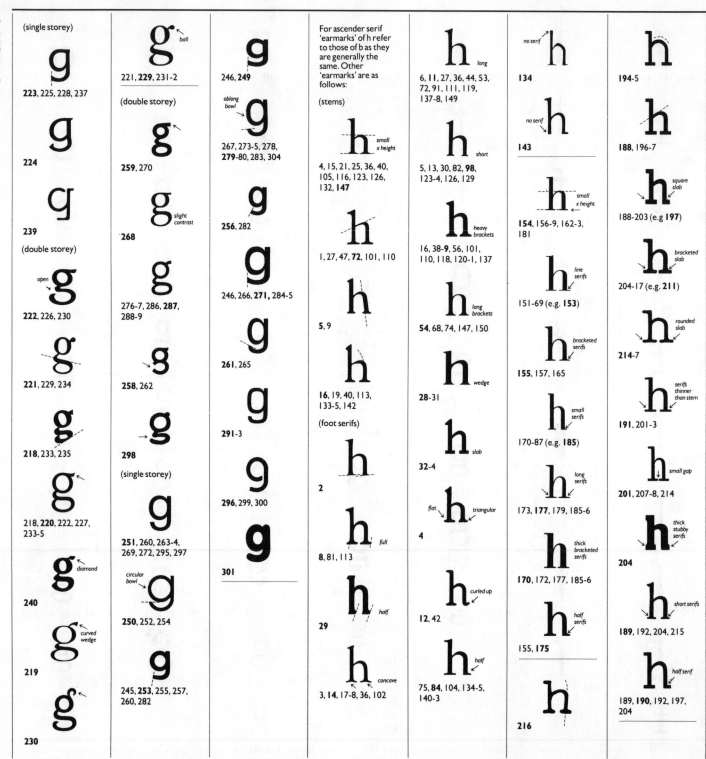

(single storey)

223, 225, 228, 237

224

239

(double storey)

open
222, 226, 230

221, **229**, 234

218, 233, 235

218, **220**, 222, 227, 233-5

diamond
240

curved wedge
219

230

ball
221, **229**, 231-2

(double storey)

259, 270

slight contrast
268

276-7, 286, **287**, 288-9

258, 262

298

(single storey)

251, 260, 263-4, 269, 272, 295, 297

circular bowl
250, 252, 254

245, **253**, 255, 257, 260, 282

246, 249

oblong bowl
267, 273-5, 278, **279**-80, 283, 304

256, 282

246, 266, **271**, 284-5

261, 265

291-3

296, 299, 300

301

For ascender serif 'earmarks' of h refer to those of b as they are generally the same. Other 'earmarks' are as follows:

(stems)

small x height
4, 15, 21, 25, 36, 40, 105, 116, 123, 126, 132, **147**

1, 27, 47, **72**, 101, 110

5, 9

16, 19, 40, 113, 133-5, 142

(foot serifs)

2

full
8, 81, 113

half
29

concave
3, **14**, 17-8, 36, 102

long
6, **11**, 27, 36, 44, 53, 72, 91, 111, 119, 137-8, 149

short
5, 13, 30, 82, **98**, 123-4, 126, 129

heavy brackets
16, 38-**9**, 56, 101, 110, 118, 120-1, 137

long brackets
54, 68, 74, 147, 150

wedge
28-31

slab
32-4

flat / *triangular*
4

curled up
12, 42

half
75, **84**, 104, 134-5, 140-3

no serif
134

no serif
143

small x height
154, 156-9, 162-3, 181

line serifs
151-69 (e.g. **153**)

bracketed serifs
155, 157, 165

small serifs
170-87 (e.g. **185**)

long serifs
173, **177**, 179, 185-6

thick bracketed serifs
170, 172, 177, 185-6

half serifs
155, **175**

216

194-5

188, 196-7

square slab
188-203 (e.g **197**)

bracketed slab
204-17 (e.g. **211**)

rounded slab
214-7

serifs thinner than stem
191, 201-3

small gap
201, 207-8, 214

thick stubby serifs
204

short serifs
189, 192, 204, 215

half serif
189, **190**, 192, 197, 204

NB. *Bold figures indicate the specimen illustrated above.*

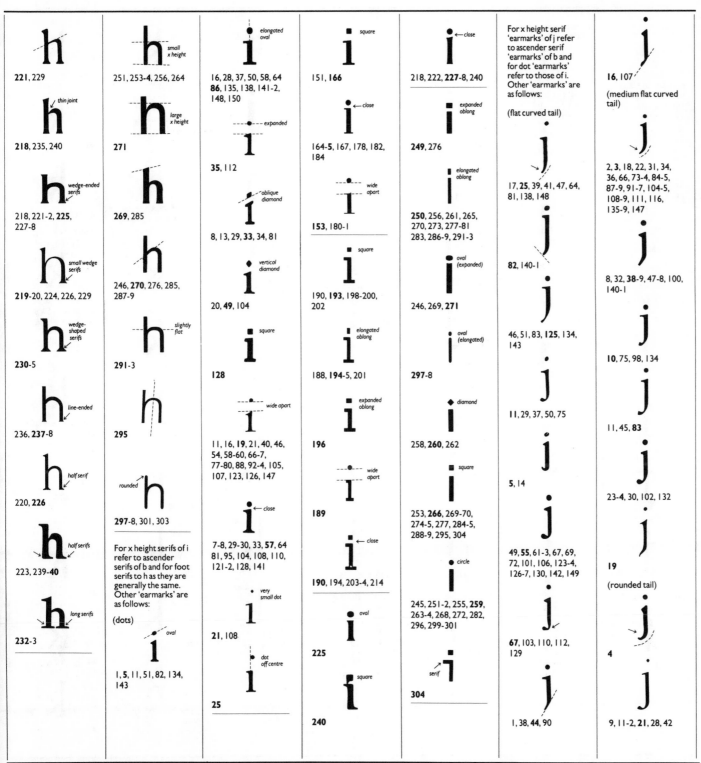

h
221, 229

h thin joint
218, 235, 240

h wedge-ended serifs
218, 221-2, **225**, 227-8

h small wedge serifs
219-20, 224, 226, 229

h wedge-shaped serifs
230-5

h line-ended
236, **237-8**

h half serif
220, **226**

h half serifs
223, 239-**40**

h long serifs
232-3

h small x height
251, 253-**4**, 256, 264

h large x height
271

h
269, 285

h
246, **270**, 276, 285, 287-9

h slightly flat
291-3

h
295

h rounded
297-8, 301, 303

For x height serifs of i refer to ascender serifs of b and for foot serifs to h as they are generally the same. Other 'earmarks' are as follows:

(dots)

i oval
1, **5**, 11, 51, 82, 134, 143

i elongated oval
16, 28, 37, 50, 58, 64 **86**, 135, 138, 141-2, 148, 150

i expanded
35, 112

i oblique diamond
8, 13, 29, **33**, 34, 81

i vertical diamond
20, **49**, 104

i square
128

i wide apart
11, 16, **19**, 21, 40, 46, 54, 58-60, 66-7, 77-80, 88, 92-4, 105, 107, 123, 126, 147

i close
7-8, 29-30, 33, **57**, 64 81, 95, 104, 108, 110, 121-2, 128, 141

i very small dot
21, 108

i dot off centre
25

i square
151, **166**

i close
164-**5**, 167, 178, 182, 184

i wide apart
153, 180-1

i square
190, **193**, 198-200, 202

i elongated oblong
188, **194-5**, 201

i expanded oblong
196

i wide apart
189

i close
190, 194, 203-4, 214

i oval
225

i square
240

i close
218, 222, **227-8**, 240

i expanded oblong
249, 276

i elongated oblong
250, 256, 261, 265, 270, 273, 277-81 283, 286-9, 291-3

i oval (expanded)
246, 269, **271**

i oval (elongated)
297-8

i diamond
258, **260**, 262

i square
253, **266**, 269-70, 274-5, 277, 284-5, 288-9, 295, 304

i circle
245, 251-2, 255, **259**, 263-4, 268, 272, 282, 296, 299-301

j serif
304

For x height serif 'earmarks' of j refer to ascender serif 'earmarks' of b and for dot 'earmarks' refer to those of i. Other 'earmarks' are as follows:

(flat curved tail)

j
17, **25**, 39, 41, 47, 64, 81, 138, 148

j
82, 140-1

j
46, 51, 83, **125**, 134, 143

j
11, 29, 37, 50, 75

j
5, 14

j
49, **55**, 61-3, 67, 69, 72, 101, 106, 123-4, 126-7, 130, 142, 149

j
67, 103, 110, 112, 129

j
1, 38, **44**, 90

j
16, 107

(medium flat curved tail)

j
2, **3**, 18, 22, 31, 34, 36, 66, 73-4, 84-5, 87-9, 91-7, 104-5, 108-9, 111, 116, 135-9, 147

j
8, 32, **38-9**, 47-8, 100, 140-1

j
10, 75, 98, 134

j
11, 45, **83**

j
23-4, 30, 102, 132

j
19

(rounded tail)

j
4

j
9, 11-2, **21**, 28, 42

'Special Earmarks'
The 'special earmarks' (or distinctive identifying features) are indicated on each letter. The general 'style' of typefaces with the same 'earmark' may vary. The figures refer to specimen numbers.

NB. *Bold figures indicate the specimen illustrated above.*

'Special Earmarks'
The 'special earmarks' (or distinctive identifying features) are indicated on each letter. The general 'style' of typefaces with the same 'earmark' may vary. The figures refer to specimen numbers.

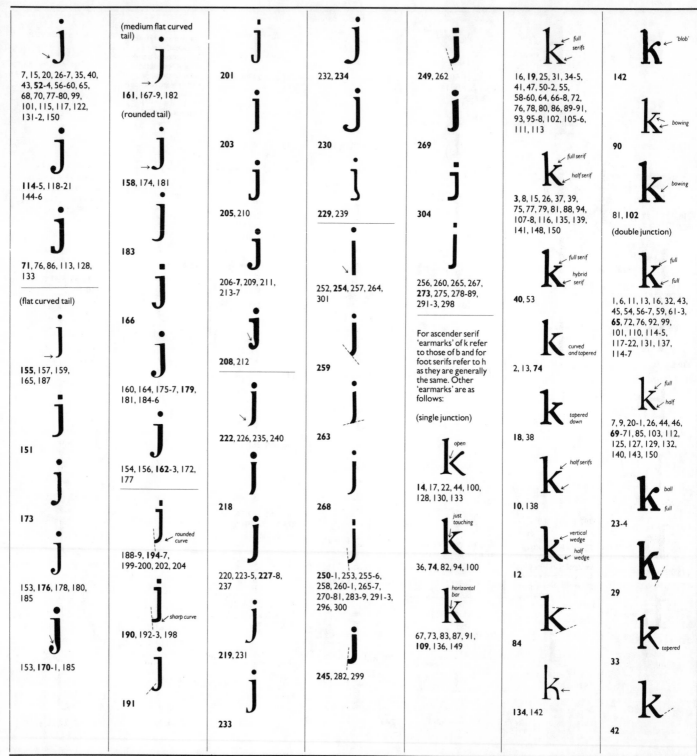

7, 15, 20, 26-7, 35, 40, 43, **52**-4, 56-60, 65, 68, 70, 77-80, 99, 101, 115, 117, 122, 131-2, 150

114-5, 118-21 144-6

71, 76, 86, 113, 128, 133

(flat curved tail)

155, 157, 159, 165, 187

151

173

153, **176**, 178, 180, 185

153, **170**-1, 185

(medium flat curved tail)

161, 167-9, 182

(rounded tail)

158, 174, 181

183

166

160, 164, 175-7, **179**, 181, 184-6

154, 156, **162**-3, 172, 177

rounded curve

188-9, **194**-7, 199-200, 202, 204

sharp curve

190, 192-3, 198

191

201

203

205, 210

206-**7**, 209, 211, 213-7

208, 212

222, 226, 235, 240

218

220, 223-5, **227**-8, 237

219, 231

233

232, **234**

230

229, 239

252, **254**, 257, 264, 301

259

263

268

250-1, 253, 255-6, 258, 260-1, 265-7, 270-81, 283-9, 291-3, 296, 300

245, 282, 299

249, 262

269

304

256, 260, 265, 267, **273**, 275, 278-89, 291-3, 298

For ascender serif 'earmarks' of k refer to those of b and for foot serifs refer to h as they are generally the same. Other 'earmarks' are as follows:

(single junction)

open

14, 17, 22, 44, 100, 128, 130, 133

just touching

36, **74**, 82, 94, 100

horizontal bar

67, 73, 83, 87, 91, **109**, 136, 149

full serifs

16, **19**, 25, 31, 34-5, 41, 47, 50-2, 55, 58-60, 64, 66-8, 72, 76, 78, 80, 86, 89-91, 93, 95-8, 102, 105-6, 111, 113

full serif / half serif

3, 8, 15, 26, 37, 39, 75, 77, 79, 81, 88, 94, 107-8, 116, 135, 139, 141, 148, 150

full serif / hybrid serif

40, 53

curved and tapered

2, 13, **74**

tapered down

18, 38

half serifs

10, 138

vertical wedge / half wedge

12

134, 142

'blob'

142

bowing

90

bowing

81, **102**

(double junction)

full / full

1, 6, 11, 13, 16, 32, 43, 45, 54, 56-7, 59, 61-3, **65**, 72, 76, 92, 99, 101, 110, 114-5, 117-22, 131, 137, 114-7

full / half

7, 9, 20-1, 26, 44, 46, **69**-71, 85, 103, 112, 125, 127, 129, 132, 140, 143, 150

ball / full

23-4

29

tapered

33

42

NB. *Bold figures indicate the specimen illustrated above.*

'Special Earmarks'
The 'special earmarks' (or distinctive identifying features) are indicated on each letter. The general 'style' of typefaces with the same 'earmark' may vary. The figures refer to specimen numbers.

Column 1 (k)

wedge
104

no serif
143

full / *full*
5

overlap
27

28

30

(single junction)

open
154, 162-**3**, 182

horizontal bar
155-6, 158, **161**, 167-8, 187

155

full / *full*
152, 154, 159, 165, 181, **183-4**

Column 2 (k)

ball
181

(double junction)

full / *full*
153, 157, 160, 164, 170-1, 173, 176-80, 185-6

full / *half*
151, 166, 169, 174-5

172

(single junction)

210

188, 194-6, 199-200, 205, 210

189, 197, 203-4

192

(double junction)

193, 198, 201-2, 206-9, 211-7

Column 3 (k)

190

(single junction)

open
222, 230, **234**, 237

horizontal bar
235

218, **220**, 226, 233, 239-40

219, 223

(double junction)

221, **224**-5, 227-9, 231-2

(single junction)

246, 254, **259**, 263, 271, 283, 285, 295

270

horizontal bar
268, 291-**2**

Column 4 (k)

246, 249, 252-3, **255**, 260, 264, 266-7, 278, 283, 304

251, 262

297-8, **301**

272

296-7

299-300

(double junction)

245, 250, 256-7, 261, 265, 269, 273-7, **279**-82, 284, 286-9, 293

long / *short*
250, 284

Column 5 (l)

For ascender serif 'earmarks' of l refer to those of b and for foot serifs to h as they are generally the same. Exceptions and other 'earmarks' are as follows:

very slight thinning
2, 8, 10-1, **19**, 36, 81, 104, 113, 130, 133

thinning
98

no serif
134

1, 36

142

14, 17, 33-4

135

143

curled in
157

Column 6 (l / m)

214-7

long
215-7

218, 227-9

220, 222-**3**, 225, 230, 237

half serif
239-40

263, 269, 285

268, 295

tail
282, 304

297-8, **301**

Column 7 (m)

For x height serif 'earmarks' of m refer to ascender serif 'earmarks' of b and for foot serifs to h. Exceptions and other 'earmarks' are as follows:

(stems)

1, 16, 19, 27, 32, 35-6, 46-7, **72**, 82, 101-2, 110, 125, 139

angular pen stroke
10, 75, 108

5, 9

11, **113**, 133

slight bowing
14-7

89

(foot serifs)

2

12, 42

half serif
75, 84, 141

NB. Bold figures indicate the specimen illustrated above.

'Special Earmarks'
The 'special earmarks' (or distinctive identifying features) are indicated on each letter. The general 'style' of typefaces with the same 'earmark' may vary. The figures refer to specimen numbers.

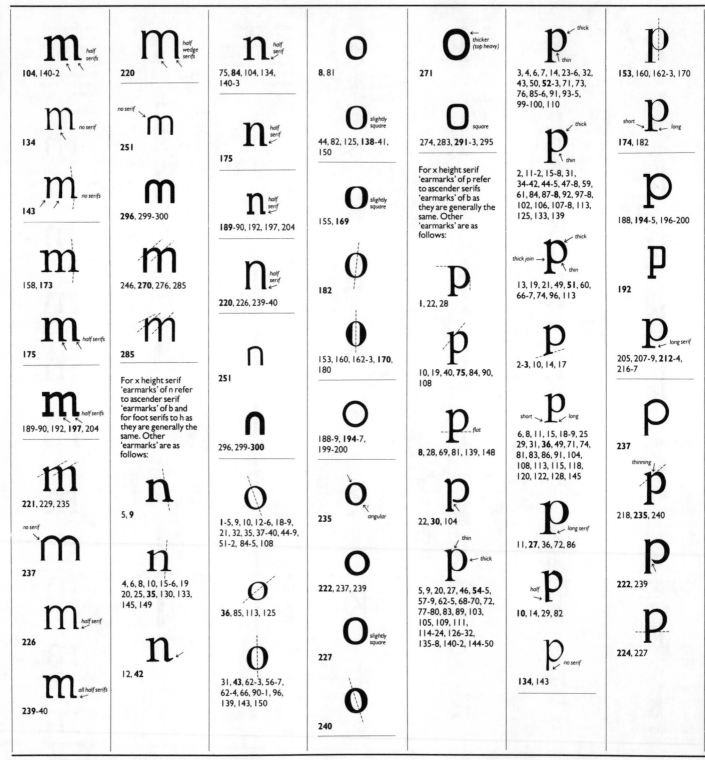

m *half serifs*
104, 140-2

m *no serif*
134

m *no serifs*
143

m
158, **173**

m *half serifs*
175

m *half serifs*
189-90, 192, **197**, 204

m
221, 229, 235

m *no serif*
237

m *half serif*
226

m *all half serifs*
239-40

---

m *half wedge serifs*
220

m *no serif*
251

m
296, 299-300

m
246, **270**, 276, 285

m
285

For x height serif 'earmarks' of n refer to ascender serif 'earmarks' of b and for foot serifs to h as they are generally the same. Other 'earmarks' are as follows:

n
5, **9**

n
4, 6, 8, 10, 15-6, 19 20, 25, **35**, 130, 133, 145, 149

n
12, **42**

---

n *half serif*
75, **84**, 104, 134, 140-3

n *half serif*
175

n *half serif*
189-90, 192, 197, 204

n *half serif*
220, 226, 239-40

n
251

n
296, 299-**300**

---

o
8, 81

o *slightly square*
44, 82, 125, **138**-41, 150

o *slightly square*
155, **169**

o
182

o
153, 160, 162-3, **170**, 180

o
188-9, **194**-7, 199-200

o *angular*
1-5, 9, 10, 12-6, 18-9, 21, 32, 35, 37-40, 44-9, 51-2, 84-5, 108

o
36, 85, 113, 125

n
12, **42**

O *thicker (top heavy)*
271

o *square*
274, 283, **291**-3, 295

For x height serif 'earmarks' of p refer to ascender serifs 'earmarks' of b as they are generally the same. Other 'earmarks' are as follows:

p
1, 22, 28

p
10, 19, 40, **75**, 84, 90, 108

p *flat*
8, 28, 69, 81, 139, 148

p
22, **30**, 104

p *thin* *thick*
5, 9, 20, 27, 46, **54**-5, 57-9, 62-5, 68-70, 72, 77-80, 83, 89, 103, 105, 109, 111, 114-24, 126-32, 135-8, 140-2, 144-50

---

p *thick* *thin*
3, 4, 6, 7, 14, 23-6, 32, **43**, 50, **52**-3, 71, 73, 76, 85-6, 91, 93-5, 99-100, 110

p *thick* *thin*
2, 11-2, 15-8, 31, 34-42, 44-5, 47-8, 59, 61, 84, 87-**8**, 92, 97-8, 102, 106, 107-8, 113, 125, 133, 139

p *thick join* *thick* *thin*
13, 19, 21, 49, **51**, 60, 66-7, 74, 96, 113

p
2-3, 10, 14, 17

p *short* *long*
6, 8, 11, 15, 18-9, 25 29, 31, **36**, 49, 71, 74, 81, 83, 86, 91, 104, 108, 113, 115, 118, 120, 122, 128, 145

p *long serif*
11, **27**, 36, 72, 86

p *half*
10, 14, 29, 82

p *no serif*
134, 143

---

p
153, 160, 162-3, 170

p *short* *long*
174, 182

p
188, **194**-5, 196-200

p
192

p *long serif*
205, 207-9, **212**-4, 216-7

p
237

p *thinning*
218, **235**, 240

p
222, 239

p
224, 227

---

o
235

o
222, 237, 239

o
227

o *slightly square*
227

o
240

NB. *Bold figures indicate the specimen illustrated above.*

'Special Earmarks'
The 'special earmarks' (or distinctive identifying features) are indicated on each letter. The general 'style' of typefaces with the same 'earmark' may vary. The figures refer to specimen numbers.

p — long serif
232

p — short / long
234

p
231

p — circular bowl
251, 253, **255**, 257-8, 262

p — no serif
251, **259**, 295, 297

p
296, 299-**300**

p
269, 296

For bowl and foot serif 'earmarks' of q refer to those of p as they are generally the same. Exceptions and other 'earmarks' are as follows:

q — no serif
8, 104, 111, 113, **116**, 133-4, 139, 148

q — half serif
3, **4**, 12-3, 23-4, 27, 36, 42, 51, 107

q — flat 'nib'
1, 28

q
125, **150**

q
22, 44, **104**

q — thick join
34

q — small 'nib'
6, 15-6, 25, 33, 40, 44, 61, 63, 66, 69, 74, 76, 83, 85, 87, 123-4, 128, 139

q
14, 17, 89, 98, 112, **131**, 136, 141-2, 147, 149

q
57, 132, **140**, 147

q
2, 3, 10, **14**, 17, 29, 81, 117, 143

q — 'nib'
29, **40**, 82, 123, 126

q — no serif
134

q
65

q — no serif
183

q — 'nib'
182

q — extended stroke
151, 166-8, 187

q
153, 160, **162**-3, 170

q
169

q
191

q
203-4, 214-7

q — no 'nib'
233

q — full serif
231

q — half serif
234, 239-40

q — 'nib'
285

For foot serif 'earmarks' of r refer to those of h as they are generally the same. Other 'earmarks' are as follows:

(angled stem)

r
23-4, 78-80, 122-4

r
30, **77**

r
8, **28**, 40

r
71
(concave x height serif)

r
27, **68**, 91, 110
(thin triangular x height serif)

r
108
(heavy triangular x height serif)

r — squashed pear
102

r — pear
6, 17, 22, 43, **53**, 55-6, 59, 61-4, 66-7, 69, 72, 74, 88, 92-3, 95-6, 99, 110

r — hanging pear
4, 7, 9, **65**, 69, 103, 109

r — club
9, 15, 26, **38**-41, 47-9, 51, 60, 70, 73, 87, 89, 94, 106-7

r — flag
16, 20, **25**, 34-5, 37, 50, 83

r
5, **32**

r
13, 33, **45**, 85

r
75, 98

r — pear
18, 27, **31**, 36, 44, 46, 52, 54, 57, 62-4, 72, 90, 97, 101, 105, 126-7, 129-30, 132, 139, 148

r — hanging pear
58, 80, 103, 106, 125, 131, 136-7, 145-6, 149-50

r — curled in
114-5, 117-21, 142, 144

r
111, 138

r
10-11, 86, 100, 106, 141, 147

r
2, **19**-20, 76, 83, 104

r
3, 12, 21, 42, 128

r
8, 81

r
14, 82, 84-5, 113, 128, 133-5, 140

r
112, 141

r
116, 143

r — ball
152-4, **159**-63, 167, 169, 171-2, 178, 180-1, 184, 186-7

r — hanging pear
156, **168**, 170, 185

r — ball
164, 175-**77**, 179

r — club
173-4, 183

r — flag
158

r — wedge
151, 157, 182

r — wedge
155, 166

r — spiked
165

NB. *Bold figures indicate the specimen illustrated above.*

'Special Earmarks'
The 'special earmarks' (or distinctive identifying features) are indicated on each letter. The general style of typefaces with the same 'earmark' may vary. The figures refer to specimen numbers.

r 189-90, 193, 196, **197**-8, 204

r 188, **194**-5, 199-200

r 205, 210

r 141, 201, **203**

r 206-9, **211**-7

r *pear* 221, 229, 231-2

r *short pear* 235, 240

r *club* 231, **234**

r 218, 222-4, 228, 233, 237

r 219, **227**

r 225

r 239-40

r 250-1, 253, 255, 258, 261, 263, 265-8, 270, 272-3, 275-89, 295-6

r 245-6, 252, 262, 264

r 271, 274

r 260

r 249, 254, 256-7, 259

r 291-2, 304

r 269

r 299-300

(full serifs)

s *steeply angled* 1, 5, 9, 25, 62

s *less steeply angled* 3, 16, 22, 25, 43, 55-7, 69, **72**, 90, 131-2

s 2, 11, 20-1, 28, 34, 36, **52**-4, 68, 73, 79-80, 116-7, 131-2, 136-7, 150

s *fine* 21, 36

s *heavy* 32, 34, 65, 70-1, 77-8, 103, **114**-5, 118-21, 127, 144-6, 150

s 51

s *full (top only)* 6, 16, **47**, 90, 108-9

(half serifs)

s *full* 35

s *blob* 4, 12

S 7, **30**, 33

s 23-4, 123-4, 126, 129, 142

S 29

S 134, 143

S *flat* 8, 14, 17-8, 64, 76, 81-2, 100, 113, 122, 138, 140-1

S 10, 26, 28, 37-9, 45-6, 48-50, 61, 63, 66-7, **74**-5, 83-5, 87, 89, 95-7, 99-100, 102, 104, 106, 125, 130, 133, 139, 147-9

S **13**, 41, 44, 88, 91, 93, 105, 109, 112, 135

s 25, 98, 107

s 15, 81

S 19, 59, 60 86, 90, 92, 94

S *fine* 40

S 31, 42, 110, 128

S *thin spikes* 10

s *bottom heavy* 46

S *top heavy* 98

S 89, 91, 93

S 10, 40, 49, 63, 66 96, 102, **148**

s 28, 67, 83-5, **95**, 99, 104, 133, 139, 147, 149

(full serifs)

S 153-**4**, 156, 160, 162-4, 170-81, 183-6

S *full (top only)* 157, 159

S *wide* 156, 164, 175, 181, 184

S *narrow* 176

S *wedge* 158

(half serifs)

S 152, **165**, 166-9, 182, 187

s 161

S 151

S *fine* 155

s *square slab serifs* 188-91, 193-203

s *bracketed slab serifs* 206-9, **211**-3

S *rounded slab serifs* 214-7

s *half serifs* 192, 204-**5**, 210

(full serifs)

S 230

(half serifs)

S 226, 233

s 234-5

S 224, 231

S 219, 221, **229**, 240

S 239

'Special Earmarks'
The 'special earmarks' (or distinctive identifying features) are indicated on each letter. The general style of typefaces with the same 'earmark' may vary. The figures refer to specimen numbers.

Column 1 (s)

218, 220, **223**, 228, 237

222

225

227, 236

— large opening
251-3, 256, 258, 260, 262, 264, **270**, 285-9, 300

245, **254**, 257, 261, 265, 276-7, 282

255, **273**, 274-5, 281

250, **267**, 278-80, 283, 304

291-2

Column 2 (s)

246, 249, **259**, 263, 266, 269, 271-2, 284

269, 272

— thick top
271

295

268

296-9

299

298, 301

(head)
2-**3**, 10

1, 29, **49**, 98

Column 3 (t)

— thickening
25, 134-5

33

— triangle
20, 39-41, 47, **52**, 59, 63, 67, 71, 73, 79, 86-90, 92, 99, 102, 108, 111

— wide
6-7, 14-6, 19, 21, 25-6, 37, 48, 60-1, 65-6, **74**, 83, 93, 105, 107, 109, 116, 132

— concave
27, 43, 55, 57, 62, 64, 69, 72, 100, 103, 106, 110, **114**-5, 118-22, 137, 144-6

— wide concave
11, 14, 27, 31, **72**, 147

1, 3, **32**

— blob
4, **142**

1, 29, **49**, 98

Column 4 (t)

36, **123**-4, 126-7, 129, 148

18, 22-4, 29, 33, 46, 75, 82, **84**, 112-3, 125, 131, 135-6, 138, 141

34
(tail)

30
(tail)

1, 8, 12, 38, 51, 71, 81, 84, **90**, 93, 104, 128, 136, 143, 150

18, 22, 39, 56, 59-**60**, 63, 66, 73-4, 123-4, 127-9, 138, 140, 148

45, 134

— curled up
114-5, 118-20, **121**, 137, 144-6

(head)
— triangle
158, **183**

Column 5 (t)

— concave
152-**3**, 159, 164, 167-8, 173, 184

— tall and concave
170, 172, 176-9, 181-2

151, **154**-5, 157, 161-3, 165, 174, 186

156, 160, 166, 169, 171, 180, **185**, 187
(tail)

— flat
151, **169**

— curled up
164-5, **175**-80, 182, 185

(head)

— concave
205-7, 210, **211**-3

— tall and concave
201, **208**-9

188, 190, 192, 194-6, **199**, 203

Column 6 (t)

189, 191, 193, **197**-8, 204

202
(tail)

188, 194-5, 199-200

189, 190, 192, **196**-7, 204

191, **203**

— curled up
193, 198, 201-2, 205-8, **209**-217

— round and curled up
214-7

(head)
— triangle
218, 220, 223, 230, 235, 237

— slightly concave
219, 231-2, **233**

— tall concave
221-2, **229**

Column 7 (t)

225, **228**

224, 226-7, 234, 240
(tail)

239

237

219

t45
222, 235, 240

227

(head)
— triangle
259

— concave
271, 280

269

'Special Earmarks'
The 'special earmarks' (or distinctive identifying features) are indicated on each letter. The general 'style' of typefaces with the same 'earmark' may vary. The figures refer to specimen numbers.

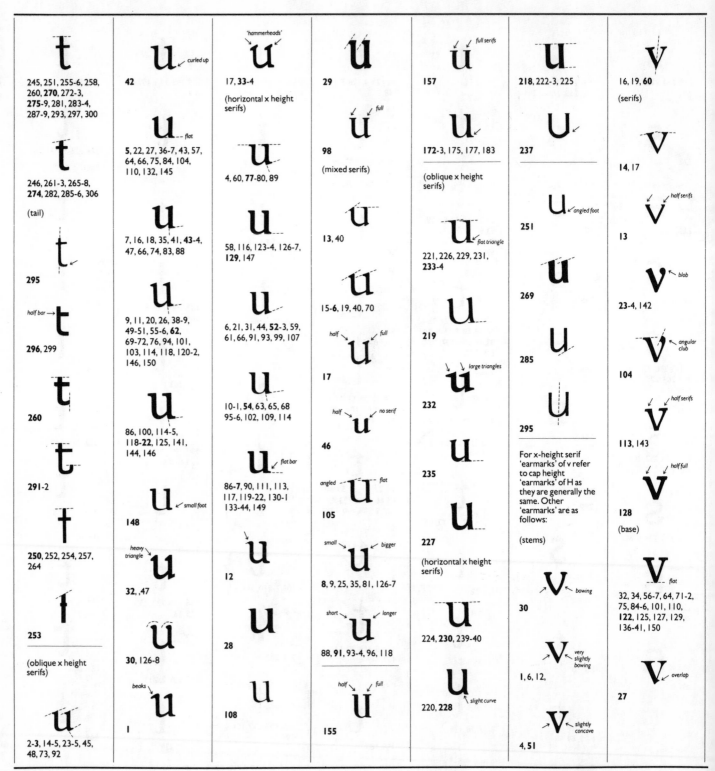

245, 251, 255-6, 258, 260, **270**, 272-3, **275**-9, 281, 283-4, 287-9, 293, 297, 300

246, 261-3, 265-8, **274**, 282, 285-6, 306

(tail)

295

half bar →

296, 299

260

291-2

250, 252, 254, 257, 264

253

(oblique x height serifs)

2-3, 14-5, 23-5, 45, 48, 73, 92

---

42 curled up

5, 22, 27, 36-7, 43, 57, 64, 66, 75, 84, 104, 110, 132, 145 — flat

7, 16, 18, 35, 41, **43**-4, 47, 66, 74, 83, 88

9, 11, 20, 26, 38-9, 49-51, 55-6, **62**, 69-72, 76, 94, 101, 103, 114, 118, 120-2, 146, 150

86, 100, 114-5, 118-**22**, 125, 141, 144, 146 — small foot

148

heavy triangle

32, ,47

30, 126-8

beaks

1

'hammerheads'

17, **33**-4

(horizontal x height serifs)

4, 60, **77**-80, 89

58, 116, 123-4, 126-7, **129**, 147

6, 21, 31, 44, **52**-3, 59, 61, 66, 91, 93, 99, 107

10-1, **54**, 63, 65, 68, 95-6, 102, 109, 114

flat bar

86-**7**, 90, 111, 113, 117, 119-22, 130-1, 133-44, 149

12

28

108

---

full serifs

29

full

98

(mixed serifs)

13, 40

15-**6**, 19, 40, 70

17

half → ← full

46

angled ← flat

105

small → ← bigger

8, 9, 25, 35, 81, 126-7

short → ← longer

88, **91**, 93-4, 96, 118

half → ← full

155

---

full serifs

157

172-3, 175, 177, 183

(oblique x height serifs)

flat triangle

221, 226, 229, 231, **233**-4

half → ← full

219

large triangles

232

235

227

(horizontal x height serifs)

224, **230**, 239-40

slight curve

220, **228**

218, 222-3, 225

237

angled foot

251

269

285

295

For x-height serif 'earmarks' of v refer to cap height 'earmarks' of H as they are generally the same. Other 'earmarks' are as follows:

(stems)

bowing

30

very slightly bowing

1, 6, 12,

slightly concave

4, **51**

16, 19, **60**

(serifs)

14, 17

half serifs

13

blob

23-4, 142

angular club

104

half serifs

113, 143

half full

128

(base)

flat

32, 34, 56-7, 64, 71-2, 75, 84-6, 101, 110, **122**, 125, 127, 129, 136-41, 150

overlap

27

NB. *Bold figures indicate the specimen illustrated above.*

'Special Earmarks'
The 'special earmarks' (or distinctive identifying features) are indicated on each letter. The general 'style' of typefaces with the same 'earmark' may vary. The figures refer to specimen numbers.

28 V wedge serif

8, 29, 81-3 V

76 V

151, 166, 169, 181-2 V

192 V half serifs

222 V

239-40 V half serifs

251-2, 254, 256, 259, 263-4 V

258, 262 V

270 V

269, 272, 297 V bowing

296, 298-9, 301 V rounded

For x height serif 'earmarks' of w refer to cap height serifs of H as they are generally the same. Other 'earmarks' are as follows:

(crossed centre strokes)

9, 89 W

(centre strokes meet at x height or stepped)

32-3, 38-9, 57, 70-2, 106, 111, 115, 118, 120, 122, 145, 150 W flat base

8, 81 W

14-16, 19, 31, 60, 135 W

30 W bowing

29, 113, 128, 143 W half serifs

5, 22, 34, 38-9, 42-3, 56-7, 64, 101, 106, 110, 120-1 W

27 W

76 W 'odd serifs'

(no centre serif)

4, 15, 18, 44-6, 54, 77-80, 98, 108, 123-4, 126-7, 134-5 W rounded bases

75, 84-6, 112, 125, 129, 133, 136-41 W flat bases

82-3 W

134 W

23-4, 142 W blob

10 W

28 W wedge serifs

(centre strokes meet at x height or stepped)

155-8, 160-1, 167-8, 170, 172-4, 177-9, 183-7 W pointed base

175 W flat base

153, 160, 170-1, 180-1 W stepped, pointed

165, 170, 174, 176, 186 W stepped, flat

(no centre serif)

154, 159, 162-4 W pointed

151-2, 166, 169, 182 W flat

(centre strokes meet at x height or stepped)

188, 196-7, 201-2, 208-9, 211, 213 W

206-7, 212 W lower join

(no centre serif)

189-91, 193, 198, 203-5, 210 W flat

194-5 W lower join

199-200, 213 W pointed

192 W

214-7 W

(centre strokes meet at x height or stepped)

231, 233 W pointed

228, 229-30 W flat

221 W blunt

223, 225 W

224, 226 W stepped

232 W half serif

222 W lower join

(no centre serif)

219, 237 W pointed

218, 220, 227 W flat

234 W

218, 227-8 W wedge serifs

239-40 W half serifs

251-2, 254, 256, 259, 263-4 W pointed

258, 262 W pointed

270 W flat

268, 272, 276 W some contrast

269, 297 W bowing

296, 299 W

298 W

304 W

295 W

4, 29, 84, 141 X all half serifs

125, 128, 143 X half / full

NB. Bold figures indicate the specimen illustrated above.

'Special Earmarks'
The 'special earmarks' (or distinctive identifying features) are indicated on each letter. The general 'style' of typefaces with the same 'earmark' may vary. The figures refer to specimen numbers.

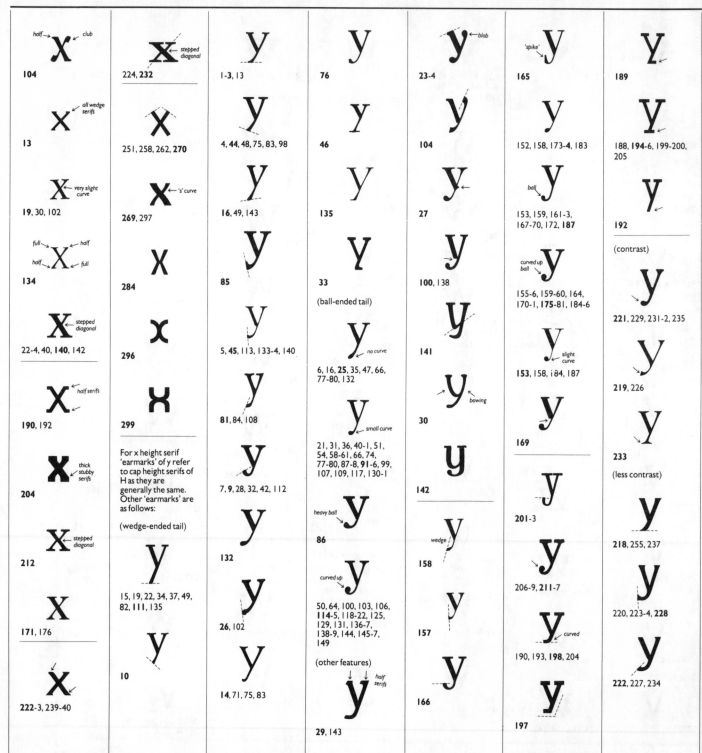

104 — half → x ← club

13 — x all wedge serifs

19, 30, 102 — x very slight curve

134 — full → X ← half, half → X ← full

22-4, 40, **140**, 142 — X stepped diagonal

190, 192 — X half serifs

204 — X thick stubby serifs

212 — X stepped diagonal

171, 176 — X

222-3, 239-40 — X

224, 232 — x stepped diagonal

251, 258, 262, 270 — X

269, 297 — X ← 's' curve

284 — X

296 — x

299 — X

For x height serif 'earmarks' of y refer to cap height serifs of H as they are generally the same. Other 'earmarks' are as follows:

(wedge-ended tail)

15, 19, 22, 34, 37, 49, 82, 111, 135 — y

10 — y

1-3, 13 — y

4, 44, 48, 75, 83, 98 — y

16, 49, 143 — y

85 — y

5, 45, 113, 133-4, 140 — y

81, 84, 108 — y

132 — y

26, 102 — y

14, 71, 75, 83 — y

76 — y

46 — y

135 — y

33 — y
(ball-ended tail)

6, 16, **25**, 35, 47, 66, 77-80, 132 — y no curve

21, 31, 36, 40-1, 51, 54, 58-61, 66, 74, 77-80, 87-8, **91-6**, 99, 107, 109, 117, 130-1 — y small curve

7, 9, 28, 32, 42, 112 — y

86 — y heavy ball

50, 64, 100, 103, 106, **114-5**, 118-22, 125, 129, 131, 136-7, 138-9, 144, 145-7, 149 — y curved up

(other features)

29, 143 — ÿ half serifs

23-4 — y ← blob

104 — y

27 — y ←

100, 138 — y ←

141 — y

30 — y ← bowing

142 — y

158 — y wedge

157 — y

166 — y

165 — 'spike' → y

152, 158, 173-**4**, 183 — y

153, 159, 161-3, 167-70, 172, **187** — y ball

155-6, 159-60, 164, 170-1, **175-81**, 184-6 — y curved up ball

153, 158, 184, 187 — y slight curve

169 — y

201-3 — y

206-9, **211-7** — y

190, 193, **198**, 204 — y curved

197 — y

189 — y

188, **194-6**, 199-200, 205 — y

192 — y
(contrast)

221, 229, 231-2, 235 — y

219, 226 — y

233 — y
(less contrast)

218, **255, 237** — y

220, 223-4, **228** — y

222, 227, 234 — y

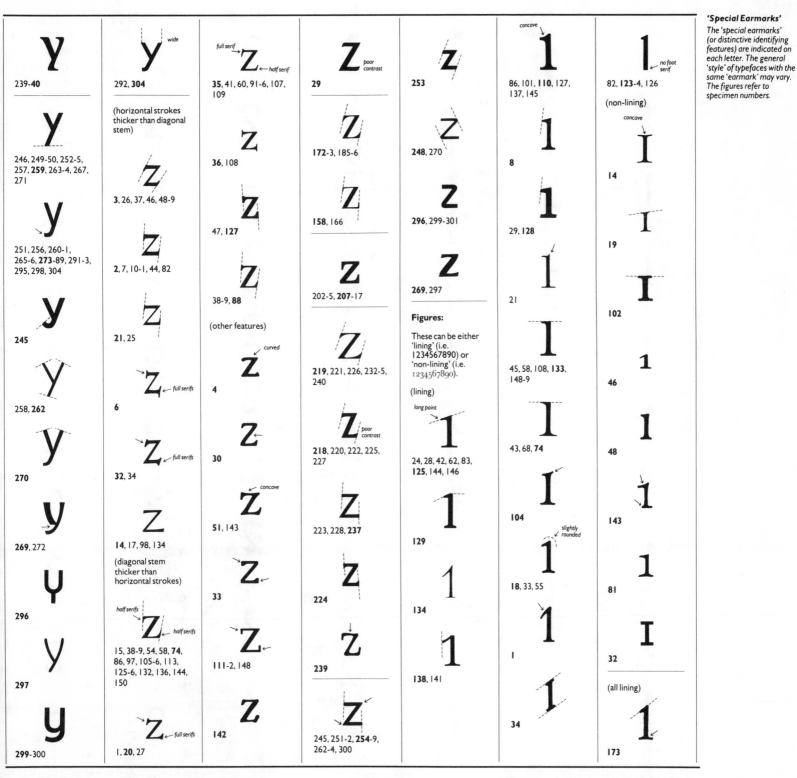

Y
239-**40**

y *wide*
292, **304**

(horizontal strokes thicker than diagonal stem)

Z *full serif* *half serif*
35, 41, 60, 91-6, 107, 109

Z *poor contrast*
29

z
253

1 *concave*
86, 101, **110**, 127, 137, 145

1 *no foot serif*
82, **123-4**, 126

(non-lining)

'Special Earmarks'
The 'special earmarks' (or distinctive identifying features) are indicated on each letter. The general 'style' of typefaces with the same 'earmark' may vary. The figures refer to specimen numbers.

y
246, 249-50, 252-5, 257, **259**, 263-4, 267, 271

Z
36, 108

Z
172-3, 185-6

z
248, 270

1
8

I *concave*
14

y
251, 256, 260-1, 265-6, **273**-89, 291-3, 295, 298, 304

Z
3, 26, 37, 46, 48-9

Z
158, 166

Z
296, 299-301

1
29, **128**

I
19

y
245

Z
2, 7, 10-1, 44, 82

Z
47, **127**

Z
269, 297

1
21

I
102

y
258, **262**

Z
21, 25

Z
38-9, **88**

(other features)

Figures:

These can be either 'lining' (i.e. 1234567890) or 'non-lining' (i.e. 1234567890).

(lining)

1
45, 58, 108, **133**, 148-9

1
46

y
270

z *curved*
4

Z
219, 221, 226, 232-5, 240

1
43, 68, **74**

1
48

y
269, 272

z *full serifs*
6

z *full serifs*
30

z *poor contrast*
218, 220, 222, 225, 227

1 *long point*
24, 28, 42, 62, 83, **125**, 144, 146

1
104

1
143

y
296

Z *full serifs*
32, 34

z *concave*
51, 143

Z
223, 228, **237**

1
129

1 *slightly rounded*
18, 33, 55

I
81

y
297

Z *half serifs* *half serifs*
15, 38-9, 54, 58, **74**, 86, 97, 105-6, 113, 125-6, 132, 136, 144, 150

z
33

z
224

1
134

1
1

I
32

(all lining)

y
299-300

Z *full serifs*
1, **20**, 27

Z
111-2, 148

Z
142

z
239

z
245, 251-2, **254**-9, 262-4, 300

1
138, 141

1
34

I
173

'Special Earmarks'
The 'special earmarks' (or distinctive identifying features) are indicated on each letter. The general 'style' of typefaces with the same 'earmark' may vary. The figures refer to specimen numbers.

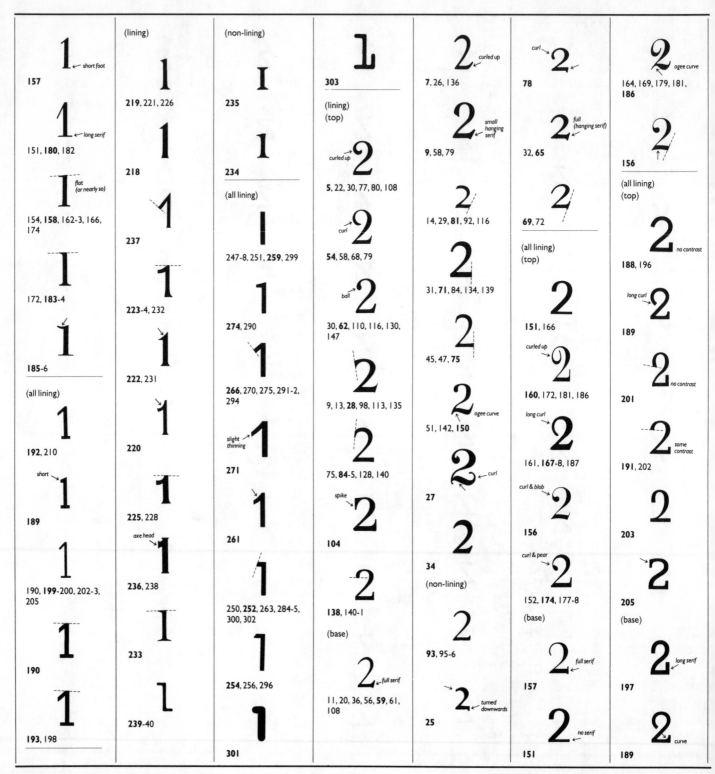

157 — short foot

151, **180**, **182** — long serif

154, **158**, 162-3, 166, 174 — flat (or nearly so)

172, **183-4**

185-6

(all lining)

192, 210

189 — short

190, **199-200**, 202-3, 205

190

193, 198

(lining)
219, 221, 226

218

237

223-4, 232

222, 231

220

225, 228 — slight thinning

236, 238 — axe head

233

239-40

(non-lining)
303

235

234

(all lining)
247-8, 251, **259**, 299

274, 290

266, 270, 275, 291-2, 294 — spike

271

261

250, **252**, 263, 284-5, 300, 302

254, 256, 296

301

7, 26, **136** — curled up

9, 58, 79 (lining) (top)

5, 22, 30, 77, 80, 108 — curled up

14, 29, **81**, 92, 116 — curl

54, 58, 68, 79 — ball

31, **71**, 84, 134, 139

30, **62**, 110, 116, 130, 147

45, 47, **75**

9, 13, **28**, 98, 113, 135

75, **84-5**, 128, 140 — spike

104

34 (non-lining)

138, 140-1 (base)

93, 95-6 — full serif

11, 20, 36, 56, **59**, 61, 108

78 — curl

32, **65** — small hanging serif

69, 72 (all lining) (top)

151, 166 — ogee curve

160, 172, 181, 186 — curled up

161, **167-8**, 187 — long curl

156 — curl & blob

152, **174**, 177-8 — curl & pear

(base)

157 — full serif

151 — no serif

164, **169**, 179, 181, 186 — ogee curve

156

(all lining) (top)

188, 196 — no contrast

189 — long curl

201 — no contrast

191, 202 — some contrast

203

205

197 — long serif

189 — curve

25 — turned downwards

27 — curl

51, 142, **150** — ogee curve

'Special Earmarks'
The 'special earmarks' (or distinctive identifying features) are indicated on each letter. The general 'style' of typefaces with the same 'earmark' may vary. The figures refer to specimen numbers.

Column 1 (numeral 2)

203

191, **213**

201-2, **205**

206

203

blob / *ogee curve*
214

(lining) (top)

218, 236-8

222, 240

239

230-1

Column 2 (numeral 2)

226

(base)

228, 236, 238

230-1, **233**, 239

238

227, 237

(non-lining)

full serif
232

half serif
234-5

(all lining) (top)

249

246, **259**-60, 266, 271, 304

Column 3 (numeral 2)

curl
265

longer curl
258, **261**-2, 296, 298

295, **297**

(base)

271

290

298

(lining) (top)

1

curved
54, 58, 68, 77-80

16, 125, 139

Column 4 (numeral 3)

82, 113, 123-4, 126

pear
86

138

13, 45

pointed wedge serif
75, 84, 98, 140

angular
6

36

flat / *spiked serifs*
104

50, 128, 147

22

Column 5 (numeral 3)

5

134

111, **135**, 141

112

9, 28

(bottom tail endings where different from top – curved top typefaces only)

12, **42**, 44, 108

17, 71

58, 68

27

Column 6 (numeral 3)

6, 20, 35, 38-9, 41, **52**-3, 55-6, 59, 61, 63, 70, 73, 87-8, 92, 94, 101, 105, 109, 125, 139

79-80

86

76

98

148

(non-lining)

65

14

78

Column 7 (numeral 3)

32

8, 81

(all lining) (top)

182

159, 173, **181**

172, 186

173

158

152, **174**

165

NB. Bold figures indicate the specimen illustrated above.

'Special Earmarks'
The 'special earmarks' (or distinctive identifying features) are indicated on each letter. The general 'style' of typefaces with the same 'earmark' may vary. The figures refer to specimen numbers.

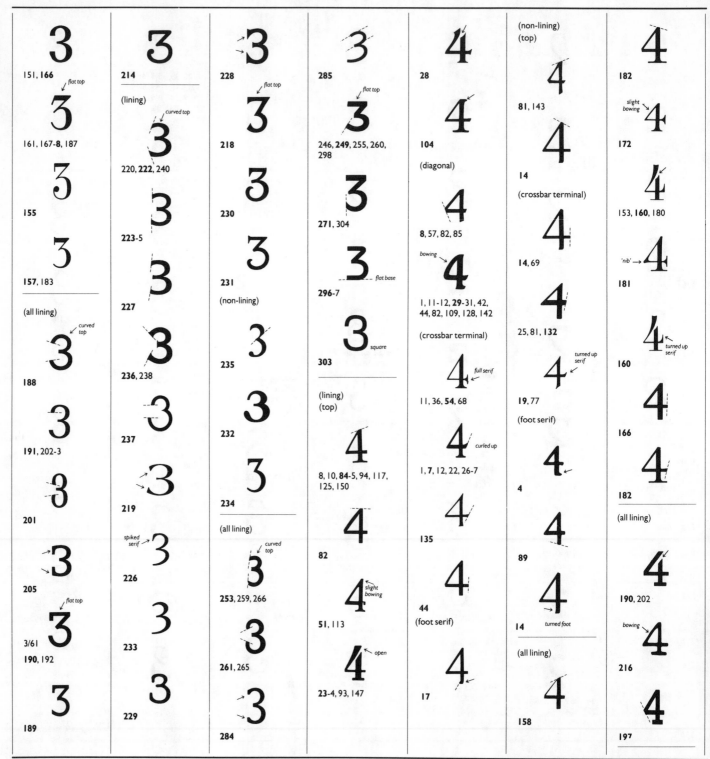

NB. *Bold figures indicate the specimen illustrated above.*

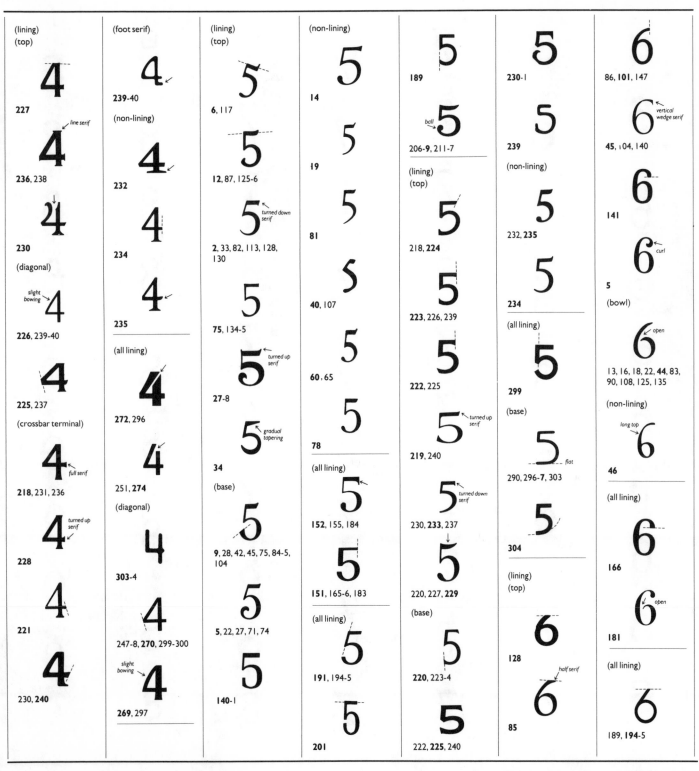

NB. *Bold figures indicate the specimen illustrated above.*

'Special Earmarks'
The 'special earmarks' (or distinctive identifying features) are indicated on each letter. The general 'style' of typefaces with the same 'earmark' may vary. The figures refer to specimen numbers.

Column 1 (6):
205
ball — **206-9**, **211-4**, **216-7**
(lining) vertical serif — **224-5**
219, 227
hook serif — **231**
228
236, 238
221, 229
240
wedge serif — **230**

Column 2 (6):
open — **222**, 239
(non-lining) — **232**
215
(all lining) — **251-2**, **254**, 258-9, 262-4
265
303
295-6
(lining) (top) — turned up serif — **44**
wedge serif — **17**, **134**

Column 3 (7):
(non-lining) — **71**, 92, 139
short top — 7
143
92
(back) bowing — 15, **21**, 51, 82
tapering — 31, **33**, 44
142
(foot) long serif — 36
82, 85, 128
bent — **108**
'nib' — 12-13, **76**

Column 4 (7):
(non-lining) wedge serif
228
turned down serif — **220**
143
81, 97
4
(all lining) bowing — **156**
ball — **153**
full serif — **157**, 165, 181
(all lining) — 191, **203**
(lining) — **240**

Column 5 (7):
thickening — **228**
bend — **220**
231
vertical half serif — **273**, 281, 290, 298, 303
298
303
(lining) open — open — 22
open — 104
bottom heavy — 29, **34**, 47, 125, 128, 142, 150

Column 6 (8):
slightly square — **140**
(non-lining)
65, 78
stepped crossover — 8, **72**
(all lining) — **151**
flattened — **169**
(all lining) bottom heavy — **194-5**
(lining) — **237**
open — **239**

Column 7 (8/9):
stepped crossover — **232**
stepped crossover — 266, **284**
bottom heavy — 265, 296, **298**-300
303
(lining) (9) — 16, **18**, 22, 90, 104, 108, 125, 135
104, 140
5
9, 28
pear — 54, 62, 77, **79**, 110, 117, 125, 130, 138, 150

NB. *Bold figures indicate the specimen illustrated above.*

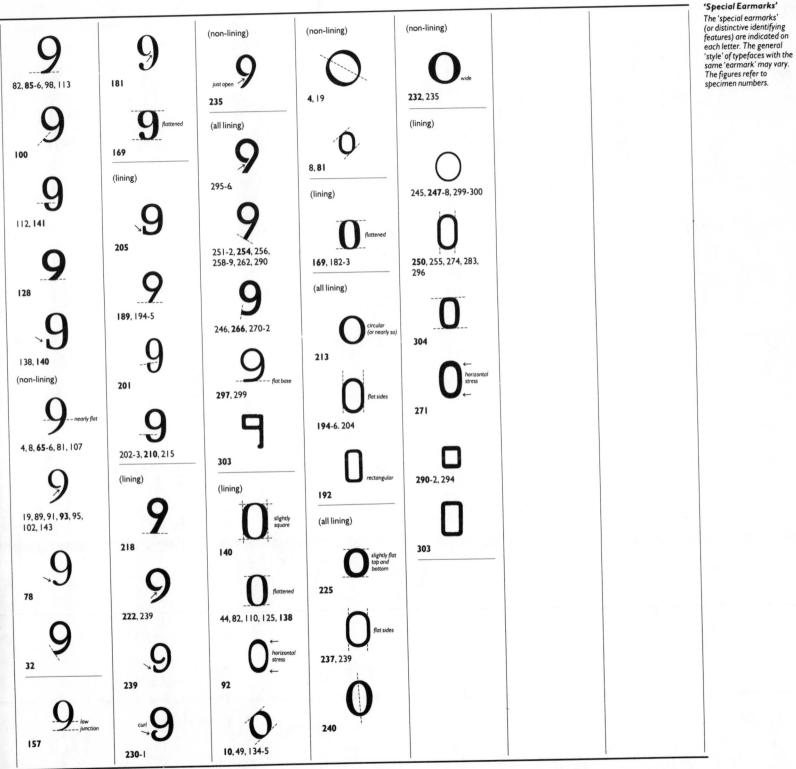

NB. Bold figures indicate the specimen illustrated above.

Part Two

DECORATIVE
(NON-CONTINUOUS TEXT)

TYPEFACES

FLOWING SCRIPTS

NON-FLOWING SCRIPTS
(INCLUDING BLACKLETTER & UNCIAL)

UNMODIFIED (FORMAL TEXT SHAPE)

UN

FAT FACE & THIN FACE (UNMODIFIED & MODIFIED)

ORNAMENTAL

MODIFIED SERIF

MODIFIED SANS SERIF

MODIFIED OUTRAGEOUS

DECORATIVE TYPEFACE CATEGORIES

THIS PART OF the book contains a cross-section of decorative typefaces, i.e. those not normally used for continuous text setting. Instead, they are used for headings and titling or in limited quantities and situations for display purposes. The characteristic features of each of the eight typeface categories are described below and are illustrated on the opposite page.

As with *Text* typefaces **the classification system and terminology is entirely new and does not follow established type classifications.** Categories are based on specific design features.

Each category is further divided into smaller groups according to more specific design features which are explained at the beginning of each section. Typeface specimens are then arranged alphabetically within each group and have an individual specimen number which is cross-referenced to the index.

NB. There is inevitably a small overlap between the *Text* and *Decorative* parts of the book. For instance, some *Decorative* typefaces in special circumstances may be used for continuous text setting and vice-versa.

Categories are as follows:

1. Flowing Scripts *Nos. 305-322*

This category includes script typefaces which, when typeset, give a 'joined up' script effect so that words appear to be 'flowing' as in handwriting. The category is divided into smaller groups of quill pen, felt or graphic pen and brush script effects. A further division is made into sloping, upright, rounded and angular forms.

2. Non-Flowing Scripts (including Blackletter & Uncial)
Nos. 323-381

As the term describes, this category includes script typefaces in which the letters remain unjoined when typeset and are, therefore, 'non-flowing'. As in the 'flowing' category there are groups for quill pen, felt or graphic pen and brush. This category includes blackletter and uncial typefaces together with a small group of roman italic typefaces based on pen scripts.

3. Unmodified (Formal Text Shape)
Nos. 382-428

This category contains typefaces that generally adhere to the formal and traditional letter shapes normally associated with continuous text typefaces but which are usually used for decorative applications. However, it excludes those typefaces which, though conforming to this criteria, are either very bold or very thin. These will be found in the next category Fat & Thin Face. The category is arranged in groups according to whether the design is roman, slab, wedge or sans serif in origin and within each of these divisions there are separate groups for outline, inline, shaded, or with background versions.

4. Fat Face & Thin Face (Unmodified & Modified)
Nos Fat 429-515, Thin 516-536

This category is divided into two parts and contains a selection of typefaces which represent the extremes in weight – very bold (Fat Face) and very light (Thin Face). As with the Unmodified Section, arrangement is by roman, slab, wedge and sans serif groups. The substantial roman serif group is further sub-divided depending on whether the typefaces have thin, medium or thick serifs. The sans serif group is also divided into typefaces of wide, medium or narrow design or of a special rounded shape. *NB. A small number of typefaces with Fat Face characteristics are to be found in the Modified Serif and Sans Serif categories as they were felt better placed there.*

5. Ornamental *Nos. 537-563*

Grouped here are typefaces of a particularly elaborate (often 'floriated') and highly decorated nature. In addition, those with 'swash style' characteristics or flourishes have been included. Consistent with the previous two sections, typefaces are arranged into roman, slab, wedge and sans serif groups. There is also a small group of script-based typefaces.

6. Modified Serif *Nos. 564-603*

The term 'modified' means non-formal or non-traditional letter shapes. Modification is by distortion, added or other subtracted elements (such as, for example, stencil letters) or by axis (sloping backwards). Arrangement is by roman, slab, wedge and sans serif groups. *NB. This category includes some typefaces with Fat Face characteristics that were felt better placed here.*

7. Modified Sans Serif *Nos. 604-665*

This section covers all 'modified' typefaces without serifs. Due to the varied and unusual nature of this typeface category new explanatory group headings have been created such as: vertical and horizontal thick and thin stress, electronic, cut, stencil or stencil effect, and striped or inline. *NB. This category includes some typefaces with Fat Face characteristics which were felt better placed here.*

8. Modified Outrageous *Nos. 666-700*

This final category includes both 'modified' serif and sans serif typefaces that are of a particularly unusual or 'way out' nature. They are highly stylised and often humorous and intended for special, very limited use only. Typeface groups include: heavy, inline or striped, dot-formed, shaded and 3D, with backgrounds and pictorial.

NB. A very small number of typeface specimens in this part of the book do not include an ampersand.

The Typefinding Process

1. To identify a typeface, first decide into which one of main categories shown opposite the typeface specimen you wish to identify belongs.

2. Using the thumb index on the edge of the page turn to the appropriate category introduction page.

3. From the listings there select the specific group within the category to which the specimen relates.

4. Read off the specimen numbers given for this group and find them in the following listings of typeface specimens.

5. Decide which of the typefaces in the group it equates to by 'scanning' the alphabetical listings until you find a typeface to which your specimen matches.

Type categories

General characteristics

1. Flowing Scripts. *Nos 305-322*

e.g. **310** Palace Script, **316** ITC Zapf Chancery, **319** Kaufmann and **322** Mistral.

quill pen sloping and rounded	quill pen upright and rounded	felt or graphic pen sloping	felt or graphic pen upright	brush
Scr	*Scr*	*Scr*	*Scr*	*Scr*

Groups include:

2. Non-Flowing Scripts. (including Blackletter & Uncial) *Nos 323-381*

e.g. **323** Bernhard Tango, **333** Bologna, **372** Old English Text and **380** Blado Italic.

Groups include:

quill pen	felt or graphic pen	brush	blackletter	uncial
Scr	*Scr*	**Scr**	**BL**	**UN**

3. Unmodified. *Nos 382-428*

e.g. **385** Engravers Roman, **392** Castellar, **412** Latin Antique No 9 and **422** Helvetica Outline.

roman serif	slab serif	wedge serif	sans serif
ROM	**SL**	WE	**SA**

4. Fat Face & Thin Face. *Nos 429-536* **(Modified & Unmodified)**

e.g. **434** Falstaff, **467** Cooper Black, **514** Harry Fat and **536** Harry Thin.

roman serif	slab serif	wedge serif	sans serif
F	**F**T	**F**T	**F**T

5. Ornamental. *Nos 537-563*

e.g. **540** Fry's Ornamented, **548** Lettres Ornées **554** Davida and **561** Ballé Initials.

roman serif	slab serif	wedge serif	sans serif	script
R	**SL**	WE	**SA**	*SCR*

6. Modified Serif. *Nos 564-603*

e.g. **566** Belwe, **575** Stencil Bold, **579** Profil and **585** Charleston.

roman serif	slab serif	wedge serif	wedge serif (sloping backwards)
ROM	**SL**	WE	

7. Modified Sans Serif. *Nos 604-665*

e.g. **608** Peignot, **619** Frankfurter Medium, **626** Countdown and **646** Neon.

Groups include:

thick and thin stress (vertical)	rounded	electronic	cut	shaded or 3D
TH	**RO**	**EL**	**CU**	3D

8. Modified Outrageous. *Nos 666-700*

e.g. **668** Litzenburg, **679** Shatter, **682** Pinball and **688** Calypso.

Groups include:

heavy distorted	inline or striped	dot-formed	shaded or 3D	pictorial
HE	**ST**	DO	3D	**PIC**

I. FLOWING SCRIPTS

Specimen nos		Basic characteristics	Secondary characteristics	
305-315	*Flow*	quill pen	sloping and rounded	e.g. **310** Palace Script
316	*Flow*	"	sloping and angular	e.g. **316** ITC Zapf Chancery
317-318	*Flow*	"	upright	e.g. **318** Linoscript
319	*Flow*	felt pen or graphic pen	sloping	e.g. **319** Kaufmann
320	*Flow*	"	upright	e.g. **320** Jiffy
321-322	*Flow*	brush		e.g. **322** Mistral

NB. *Typefaces in each group are arranged in alphabetical order.*

FLOWING
SCRIPTS

Scr

Ariston Light Script
Bank Script
Commercial Script
Diskus
 Künstler Schreibschrift
Palace Script
Park Avenue
Shelley Allegro Script
 Shelley Andante Script
Snell Roundhand

*quill pen
sloping
and rounded*

305 Ariston Light Script

ABCDEFGHIJKLMNOPQRSTUVWXYZ&

306 Bank Script

ABCDEFGHIJKLMNOPQRSTUVWXYZ

307 Commercial Script

ABCDEFGHIJKLMNOPQRSTUVWXYZ&

308 Diskus

ABCDEFGHIJKLMNOPQRSTUVWXYZ&

309 Künstler Schreibschrift

ABCDEFGHIJKLMNOPQRSTUVWXYZ&

310 Palace Script

ABCDEFGHIJKLMNOPQRSTUVWXYZ&

311 Park Avenue

ABCDEFGHIJKLMNOPQRSTUVWXYZ&

312 Shelley Allegro Script

ABCDEFGHIJKLMNOPQRSTUVWXYZ&

313 Shelley Andante Script

ABCDEFGHIJKLMNOPQRSTUVWXYZ&

314 Snell Roundhand

ABCDEFGHIJKLMNOPQRSTUVWXYZ&

FLOWING
SCRIPTS

Ariston Light Script
Bank Script
Commercial Script
Diskus
Künstler Schreibschrift
Palace Script
Park Avenue
Shelley Allegro Script
Shelley Andante Script
Snell Roundhand

Ariston Light Script **305**

abcdefghijklmnopqrstuvwxyz1234567890

Bank Script **306**

abcdefghijklmnopqrstuvwxyz1234567890

Commercial Script **307**

abcdefghijklmnopqrstuvwxyz 1234567890

Diskus **308**

abcdefghijklmnopqrstuvwxyz1234567890

Künstler Schreibschrift **309**

abcdefghijklmnopqrstuvwxyz1234567890

Palace Script **310**

abcdefghijklmnopqrstuvwxyz 1234567890

Park Avenue **311**

abcdefghijklmnopqrstuvwxyz1234567890

Shelley Allegro Script **312**

abcdefghijklmnopqrstuvwxyz1234567890

Shelley Andante Script **313**

abcdefghijklmnopqrstuvwxyz1234567890

Snell Roundhand **314**

abcdefghijklmnopqrstuvwxyz 1234567890

**FLOWING
SCRIPTS**

Yale Script
ITC Zapf Chancery
Gando Ronde Script
Linoscript
Kaufmann
Jiffy
Brush Script
Mistral

315 Yale Script

quill pen
sloping
and angular

ABCDEFGHIJKLMNOPQRSTUVWXYZ

316 ITC Zapf Chancery

felt or
graphic per.
upright

ABCDEFGHIJKLMNOPQRSTUVWXYZ&

317 Gando Ronde Script

quill pen
upright
rounded

ABCDEFGHIJKLMNOPQRSTUVWXYZ &

318 Linoscript

felt or
graphic pen
sloping

ABCDEFGHIJKLMNOPQRSTUVWXYZ &

319 Kaufmann

ABCDEFGHIJKLMNOP2RSTUVWXYZ&

320 Jiffy

brush

ABCDEFGHIJKLMNOPQRSTUVWXYZ&

321 Brush Script

ABCDEFGHIJKLMNOP2RSTUVWXYZ&

322 Mistral

ABCDEFGHIJKLMNOPQRSTUVWXYZ&

Yale Script
ITC Zapf Chancery
Gando Ronde Script
Linoscript
Kaufmann
Jiffy
Brush Script
Mistral

Yale Script **315**

abcdefghijklmnopqrstuvwxyz1234567890

ITC Zapf Chancery **316**

abcdefghijklmnopqrstuvwxyz1234567890

Gando Ronde Script **317**

abcdefghijklmnopqrstuvwxyz1234567890

Linoscript **318**

abcdefghijklmnopqrstuvwxyz1234567890

Kaufmann **319**

abcdefghijklmnopqrstuvwxyz1234567890

Jiffy **320**

abcdefghijklmnopqrstuvwxyz1234567890

Brush Script **321**

abcdefghijklmnopqrstuvwxyz1234567890

Mistral **322**

abcdefghijklmnopqrstuvwxyz1234567890

2. NON-FLOWING SCRIPTS
(INCLUDING BLACKLETTER & UNCIAL)

Specimen nos		Basic characteristics	Secondary characteristics	
323-326	*Nofl*	quill pen	sloping and rounded	e.g. **323** Bernhard Tango
327-331	*Nofl*	„	sloping and angular	e.g. **330** Noris Script
332	*Nofl*	„	upright and rounded	e.g. **332** Murray Hill Bold
333-336	Nofl	„	upright and angular	e.g. **333** Bologna
337-338	**Nofl**	„	'oriental'	e.g. **337** Auriol
339-343	*Nofl*	„	decorative sloping	e.g. **343** Vivaldi
344-345	Nofl	„	decorative upright	e.g. **344** Delphin No I
346-352	*Nofl*	felt or graphic pen	sloping	e.g. **350** Sallwey Script
353-356	Nofl	„	upright	e.g. **353** Artic
357-362	**Nofl**	brush		e.g. **359** Flash

NB. *Typefaces in each group are arranged in alphabetical order.*

continued on next page

continued from previous page

Specimen nos

363-374	𝕹𝖔𝖋𝖑	blackletter	text	e.g. **372** Old English Text
375-376	𝕹𝖔𝖋𝖑	„	decorative	e.g. **376** St. Clair
377-378	nofl	uncial		e.g. **378** Libra
379-381	*Nofl*	roman italic (based on pen scripts)		e.g. **380** Blado Italic

NB. *Typefaces in each group are arranged in alphabetical order.*

NON-FLOWING
SCRIPTS
(INCLUDING
BLACKLETTER & UNCIAL)

Scr

quill pen
sloping
and rounded

323 Bernhard Tango

ABCDEFGHIJKLMNOPQRSTUVWXYZ&

324 Dorchester Script

ABCDEFGHIJKLMNOPQRSTUVWXYZ&

325 Nuptial Script

ABCDEFGHIJKLMNOPQRSTUVWXYZ&

326 Stradivarius

ABCDEFGHIJKLMNOPQRSTUVWXYZ&

quill pen
sloping
and angular

327 Cascade

ABCDEFGHIJKLMNOPQRSTUVWXYZ&

328 Klang

ABCDEFGHIJKLMNOPQRSTUVWXYZ&

329 Medici Script

ABCDEFGHIJKLMNOPQRSTUVWXYZ&

330 Noris Script

ABCDEFGHIJKLMNOPQRSTUVWXYZ&

331 Temple Script

ABCDEFGHIJKLMNOPQRSTUVWXYZ&

quill pen
upright
and rounded

332 Murray Hill Bold

ABCDEFGHIJKLMNOPQRSTUVWXYZ&

Bernhard Tango **323**

abcdefghijklmnopqrstuvwxyz 1234567890

Dorchester Script **324**

abcdefghijklmnopqrstuvwxyz1234567890

Nuptial Script **325**

abcdefghijklmnopqrstuvwxyz1234567890

Stradivarius **326**

abcdefghijklmnopqrstuvwxyz1234567890

Cascade **327**

abcdefghijklmnopqrstuvwxyz 1234567890

Klang **328**

abcdefghijklmnopqrstuvwxyz1234567890

Medici Script **329**

abcdefghijklmnopqrstuvwxyz1234567890

Noris Script **330**

abcdefghijklmnopqrstuvwxyz1234567890

Temple Script **331**

abcdefghijklmnopqrstuvwxyz1234567890

Murray Hill Bold **332**

abcdefghijklmnopqrstuvwxyz 1234567890

NON-FLOWING
SCRIPTS
(INCLUDING
BLACKLETTER & UNCIAL)

Scr

Bernhard Tango
Dorchester Script
Nuptial Script
Stradivarius
Cascade
Klang
Medici Script
Noris Script
Temple Script
Murray Hill Bold

**NON-FLOWING
SCRIPTS**
(INCLUDING
BLACKLETTER & UNCIAL)

Scr

Bologna
Codex
Lydian
Ondine
Auriol
Boutique
Crayonette
Kalligraphia
Le Griffe
Treasury Open

*quill pen
upright
and angular*

333 Bologna

ABCDEFGHIJKLMNOPQRSTUVWXYZ&

334 Codex

ABCDEFGHIJKLMNOPQRSTUVWXYZ&

335 Lydian

ABCDEFGHIJKLMNOPQRSTUVWXYZ&

336 Ondine

ABCDEFGHIJKLMNOPQRSTUVWXYZ

*quill pen
'oriental'*

337 Auriol

ABCDEFGHIJKLMNOPQRSTUVWXYZ&

338 Boutique

ABCDEFGHIJKLMNOPQRSTUVWXYZ&

*quill pen
decorative
sloping*

339 Crayonette

ABCDEFGHIJKLMNOPQRSTUVWXYZ&

340 Kalligraphia

ABCDEFGHIJKLMNOPQRSTUVWXYZ&

341 Le Griffe

ABCDEFGHIJKLMNOPQRSTUVWXYZ&

342 Treasury Open

ABCDEFGHIJKLMNOPQRSTUVWXYZ&

Bologna **333**

abcdefghijklmnopqrstuvwxyz1234567890

Codex **334**

abcdefghijklmnopqrstuvwxyz 1234567890

Lydian **335**

abcdefghijklmnopqrstuvwxyz 1234567890

Ondine **336**

abcdefghijklmnopqrstuvwxyz 1234567890

Auriol **337**

abcdefghijklmnopqrstuvwxyz 1234567890

Boutique **338**

abcdefghijklmnopqrstuvwxyz 1234567890

Crayonette **339**

abcdefghijklmnopqrstuvwxyz 1234567890

Kalligraphia **340**

abcdefghijklmnopqrstuvwxyz 1234567890

Le Griffe **341**

abcdefghijklmnopqrstuvwxyz 1234567890

Treasury Open **342**

abcdefghijklmnopqrstuvwxyz 1234567890

**NON-FLOWING
SCRIPTS**
(INCLUDING
BLACKLETTER & UNCIAL)

Scr

Bologna
Codex
Lydian
Ondine
Auriol
Boutique
Crayonette
Kalligraphia
Le Griffe
Treasury Open

NON-FLOWING SCRIPTS
(INCLUDING BLACKLETTER & UNCIAL)

Scr

Vivaldi
Delphin No I
Matura
Balloon Extra Bold
Caprice
Gillies Extra Bold
Lateinische Ausgangsschrift
Sallwey Script
Venture
Vertex

343 Vivaldi

ABCDEFGHIJKLMNOPQRSTUVWXYZ&

quill pen decorative upright

344 Delphin No I

ABCDEFGHIJKLMNOPQRSTUVWXYZ&

345 Matura

ABCDEFGHIJKLMNOPQRSTUVWXYZ&

felt or graphic pen sloping

346 Balloon Extra Bold

ABCDEFGHIJKLMNOPQRSTUVWXYZ&

347 Caprice

ABCDEFGHIJKLMNOPQRSTUVWXYZ&

348 Gillies Extra Bold

ABCDEFGHIJKLMNOPQRSTUVWXYZ&

349 Lateinische Ausgangsschrift

ABCDEFGHIJKLMNOPQRSTUVWXYZ

350 Sallwey Script

ABCDEFGHIJKLMNOPQRSTUVWXYZ&

351 Venture

ABCDEFGHIJKLMNOPQRSTUVWXYZ&

352 Vertex

ABCDEFGHIJKLMNOPQRSTUVWXYZ&

Vivaldi **343**

abcdefghijklmnopqrstuvwxyz1234567890

Delphin No 1 **344**

abcdefghijklmnopqrstuvwxyz1234567890

Matura **345**

abcdefghijklmnopqrstuvwxyz1234567890

Balloon Extra Bold **346**

1234567890 no lower case

Caprice **347**

abcdefghijklmnopqrstuvwxyz1234567890

Gillies Extra Bold **348**

abcdefghijklmnopqrstuvwxyz1234567890

Lateinische Ausgangsschrift **349**

abcdefghijklmnopqrstuvwxyz1234567890

Sallwey Script **350**

abcdefghijklmnopqrstuvwxyz1234567890

Venture **351**

abcdefghijklmnopqrstuvwxyz1234567890

Vertex **352**

abcdefghijklmnopqrstuvwxyz1234567890

**NON-FLOWING
SCRIPTS**
(INCLUDING
BLACKLETTER & UNCIAL)

Scr

Vivaldi
Delphin No 1
Matura
Balloon Extra Bold
Caprice
Gillies Extra Bold
Lateinische
Ausgangsschrift
Sallwey Script
Venture
Vertex

felt or graphic pen upright

353 Artic

ABCDEFGHIJKLMNOPQRSTUVWXYZ&

354 Dom Casual

ABCDEFGHIJKLMNOPQRSTUVWXYZ&

355 Present

ABCDEFGHIJKLMNOPQRSTUVWXYZ&

356 Studio

ABCDEFGHIJKLMNOPQRSTUVWXYZ&

brush

357 Ashley Script

ABCDEFGHIJKLMNOPQRSTUVWXYZ&

358 Bison

ABCDEFGHIJKLMNOPQRSTUVWXYZ&

359 Flash

ABCDEFGHIJKLMNOPQRSTUVWXYZ&

360 Forte

ABCDEFGHIJKLMNOPQRSTUVWXYZ&

361 Pepita

ABCDEFGHIJKLMNOPQRSTUVWXYZ&

362 Reporter No 2

ABCDEFGHIJKLMNOPQRSTUVWXYZ&

Artic **353**

abcdefghijklmnopqrstuvwxyz1234567890

Dom Casual **354**

abcdefghijklmnopqrstuvwxyz1234567890

Present **355**

abcdefghijklmnopqrstuvwxyz1234567890

Studio **356**

abcdefghijkl mnopqrstuvwxyz1234567890

Ashley Script **357**

abcdefghijklmnopqrstuvwxyz*1234567890*

Bison **358**

abcdefghijklmnopqrstuvwxyz1234567890

Flash **359**

abcdefghijklmnopqrstuvwxyz1234567890

Forte **360**

abcdefghijklmnopqrstuvwxyz1234567890

Pepita **361**

abcdefghijklmnopqrstuvwxyz1234567890

Reporter No 2 **362**

abcdefghijklmnopqrstuvwxyz1234567890

**NON-FLOWING
SCRIPTS**
(INCLUDING
BLACKLETTER & UNCIAL)

Scr

Artic
Dom Casual
Present
Studio
Ashley Script
Bison
Flash
Forte
Pepita
Reporter No 2

NON-FLOWING
SCRIPTS
(INCLUDING
BLACKLETTER & UNCIAL)

Scr

Caligra
Cloister Black
Fette Fraktur
Fraktur Bold
Gothique
Goudy Text
ITC Honda
Linotext
Luthersche Fraktur
Old English Text

*blackletter
text*

363 Caligra

ABCDEFGHIJKLMNOPQRSTUVWXYZ

364 Cloister Black

ABCDEFGHIJKLMNOPQRSTUVWXYZ&

365 Fette Fraktur

ABCDEFGHIJKLMNOPQRSTUVWXYZ&

366 Fraktur Bold

ABCDEFGHIJKLMNOPQRSTUVWXYZ&

367 Gothique

ABCDEFGHIJKLMNOPQRSTUVWXYZ&

368 Goudy Text

ABCDEFGHIJKLMNOPQRSTUVWXYZ&

369 ITC Honda

ABCDEFGHIJKLMNOPQRSTUVWXYZ&

370 Linotext

ABCDEFGHIJKLMNOPQRSTUVWXYZ&

371 Luthersche Fraktur

ABCDEFGHIJKLMNOPQRSTUVWXYZ&

372 Old English Text

ABCDEFGHIJKLMNOPQRSTUVWXYZ&

Caligra **363**

abcdefghijklmnopqrstuvwxyz1234567890

Cloister Black **364**

abcdefghijklmnopqrstubwxyz1234567890

Fette Fraktur **365**

abcdefghijklmnopqrstuvwxyz1234567890

Fraktur Bold **366**

abcdefghijflmnopqrsstuvwrhz1234567890

Gothique **367**

abcdefghijklmnopqrstuvwrhz1234567890

Goudy Text **368**

abcdefghijklmnopqrstuvwxyz1234567890

ITC Honda **369**

abcdefghijklmnopqrstuvwxyz1234567890

Linotext **370**

abcdefghijklmnopqrstubwxyz1234567890

Luthersche Fraktur **371**

abcdefghijklmnopqrstuvwxhz1234567890

Old English Text **372**

abcdefghijklmnopqrstubwxyz1234567890

NON-FLOWING
SCRIPTS
(INCLUDING
BLACKLETTER & UNCIAL)

Scr

Venetian Text
Condensed

Wilhelm Klingspor
Gotisch

Pamela

St. Clair

American Uncial

Libra

Arrighi Italic
(Centaur Italic)

Blado Italic

Cancelleresca
Bastarda

373 Venetian Text Condensed

ABCDEFGHIJKLMNOPQRSTUVWXYZ&

374 Wilhelm Klingspor Gotisch

ABCDEFGHIJKLMNOPQRSTUVWXYZ&

*blackletter
decorative*

375 Pamela

ABCDEFGHIJKLMNOPQRSTUVWXYZ&

376 St. Clair

ABCDEFGHIJKLMNOPQRSTUVWXYZ&

uncial

377 American Uncial

abcdefghijklmnopqrstuvwxyz&

378 Libra

abcdefghijklmnopqrstuvwxyz

*roman italic
(based on
pen scripts)*

379 Arrighi Italic (Centaur Italic)

ABCDEFGHIJKLMNOPQRSTUVWXYZ&

380 Blado Italic

ABCDEFGHIJKLMNOPQRSTUVWXYZ&

381 Cancelleresca Bastarda

ABCDEFGHIJKLMNOPQRSTUVWXYZ

Venetian Text Condensed **373**

abcdefghijklmnopqrstuvwxyz 1234567890

Wilhelm Klingspor Gotisch **374**

abcdefghijklmnopqrstuvwxyz1234567890

Pamela **375**

abcdefghijklmnopqrstuvwxyz *no figures*

St. Clair **376**

abcdefghijklmnopqrstuvwxyz1234567890

American Uncial **377**

1234567890 *no lower case*

Libra **378**

1234567890 *no lower case*

Arrighi Italic (Centaur Italic) **379**

abcdefghijklmnopqrstuvwxyz 1234567890

Blado Italic **380**

abcdefghijklmnopqrstuvwxyz 1234567890

Cancelleresca Bastarda **381**

abcdefghijklmnopqrstuvwxyz1234567890

NON-FLOWING
SCRIPTS
(INCLUDING
BLACKLETTER & UNCIAL)

Scr

Venetian Text
Condensed
Wilhelm Klingspor
Gotisch
Pamela
St. Clair
American Uncial
Libra
Arrighi Italic
(Centaur Italic)
Blado Italic
Cancelleresca
Bastarda

3. UNMODIFIED
(FORMAL TEXT SHAPE)

Specimen nos		Basic characteristics	Secondary characteristics	
382-390	R	roman serif		e.g. **385** Engravers Roman
391-399	R	,,	inline and outline	e.g. **392** Castellar
400-402	R	,,	shaded	e.g. **402** Thorne Shaded
403	SL	slab serif		e.g. **403** Hellenic Wide
404-405	SL	,,	inline and outline	e.g. **405** Egyptian Outline
406-408	SL	,,	shaded	e.g. **407** Gold Rush
409-415	W	wedge serif		e.g. **412** Latin Antique No 9
416-419	W	,,	inline	e.g. **417** Chisel
420-421	SA	sans serif		e.g. **420** Fleet
422	SA	,,	outline	e.g. **422** Helvetica Outline

NB. *Typefaces in each group are arranged in alphabetical order.*

continued on next page

continued from previous page

423-426		*(sans serif)*	*inline and outline shaded*	e.g. **425** Gill Sans Shadow 408
427-428		,,	*with backgrounds*	e.g. **427** Gill Cameo

NB. *Typefaces in each group are arranged in alphabetical order.*

roman serif

382 Bauer Classic Roman

ABCDEFGHIJKLMNOPQRSTUVWXYZ&

383 Caslon Antique

ABCDEFGHIJKLMNOPQRSTUVWXYZ&

384 Elizabeth Roman

ABCDEFGHIJKLMNOPQRSTUVWXYZ&

385 Engravers Roman

ABCDEFGHIJKLMNOPQRSTUVWXYZ&

386 Engravers Roman Bold

ABCDEFGHIJKLMNOPQRSTUVWXYZ&

387 Felix Titling

ABCDEFGHIJKLMNOPQRSTUVWXYZ

388 Fleet Titling

ABCDEFGHIJKLMNOPQRSTUVWXYZ&

389 Horizon

ABCDEFGHIJKLMNOPQRSTUVWXYZ&

390 Victoria Titling

ABCDEFGHIJKLMNOPQRSTUVWXYZ&

roman serif
inline and
outline

391 Caslon Open Face

ABCDEFGHIJKLMNOPQRSTUVWXYZ&

UNMODIFIED
(FORMAL TEXT SHAPE)

UN

Bauer Classic Roman
Caslon Antique
Elizabeth Roman
Engravers Roman
Engravers Roman Bold
Felix Titling
Fleet Titling
Horizon
Victoria Titling
Caslon Open Face

Bauer Classic Roman **382**

abcdefghijklmnopqrstuvwxyz1234567890

Caslon Antique **383**

abcdefghijklmnopqrstuvwxyz1234567890

Elizabeth Roman **384**

abcdefghijklmnopqrstuvwxyz 1234567890

small capitals (no lower case) Engravers Roman **385**

ABCDEFGHIJKLMNOPQRSTUVWXYZ1234567890

small capitals (no lower case) Engravers Roman Bold **386**

ABCDEFGHIJKLMNOPQRSTUVWXYZ1234567890

Felix Titling **387**

1234567890 *no lower case*

Fleet Titling **388**

1234567890 *no lower case*

Horizon **389**

abcdefghijklmnopqrstuvwxyz1234567890

Victoria Titling **390**

1234567890 *no lower case*

Caslon Open Face **391**

abcdefghijklmnopqrstuvwxyz1234567890

UNMODIFIED
(FORMAL TEXT SHAPE)

Bauer Classic Roman
Caslon Antique
Elizabeth Roman
Engravers Roman
Engravers Roman Bold
Felix Titling
Fleet Titling
Horizon
Victoria Titling
Caslon Open Face

392 Castellar

ABCDEFGHIJKLMNOPQRSTUVWXYZ&

393 Cloister Open Face

ABCDEFGHIJKLMNOPQRSTUVWXYZ&

394 Goudy Handtooled

ABCDEFGHIJKLMNOPQRSTUVWXYZ

395 Hadriano Stonecut

ABCDEFGHIJKLMNOPQRSTUVWXYZ&

396 Old Style Bold Outline

ABCDEFGHIJKLMNOPQRSTUVWXYZ&

397 Times English Black Outline

ABCDEFGHIJKLMNOPQRSTUVWXYZ&

398 Windsor Bold Outline

ABCDEFGHIJKLMNOPQRSTUVWXYZ&

399 Windsor Elongated

ABCDEFGHIJKLMNOPQRSTUVWXYZ&

400 Bank Note

ABCDEFGHIJKLMNOPQRSTUVWXYZ&

401 Cheque

ABCDEFGHIJKLMNOPQRSTUVWXYZ&

UNMODIFIED
(FORMAL TEXT SHAPE)

UN

Castellar
Cloister Open Face
Goudy Handtooled
Hadriano Stonecut
Old Style Bold Outline
Times English
Black Outline
Windsor Bold Outline
Windsor Elongated
Bank Note
Cheque

*roman serif
shaded*

Castellar **392**

1234567890 *no lower case*

Cloister Open Face **393**

abcdefghijklmnopqrstuvwxyz1234567890

Goudy Handtooled **394**

abcdefghijklmnopqrstuvwxyz1234567890

Hadriano Stonecut **395**

1234567890 *no lower case*

Old Style Bold Outline **396**

abcdefghijklmnopqrstuvwxyz1234567890

Times English Black Outline **397**

abcdefghijklmnopqrstuvwxyz1234567890

Windsor Bold Outline **398**

abcdefghijklmnopqrstuvwxyz1234567890

Windsor Elongated **399**

abcdefghijklmnopqrstuvwxyz 1234567890

Bank Note **400**

1234567890 *no lower case*

Cheque **401**

1234567890 *no lower case*

UNMODIFIED
(FORMAL TEXT SHAPE)

UN

Castellar
Cloister Open Face
Goudy Handtooled
Hadriano Stonecut
Old Style Bold Outline
Times English
Black Outline
Windsor Bold Outline
Windsor Elongated
Bank Note
Cheque

402 Thorne Shaded

ABCDEFGHIJKLMNOPQRSTUVWXYZ

slab serif inline and outline

403 Hellenic Wide

ABCDEFGHIJKLMNOPQRSTUVWXYZ&

slab serif

404 ITC American Typewriter Bold Outline

ABCDEFGHIJKLMNOPQRSTUVWXYZ&

405 Egyptian Outline

ABCDEFGHIJKLMNOPQRSTUVWXYZ&

slab serif shaded or 3D

406 Egyptienne Filette

ABCDEFGHIJKLMNOPQRSTUVWXYZ

407 Gold Rush

ABCDEFGHIJKLMNOPQRSTUVWXYZ&

408 Rockwell Shadow

ABCDEFGHIJKLMNOPQRSTUVWXYZ&

wedge serif

409 Augustea Nova

ABCDEFGHIJKLMNOPQRSTUVWXYZ&

410 Columna

ABCDEFGHIJKLMNOPQRSTUVWXYZ&

411 Jana

ABCDEFGHIJKLMNOPQRSTUVWXYZ&

UNMODIFIED
(FORMAL TEXT SHAPE)

UN

Thorne Shaded
Hellenic Wide
ITC American Typewriter Bold Outline
Egyptian Outline
Egyptienne Filette
Gold Rush
Rockwell Shadow
Augustea Nova
Columna
Jana

Thorne Shaded **402**

1234567890 *no lower case*

Hellenic Wide **403**

abcdefghijklmnopqrstuvwxyz1234567890

ITC American Typewriter Bold Outline **404**

abcdefghijklmnopqrstuvwxyz1234567890

Egyptian Outline **405**

1234567890 *no lower case*

Egyptienne Filette **406**

no lower case or figures

Gold Rush **407**

1234567890 *no lower case*

Rockwell Shadow **408**

1234567890 *no lower case*

Augustea Nova **409**

abcdefghijklmnopqrstuvwxyz1234567890

Columna **410**

1234567890 *no lower case*

Jana **411**

abcdefghijklmnopqrstuvwxyz1234567890

UNMODIFIED
(FORMAL TEXT SHAPE)

UN

Thorne Shaded
Hellenic Wide
ITC American
Typewriter
Bold Outline
Egyptian Outline
Egyptienne Filette
Gold Rush
Rockwell Shadow
Augustea Nova
Columna
Jana

412 Latin Antique No 9

ABCDEFGHIJKLMNOPQRSTUVWXYZ&

413 Latin Condensed No 2

ABCDEFGHIJKLMNOPQRSTUVWXYZ&

414 Latin Wide

ABCDEFGHIJKLMNOPQRSTUVWXYZ&

415 Runic Condensed

ABCDEFGHIJKLMNOPQRSTUVWXYZ&

416 Augustea Inline

ABCDEFGHIJKLMNOPQRSTUVWXYZ&

417 Chisel

ABCDEFGHIJKLMNOPQRSTUVWXYZ&

418 Contura

ABCDEFGHIJKLMNOPQRSTUVWXYZ&

419 Crystal

ABCDEFGHIJKLMNOPQRSTUVWXYZ&

420 Fleet

ABCDEFGHIJKLMNOPQRSTUVWXYZ&

421 Hanseatic Bold

ABCDEFGHIJKLMNOPQRSTUVWXYZ&

UNMODIFIED
(FORMAL TEXT SHAPE)

Latin Antique No 9
Latin Condensed No 2
Latin Wide
Runic Condensed
Augustea Inline
Chisel
Contura
Crystal
Fleet
Hanseatic Bold

wedge serif
inline and
outline

sans serif

Latin Antique No 9 **412**

abcdefghijklmnopqrstuvwxyz1234567890

Latin Condensed No 2 **413**

abcdefghijklmnopqrstuvwxyz1234567890

Latin Wide **414**

abcdefghijklmnopqrstuvwxyz 1234567890

Runic Condensed **415**

abcdefghijklmnopqrstuvwxyz1234567890

Augustea Inline **416**

1234567890 *no lower case*

Chisel **417**

abcdefghijklmnopqrstuvwxyz1234567890

Contura **418**

abcdefghijklmnopqrstuvwxyz1234567890

Crystal **419**

1234567890 *no lower case*

Fleet **420**

abcdefghijklmnopqrstuvwxyz1234567890

Hanseatic Bold **421**

abcdefghijklmnopqrstuvwxyz1234567890

UNMODIFIED
(FORMAL TEXT SHAPE)

UN

Latin Antique No 9
Latin Condensed No 2
Latin Wide
Runic Condensed
Augustea Inline
Chisel
Contura
Crystal
Fleet
Hanseatic Bold

sans serif outline

422 Helvetica Outline

ABCDEFGHIJKLMNOPQRSTUVWXYZ&

sans serif inline and outline shaded

423 Festival Titling

ABCDEFGHIJKLMNOPQRSTUVWXYZ&

424 Gill Sans Shadow Line 290

ABCDEFGHIJKLMNOPQRSTUVWXYZ&

425 Gill Sans Shadow 408

ABCDEFGHIJKLMNOPQRSTUVWXYZ&

426 Sans Serif Shaded

ABCDEFGHIJKLMNOPQRSTUVWXYZ&

sans serif with backgrounds

427 Gill Cameo

ABCDEFGHIJKLMNOPQRSTUVWXYZ&

428 Gill Cameo Ruled

ABCDEFGHIJKLMNOPQRSTUVWXYZ&

Helvetica Outline **422**

abcdefghijklmnopqrstuvwxyz1234567890

Festival Titling **423**

1234567890 *no lower case*

Gill Sans Shadow Line 290 **424**

abcdefghijklmnopqrstuvwxyz1234567890

Gill Sans Shadow 408 **425**

1234567890 *no lower case*

Sans Serif Shaded **426**

1234567890 *no lower case*

Gill Cameo **427**

1234567890 *no lower case*

Gill Cameo Ruled **428**

1234567890 *no lower case*

UNMODIFIED
(FORMAL TEXT SHAPE)

UN

Helvetica Outline
Festival Titling
Gill Sans Shadow
Line 290
Gill Sans Shadow 408
Sans Serif Shaded
Gill Cameo
Gill Cameo Ruled

4. FAT & THIN FACE
(UNMODIFIED & MODIFIED)

FAT FACE

Specimen nos		Basic characteristics	Secondary characteristics	
429-443	**R**	roman serif	thin serifs	e.g. **434** Falstaff
444-449	**R**	,,	medium weight serifs	e.g. **445** Caslon Black
450-452	**R**	,,	heavy serifs	e.g. **451** Kompakt
453-458	**SL**	slab serif		e.g. **453** Figaro
459-466	**W**	wedge serif	thin/medium serifs	e.g. **459** Americana True
467-469	**W**	,,	heavy serifs	e.g. **467** Cooper Black
470-471	**W**	,,	heavy serifs and outline	e.g. **471** ITC Souvenir Bold Outline
472-481	**SA**	sans serif	wide	e.g. **472** Annonce Grotesque
482	**SA**	,,	wide outline	e.g. **482** Gill Kayo Outline
483-498	**SA**	,,	medium width	e.g. **493** Helvetica Heavy

NB. *Typefaces in each group are arranged in alphabetical order.*

continued on next page

continued from previous page

499-506	**SA** *(sans serif)*	narrow	e.g. **501** Compacta Bold
507-509	SA ,,	narrow outline	e.g. **508** Impact Outline
510-514	**SA** ,,	rounded shape	e.g. **514** Harry Fat
515	SA ,,	rounded shape outline	e.g. **515** ITC Bauhaus Heavy Outline

THIN FACE

516-519	LS *slab serif*		e.g. **519** ITC Stymie Hairline
520-521	W *wedge serif*		e.g. **520** ITC Newtext Light
522-533	SA *sans serif*		e.g. **530** Helvetica Ultra Light
534-536	SA ,,	rounded shape	e.g. **535** Churchward 70 Hairline

NB. *Typefaces in each group are arranged in alphabetical order.*

FAT FACE
& THIN FACE
(UNMODIFIED & MODIFIED)

roman serif with thin serifs

429 Annlie Extra Bold

ABCDEFGHIJKLMNOPQRSTUVWXYZ&

430 Brace Condensed

ABCDEFGHIJKLMNOPQRSTUVWXYZ&

431 Carousel

ABCDEFGHIJKLMNOPQRSTUVWXYZ&

432 ITC Didi

ABCDEFGHIJKLMMNOPQRSTUVWXYZ&

433 Elongated Roman

ABCDEFGHIJKLMNOPQRSTUVWXYZ&

434 Falstaff

ABCDEFGHIJKLMNOPQRSTUVWXYZ&

435 ITC Firenze

ABCDEFGHIJKLMNOPQRSTUVWXYZ&

436 Normande

ABCDEFGHIJKLMNOPQRSTUVWXYZ&

437 Orator

ABCDEFGHIJKLMNOPQRSTUVWXYZ&

438 Perpetua Black

ABCDEFGHIJKLMNOPQRSTUVWXYZ&

**FAT FACE
& THIN FACE**
(UNMODIFIED & MODIFIED)

Annlie Extra Bold
Brace Condensed
Carousel
ITC Didi
Elongated Roman
Falstaff
ITC Firenze
Normande
Orator
Perpetua Black

Annlie Extra Bold **429**

abcdefghijklmnopqrstuvwxyz**1234567890**

Brace Condensed **430**

abcdefghijklmnopqrstuvwxyz 1234567890

Carousel **431**

abcdefghijklmnopqrstuvwxyz**1234567890**

ITC Didi **432**

abcdefghijklmnopqrstuvwxyz1234567890

Elongated Roman **433**

1234567890 *no lower case*

Falstaff **434**

abcdefghijklmnopqrstuvwxyz**1234567890**

ITC Firenze **435**

abcdefghijklmnopqrstuvwxyz**1234567890**

Normande **436**

abcdefghijklmnopqrstuvwxyz**1234567890**

Orator **437**

abcdefghijklmnopqrstuvwxyz**1234567890**

Perpetua Black **438**

abcdefghijklmnopqrstuvwxyz1234567890

**FAT FACE
& THIN FACE**
(UNMODIFIED & MODIFIED)

Annlie Extra Bold
Brace Condensed
Carousel
ITC Didi
Elongated Roman
Falstaff
ITC Firenze
Normande
Orator
Perpetua Black

439 Pistilli Roman

ABCDEFGHIJKLMNOPQRSTUVWXYZ&

440 Poster Bodoni

ABCDEFGHIJKLMNOPQRSTUVWXYZ&

441 Thorowgood

ABCDEFGHIJKLMNOPQRSTUVWXYZ&

442 ITC Tiffany Heavy

ABCDEFGHIJKLMNOPQRSTUVWXYZ&

443 ITC Zapf Book Heavy

ABCDEFGHIJKLMNOPQRSTUVWXYZ&

**FAT FACE
& THIN FACE**
(UNMODIFIED & MODIFIED)

Pistilli Roman
Poster Bodoni
Thorowgood
ITC Tiffany Heavy
ITC Zapf Book Heavy
Aetna
Caslon Black
ITC Century Ultra
ITC Galliard Ultra
ITC Garamond Ultra

*roman serif
with medium
thickness serifs*

444 Aetna

ABCDEFGHIJKLMNOPQRSTUVWXYZ&

445 Caslon Black

ABCDEFGHIJKLMNOPQRSTUVWXYZ&

446 ITC Century Ultra

ABCDEFGHIJKLMNOPQRSTUVWXYZ&

447 ITC Galliard Ultra

ABCDEFGHIJKLMNOPQRSTUVWXYZ&

448 ITC Garamond Ultra

ABCDEFGHIJKLMNOPQRSTUVWXYZ&

Pistilli Roman **439**

abcdefghijklmnopqrstuvwxyz1234567890

Poster Bodoni **440**

abcdefghijklmnopqrstuvwxyz1234567890

Thorowgood **441**

abcdefghijklmnopqrstuvwxyz1234567890

ITC Tiffany Heavy **442**

abcdefghijklmnopqrstuvwxyz1234567890

ITC Zapf Book Heavy **443**

abcdefghijklmnopqrstuvwxyz1234567890

Aetna **444**

1234567890 *no lower case*

Caslon Black **445**

abcdefghijklmnopqrstuvwxyz1234567890

ITC Century Ultra **446**

abcdefghijklmnopqrstuvwxyz1234567890

ITC Galliard Ultra **447**

abcdefghijklmnopqrstuvwxyz1234567890

ITC Garamond Ultra **448**

abcdefghijklmnopqrstuvwxyz1234567890

**FAT FACE
& THIN FACE**
(UNMODIFIED & MODIFIED)

Pistilli Roman
Poster Bodoni
Thorowgood
ITC Tiffany Heavy
ITC Zapf Book Heavy
Aetna
Caslon Black
ITC Century Ultra
ITC Galliard Ultra
ITC Garamond Ultra

449 ITC Grouch

ABCDEFGHIJKLMNOPQRSTUVWXYZ&

roman serifs with heavy serifs

450 ITC Cheltenham Ultra

ABCDEFGHIJKLMNOPQRSTUVWXYZ&

451 Kompakt

ABCDEFGHIJKLMNOPQRSTUVWXYZ&

452 Whitin Black

ABCDEFGHIJKLMNOPQRSTUVWXYZ&

slab serif

453 Figaro

ABCDEFGHIJKLMNOPQRSTUVWXYZ&

454 Hidalgo

ABCDEFGHIJKLMNOPQRSTUVWXYZ&

455 Karnak Black

ABCDEFGHIJKLMNOPQRSTUVWXYZ&

456 Memphis Extra Bold

ABCDEFGHIJKLMNOPQRSTUVWXYZ&

457 Playbill

ABCDEFGHIJKLMNOPQRSTUVWXYZ&

458 Rockwell Extra Bold

ABCDEFGHIJKLMNOPQRSTUVWXYZ&

**FAT FACE
& THIN FACE
(UNMODIFIED & MODIFIED)**

ITC Grouch
ITC Cheltenham Ultra
Kompakt
Whitin Black
Figaro
Hidalgo
Karnak Black
Memphis Extra Bold
Playbill
Rockwell Extra Bold

ITC Grouch **449**

abcdefghijklmnopqrstuvwxyz1234567890

ITC Cheltenham Ultra **450**

abcdefghijklmnopqrstuvwxyz1234567890

Kompakt **451**

abcdefghijklmnopqrstuvwxyz1234567890

Whitin Black **452**

abcdefghijklmnopqrstuvwxyz1234567890

Figaro **453**

abcdefghijklmnopqrstuvwxyz1234567890

Hidalgo **454**

1234567890 *no lower case*

Karnak Black **455**

abcdefghijklmnopqrstuvwxyz1234567890

Memphis Extra Bold **456**

abcdefghijklmnopqrstuvwxyz1234567890

Playbill **457**

abcdefghijklmnopqrstuvwxyz1234567890

Rockwell Extra Bold **458**

abcdefghijklmnopqrstuvwxyz1234567890

FAT FACE & THIN FACE
(UNMODIFIED & MODIFIED)

ITC Grouch
ITC Cheltenham Ultra
Kompakt
Whitin Black
Figaro
Hidalgo
Karnak Black
Memphis Extra Bold
Playbill
Rockwell Extra Bold

wedge serif with thin or medium serifs

459 Americana True

ABCDEFGHIJKLMNOPQRSTUVWXYZ&

460 Hawthorn

ABCDEFGHIJKLMNOPQRSTUVWXYZ&

461 Hess Neobold

ABCDEFGHIJKLMNOPQRSTUVWXYZ&

462 Las Vegas

ABCDEFGHIJKLMNOPQRSTUVWXYZ&

463 Macbeth

ABCDEFGHIJKLMNOPQRSTUVWXYZ&

464 ITC Novarese Ultra

ABCDEFGHIJKLMNOPQRSTUVWXYZ&

465 ITC Serif Gothic Heavy

ABCDEFGHIJKLMNOPQRSTUVWXYZ&

466 Trooper Black

ABCDEFGHIJKLMNOPQRSTUVWXYZ&

wedge serif with heavy serifs

467 Cooper Black

ABCDEFGHIJKLMNOPQRSTUVWXYZ&

468 Pabst

ABCDEFGHIJKLMNOPQRSTUVWXYZ&

**FAT FACE
& THIN FACE**
(UNMODIFIED & MODIFIED)

Americana True
Hawthorn
Hess Neobold
Las Vegas
Macbeth
ITC Novarese Ultra
ITC Serif Gothic Heavy
Trooper Black
Cooper Black
Pabst

Americana True **459**

abcdefghijklmnopqrstuvwxyz1234567890

Hawthorn **460**

abcdefghijklmnopqrstuvwxyz1234567890

Hess Neobold **461**

1234567890 *no lower case*

Las Vegas **462**

abcdefghijklmnopqrstuvwxyz1234567890

Macbeth **463**

abcdefghijklmnopqrstuvwxyz1234567890

ITC Novarese Ultra **464**

abcdefghijklmnopqrstuvwxyz1234567890

ITC Serif Gothic Heavy **465**

abcdefghijklmnopqrstuvwxyz1234567890

Trooper Black **466**

abcdefghijklmnopqrstuvwxyz1234567890

Cooper Black **467**

abcdefghijklmnopqrstuvwxyz1234567890

Pabst **468**

abcdefghijklmnopqrstuvwxyz1234567890

FAT FACE
& THIN FACE
(UNMODIFIED & MODIFIED)

Americana True
Hawthorn
Hess Neobold
Las Vegas
Macbeth
ITC Novarese Ultra
ITC Serif Gothic Heavy
Trooper Black
Cooper Black
Pabst

469 ITC Souvenir Bold

ABCDEFGHIJKLMNOPQRSTUVWXYZ&

wedge serif with heavy serifs and outline

470 Cooper Black Outline

ABCDEFGHIJKLMNOPQRSTUVWXYZ&

471 ITC Souvenir Bold Outline

ABCDEFGHIJKLMNOPQRSTUVWXYZ&

sans serif wide

472 Annonce Grotesque

ABCDEFGHIJKLMNOPQRSTUVWXYZ&

473 Antique Olive Nord

ABCDEFGHIJKLMNOPQRSTUVWXYZ&

474 ITC Bolt Bold

ABCDEFGHIJKLMNOPQRSTUVWXYZ&

475 Fehrle Display

ABCDEFGHIJKLMNOPQRSTUVWXYZ&

476 Gill Kayo

ABCDEFGHIJKLMNOPQRSTUVWXYZ&

477 Helvetica Bold Extended

ABCDEFGHIJKLMNOPQRSTUVWXYZ&

478 Information Black Extended

ABCDEFGHIJKLMNOPQRSTUVWXYZ&

**FAT FACE
& THIN FACE**
(UNMODIFIED & MODIFIED)

ITC Souvenir Bold
Cooper Black Outline
ITC Souvenir Bold Outline
Annonce Grotesque
Antique Olive Nord
ITC Bolt Bold
Fehrle Display
Gill Kayo
Helvetica Bold Extended
Information Black
Extended

ITC Souvenir Bold **469**

abcdefghijklmnopqrstuvwxyz**1234567890**

Cooper Black Outline **470**

abcdefghijklmnopqrstuvwxyz1234567890

ITC Souvenir Bold Outline **471**

abcdefghijklmnopqrstuvwxyz1234567890

Annonce Grotesque **472**

abcdefghijklmnopqrstuvwxyz1234567890

Antique Olive Nord **473**

abcdefghijklmnopqrstuvwxyz1234567890

ITC Bolt Bold **474**

abcdefghijklmnopqrstuvwxyz1234567890

Fehrle Display **475**

abcdefghijklmnopqrstuvwxyz1234567890

Gill Kayo **476**

abcdefghijklmnopqrstuvwxyz1234567890

Helvetica Bold Extended **477**

abcdefghijklmnopqrstuvwxyz1234567890

Information Black Extended **478**

abcdefghijklmnopqrstuvwxyz1234567890

**FAT FACE
& THIN FACE**
(UNMODIFIED & MODIFIED)

ITC Souvenir Bold
Cooper Black Outline
ITC Souvenir Bold Outline
Annonce Grotesque
Antique Olive Nord
ITC Bolt Bold
Fehrle Display
Gill Kayo
Helvetica Bold Extended
Information Black
Extended

479 Koloss

ABCDEFGHIJKLMNOPQRSTUVWXYZ&

480 Spartan Extra Black

ABCDEFGHIJKLMNOPQRSTUVWXYZ&

481 Univers 83

ABCDEFGHIJKLMNOPQRSTUVWXYZ&

*sans serif
wide
outline*

482 Gill Kayo Outline

ABCDEFGHIJKLMNOPQRSTUVWXYZ&

*sans serif
medium
width*

483 Antique Olive Compact

ABCDEFGHIJKLMNOPQRSTUVWXYZ&

484 Broadway

ABCDEFGHIJKLMNOPQRSTUVWXYZ&

485 Broadway Engraved

ABCDEFGHIJKLMNOPQRSTUVWXYZ&

486 Bullion Solid

ABCDEFGHIJKLMNOPQRSTUVWXYZ &

487 Dynamo

ABCDEFGHIJKLMNOPQRSTUVWXYZ&

488 Folio Extra Bold

ABCDEFGHIJKLMNOPQRSTUVWXYZ&

**FAT FACE
& THIN FACE**
(UNMODIFIED & MODIFIED)

Koloss
Spartan Extra Black
Univers 83
Gill Kayo Outline
Antique Olive Compact
Broadway
Broadway Engraved
Bullion Solid
Dynamo
Folio Extra Bold

Koloss **479**

abcdefghijklmnopqrstuvwxyz1234567890

Spartan Extra Black **480**

abcdefghijklmnopqrstuvwxyz1234567890

Univers 83 **481**

abcdefghijklmnopqrstuvwxyz1234567890

Gill Kayo Outline **482**

abcdefghijklmnopqrstuvwxyz1234567890

Antique Olive Compact **483**

abcdefghijklmnopqrstuvwxyz1234567890

Broadway **484**

abcdefghijklmnopqrstuvwxyz1234567890

Broadway Engraved **485**

abcdefghijklmnopqrstuvwxyz1234567890

Bullion Solid **486**

1234567890 *no lower case*

Dynamo **487**

abcdefghijklmnopqrstuvwxyz1234567890

Folio Extra Bold **488**

abcdefghijklmnopqrstuvwxyz1234567890

FAT FACE
& THIN FACE
(UNMODIFIED & MODIFIED)

Koloss
Spartan Extra Black
Univers 83
Gill Kayo Outline
Antique Olive Compact
Broadway
Broadway Engraved
Bullion Solid
Dynamo
Folio Extra Bold

489 Frutiger 75 Black

ABCDEFGHIJKLMNOPQRSTUVWXYZ&

490 Gothic No 16

ABCDEFGHIJKLMNOPQRSTUVWXYZ&

491 ITC Grizzly

ABCDEFGHIJKLMNOPQRSTUVWXYZ&

492 Haas Unica Black

ABCDEFGHIJKLMNOPQRSTUVWXYZ&

493 Helvetica Heavy

ABCDEFGHIJKLMNOPQRSTUVWXYZ&

494 Helvetica No 2 Bold

ABCDEFGHIJKLMNOPQRSTUVWXYZ&

495 Neil Bold

ABCDEFGHIJKLMNOPQRSTUVWXYZ&

496 Plak Heavy

ABCDEFGHIJKLMNOPQRSTUVWXYZ&

497 Syntax Ultra Black

ABCDEFGHIJKLMNOPQRSTUVWXYZ&

498 Univers 75

ABCDEFGHIJKLMNOPQRSTUVWXYZ&

**FAT FACE
& THIN FACE**
(UNMODIFIED & MODIFIED)

Frutiger 75 Black
Gothic No 16
ITC Grizzly
Haas Unica Black
Helvetica Heavy
Helvetica No 2 Bold
Neil Bold
Plak Heavy
Syntax Ultra Black
Univers 75

Frutiger 75 Black **489**

abcdefghijklmnopqrstuvwxyz1234567890

Gothic No 16 **490**

abcdefghijklmnopqrstuvwxyz1234567890

ITC Grizzly **491**

abcdefghijklmnopqrstuvwxyz1234567890

Haas Unica Black **492**

abcdefghijklmnopqrstuvwxyz1234567890

Helvetica Heavy **493**

abcdefghijklmnopqrstuvwxyz1234567890

Helvetica No 2 Bold **494**

abcdefghijklmnopqrstuvwxyz1234567890

Neil Bold **495**

abcdefghijklmnopqrstuvwxyz1234567890

Plak Heavy **496**

abcdefghijklmnopqrstuvwxyz1234567890

Syntax Ultra Black **497**

abcdefghijklmnopqrstuvwxyz1234567890

Univers 75 **498**

abcdefghijklmnopqrstuvwxyz1234567890

**FAT FACE
& THIN FACE**
(UNMODIFIED & MODIFIED)

Frutiger 75 Black
Gothic No 16
ITC Grizzly
Haas Unica Black
Helvetica Heavy
Helvetica No 2 Bold
Neil Bold
Plak Heavy
Syntax Ultra Black
Univers 75

499-508

sans serif narrow

499 Anzeigen Grotesque

ABCDEFGHIJKLMNOPQRSTUVWXYZ&

500 Block Black Condensed

ABCDEFGHIJKLMNOPQRSTUVWXYZ&

501 Compacta Bold

ABCDEFGHIJKLMNOPQRSTUVWXYZ&

502 Futura Display

ABCDEFGHIJKLMNOPQRSTUVWXYZ&

503 Headline Bold

ABCDEFGHIJKLMNOPQRSTUVWXYZ&

504 Impact

ABCDEFGHIJKLMNOPQRSTUVWXYZ&

505 ITC Machine

ABCDEFGHIJKLMNOPQRSTUVWXYZ&

506 Placard Extra Bold Condensed

ABCDEFGHIJKLMNOPQRSTUVWXYZ&

sans serif narrow outline or inline

507 Compacta Bold Outline

ABCDEFGHIJKLMNOPQRSTUVWXYZ&

508 Impact Outline

ABCDEFGHIJJKLMNOPQRSTUVWXYZ&

**FAT FACE
& THIN FACE**
(UNMODIFIED & MODIFIED)

Anzeigen Grotesque
Block Black Condensed
Compacta Bold
Futura Display
Headline Bold
Impact
ITC Machine
Placard Extra Bold
Condensed
Compacta Bold Outline
Impact Outline

212

Anzeigen Grotesque **499**

abcdefghijklmnopqrstuvwxyz1234567890

Block Black Condensed **500**

abcdefghijklmnopqrstuvwxyz1234567890

Compacta Bold **501**

abcdefghijklmnopqrstuvwxyz1234567890

Futura Display **502**

abcdefghijklmnopqrstuvwxyz1234567890

Headline Bold **503**

abcdefghijklmnopqrstuvwxyz1234567890

Impact **504**

abcdefghijklmnopqrstuvwxyz1234567890

ITC Machine **505**

1234567890 no lower case

Placard Extra Bold Condensed **506**

abcdefghijklmnopqrstuvwxyz1234567890

Compacta Bold Outline **507**

1234567890 no lower case

Impact Outline **508**

abcdefghijklmnopqrstuvwxyz1234567890

FAT FACE
& THIN FACE
(UNMODIFIED & MODIFIED)

Anzeigen Grotesque
Block Black Condensed
Compacta Bold
Futura Display
Headline Bold
Impact
ITC Machine
Placard Extra Bold
Condensed
Compacta Bold Outline
Impact Outline

509 Superstar

ABCDEFGHIJKLMNOPQRSTUVWXYZ&

sans serif
rounded
shape

510 ITC Bauhaus Heavy

ABCDEFGHIJKLMNOPQRSTUVWXYZ&

511 Blippo Black

ABCDEFGHIJKLMNOPQRSTUVWXYZ&

512 Cable Heavy (Klingspor)

ABCDEFGHIJKLMNOPQRSTUVWXYZ&

513 Churchward 70 Ultra Black

ABCDEFGHIJKLMNOPQRSTUVWXYZ&

514 Harry Fat

ABCDEFGHIJKLMNOPQRSTUVWXYZ&

sans serif
rounded
shape
outline

515 ITC Bauhaus Heavy Outline

ABCDEFGHIJKLMNOPQRSTUVWXYZ&

slab serif

516 ITC American Typewriter Light

ABCDEFGHIJKLMNOPQRSTUVWXYZ&

517 Glypha 35 Thin

ABCDEFGHIJKLMNOPQRSTUVWXYZ&

518 Serifa 35 Thin

ABCDEFGHIJKLMNOPQRSTUVWXYZ&

FAT FACE
& THIN FACE
(UNMODIFIED & MODIFIED)

Superstar
ITC Bauhaus Heavy
Blippo Black
Cable Heavy (Klingspor)
Churchward 70
Ultra Black
Harry Fat
ITC Bauhaus
Heavy Outline
ITC American
Typewriter Light
Glypha 35 Thin
Serifa 35 Thin

Superstar **509**

1234567890 *no lower case*

ITC Bauhaus Heavy **510**

abcdefghijklmnopqrstuvwxyz1234567890

Blippo Black **511**

abcdefghijklmnopqrstuvwxyz1234567890

Cable Heavy (Klingspor) **512**

abcdefghijklmnopqrstuvwxyz1234567890

Churchward 70 Ultra Black **513**

abcdefghijklmnopqrstuvwxyz1234567890

Harry Fat **514**

abcdefghijklmnopqrstuvwxyz1234567890

ITC Bauhaus Heavy Outline **515**

abcdefghijklmnopqrstuvwxyz1234567890

ITC American Typewriter Light **516**

abcdefghijklmnopqrstuvwxyz1234567890

Glypha 35 Thin **517**

abcdefghijklmnopqrstuvwxyz1234567890

Serifa 35 Thin **518**

abcdefghijklmnopqrstuvwxyz1234567890

FAT FACE & THIN FACE
(UNMODIFIED & MODIFIED)

Superstar
ITC Bauhaus Heavy
Blippo Black
Cable Light (Klingspor)
Churchward 70
Ultra Black
Harry Fat
ITC Bauhaus
Heavy Outline
ITC American
Typewriter Light
Glypha 35 Thin
Serifa 35 Thin

519 ITC Stymie Hairline

ABCDEFGHIJKLMNOPQRSTUVWXYZ&

wedge serif

520 ITC Newtext Light

ABCDEFGHIJKLMNOPQRSTUVWXYZ&

521 Virgin Roman

ABCDEFGHIJKLMNOPQRSTUVWXYZ&

sans serif

522 ITC Avant Garde Gothic Extra Light

ABCDEFGHIJKLMNOPQRSTUVWXYZ&

523 Cable Light (Klingspor)

ABCDEFGHIJKLMNOPQRSTUVWXYZ&

524 Empire

ABCDEFGHIJKLMNOPQRSTUVWXYZ&

525 ITC Eras Light

ABCDEFGHIJKLMNOPQRSTUVWXYZ&

526 Futura Light

ABCDEFGHIJKLMNOPQRSTUVWXYZ&

527 Gill Sans Light

ABCDEFGHIJKLMNOPQRSTUVWXYZ&

528 Grotesque 126

ABCDEFGHIJKLMNOPQRSTUVWXYZ&

**FAT FACE
& THIN FACE**
(UNMODIFIED & MODIFIED)

ITC Stymie Hairline
ITC Newtext Light
Virgin Roman
ITC Avant Garde Gothic
Extra Light
Cable Light (Klingspor)
Empire
ITC Eras Light
Futura Light
Gill Sans Light
Grotesque 126

ITC Stymie Hairline **519**

abcdefghijklmnopqrstuvwxyz 1234567890

ITC Newtext Light **520**

abcdefghijklmnopqrstuvwxyz1234567890

Virgin Roman **521**

abcdefghijklmnopqrstuvwxyz1234567890

ITC Avant Garde Gothic Extra Light **522**

abcdefghijklmnopqrstuvwxyz1234567890

Cable Light (Klingspor) **523**

abcdefghijklmnopqrstuvwxyz1234567890

Empire **524**

1234567890 *no lower case*

ITC Eras Light **525**

abcdefghijklmnopqrstuvwxyz1234567890

Futura Light **526**

abcdefghijklmnopqrstuvwxyz1234567890

Gill Sans Light **527**

abcdefghijklmnopqrstuvwxyz1234567890

Grotesque 126 **528**

abcdefghijklmnopqrstuvwxyz1234567890

**FAT FACE
& THIN FACE**
(UNMODIFIED & MODIFIED)

ITC Stymie Hairline
ITC Newtext Light
Virgin Roman
ITC Avant Garde Gothic
Extra Light
Cable Light (Klingspor)
Empire
ITC Eras Light
Futura Light
Gill Sans Light
Grotesque 126

529 Helvetica Thin

ABCDEFGHIJKLMNOPQRSTUVWXYZ&

530 Helvetica Ultra Light

ABCDEFGHIJKLMNOPQRSTUVWXYZ&

531 L & C Hairline

ABCDEFGHIJKLMNOPQRSTUVWXYZ &

532 Penny Bee

ABCDEFGHIJKLMNOPQRSTUVWXYZ &.

533 Stark Debonair

ABCDEFGHIJKLMNOPQRSTUVWXYZ &.

sans serif rounded shape

534 ITC Busorama Light

ABCDEFGHIJKLMNOPQRSTUVWXYZ&

535 Churchward 70 Hairline

ABCDEFGHIJKLMNOPQRSTUVWXYZ&

536 Harry Thin

ABCDEFGHIJKLMNOPQRSTUVWXYZ&

**FAT FACE
& THIN FACE**
(UNMODIFIED & MODIFIED)

F

Helvetica Thin
Helvetica Ultra Light
L & C Hairline
Penny Bee
Stark Debonair
ITC Busorama Light
Churchward 70
Hairline
Harry Thin

Helvetica Thin **529**

abcdefghijklmnopqrstuvwxyz1234567890

Helvetica Ultra Light **530**

abcdefghijklmnopqrstuvwxyz1234567890

L & C Hairline **531**

abcdefghijklmnopqrstuvwxyz1234567890

Penny Bee **532**

1234567890 *no lower case*

Stark Debonair **533**

abcdefghijklmnopqrstuvwxyz1234567890

ITC Busorama Light **534**

1234567890 *no lower case*

Churchward 70 Hairline **535**

abcdefghijklmnopqrstuvwxyz1234567890

Harry Thin **536**

abcdefghijklmnopqrstuvwxyz1234567890

**FAT FACE
& THIN FACE**
(UNMODIFIED & MODIFIED)

Helvetica Thin
Helvetica Ultra Light
L & C Hairline
Penny Bee
Stark Debonair
ITC Busorama Light
Churchward 70
Hairline
Harry Thin

5. ORNAMENTAL

Specimen nos		Basic characteristics	Secondary characteristics	
537-546	R	roman serif		e.g. **540** Fry's Ornamented
547	R	„	sloping	e.g. **547** Goudy Fancy
548-551	SL	slab serif		e.g. **548** Lettres Ornées
552-559	W	wedge serif		e.g. **554** Davida
560	SA	sans serif		e.g. **560** Abramesque
561-563	SCR	script		e.g. **561** Ballé Initials

NB. *Typefaces in each group are arranged in alphabetical order.*

ORNAMENTAL

roman serif

537 Flirt

ABCDEFGHIJKLMNOPQRSTUVWXYZ&

538 Floriated Capitals

ABCDEFGHIJKLMNOPQRSTUVWXYZ

539 Fontanesi

ABCDEFGHIJKLMNOPQRSTUVWXYZ&

540 Fry's Ornamented

ABCDEFGHIJKLMNOPQRSTUVWXYZ &

541 Gallia

ABCDEFGHIJKLMNOPQRSTUVWXYZ&

542 Lexington

ABCDEFGHIJKLMNOPQRSTUVWXYZ&

543 Modernistic

ABCDEFGHIJKLMNOPQRSTUVWXYZ&

544 Mole Foliate

ABCDEFGHIJKLMNOPQRSTUVWXYZ&

545 Nymphic

ABCDEFGHIJKLMNOPQRSTUVWXYZ&

546 Sapphire

ABCDEFGHIJKLMNOPQRSTUVWXYZ&

ORNAMENTAL

ORR

Flirt
Floriated Capitals
Fontanesi
Fry's Ornamented
Gallia
Lexington
Modernistic
Mole Foliate
Nymphic
Sapphire

Flirt **537**

abcdefghijklmnopqrstuvwxyz1234567890

Floriated Capitals **538**

no lower case or figures

Fontanesi **539**

1234567890 *no lower case*

Fry's Ornamented **540**

no lower case or figures

Gallia **541**

1234567890 *no lower case*

Lexington **542**

1234567890 *no lower case*

Modernistic **543**

1234567890 *no lower case*

Mole Foliate **544**

1234567890 *no lower case*

Nymphic **545**

abcdefghijklmnopqrstuvwxyz 1234567890

Sapphire **546**

1234567890 *no lower case*

ORNAMENTAL

roman serif
sloping

547 Goudy Fancy

ABCDEFGHIJKLMNOPQRSTUVWXYZ&

slab serif

548 Lettres Ornées

ABCDEFGHIJKLMNOPQRSTUVWXYZ

549 Quentin

ABCDEFGHIJKLMNOPQRSTUVWXYZ&

550 Romantiques No 5

ABCDEFGHIJKLMNOPQRSTUVWXYZ&

551 Trocadero

ABCDEFGHIJKLMNOPQRSTUVWXYZ&

wedge serif

552 Aesthetic Ornamented

ABCDEFGHIJKLMNOPQRSTUVWXYZ&

553 Arnold Böcklin

ABCDEFGHIJKLMNOPQRSTUVWXYZ&

554 Davida

ABCDEFGHIJKLMNOPQRSTUVWXYZ&

555 Karnac

ABCDEFGHIJKLMNOPQRSTUVWXYZ&

556 Kismet

ABCDEFGHIJKLMNOPQRSTUVWXYZ&

ORNAMENTAL

Goudy Fancy
Lettres Ornées
Quentin
Romantiques No 5
Trocadero
Aesthetic
Ornamented
Arnold Böcklin
Davida
Karnac
Kismet

Goudy Fancy **547**

abcdefghijklmnopqrstuvwxyz1234567890

Lettres Ornées **548**

no lower case or figures

Quentin **549**

1234567890 *no lower case*

Romantiques No 5 **550**

123456789 *no lower case*

Trocadero **551**

1234567890 *no lower case*

Aesthetic Ornamented **552**

ABCDEFGHIJKLMNOPQRSTUVWXYZ1234567890 *small capitals (no lower case)*

Arnold Böcklin **553**

abcdefghijklmnopqrstuvwxyz1234567890

Davida **554**

1234567890 *no lower case*

Karnac **555**

abcdefghijklmnopqrstuvwxyz1234567890

Kismet **556**

abcdefghijklmnopqrstuvwxyz1234567890

ORNAMENTAL

Goudy Fancy
Lettres Ornées
Quentin
Romantiques No 5
Trocadero
Aesthetic
Ornamented
Arnold Böcklin
Davida
Karnac
Kismet

225

557 Recherche

ABCDEFGHIJKLMNOPQRSTUVWXYZ&

558 Ringlet

ABCDEFGHIJKLMNOPQRSTUVWXYZ

559 Victorian

ABCDEFGHIJKLMNOPQRSTUVWXYZ&

sans serif

560 Abramesque

ABCDEFGHIJKLMNOPQRSTUVWXYZ&

script

561 Ballé Initials

ABCDEFGHIJKLMNOPQRSTUVWXYZ

562 Lilith

ABCDEFGHIJKLMNOPQRSTUVWXYZ&

563 Raffia Initials

ABCDEFGHIJKLMNOPQRSTUVWXYZ

ORNAMENTAL

Recherche
Ringlet
Victorian
Abramesque
Ballé Initials
Lilith
Raffia Initials

Recherche **557**

abcdefghijklmnopqrstuvwxyz1234567890

Ringlet **558**

abcdefghijklmnopqrstuvwxyz1234567890

Victorian **559**

abcdefghijklmnopqrstuvwxyz1234567890

Abramesque **560**

no lower case or figures

Ballé Initials **561**

no lower case or figures

Lilith **562**

abcdefghijklmno pqrstuvwxyz1234567890

Raffia Initials **563**

1234567890 *no lower case*

ORNAMENTAL

Recherche
Ringlet
Victorian
Abramesque
Ballé Initials
Lilith
Raffia Initials

6. MODIFIED SERIF

Specimen nos		Basic characteristics	Secondary characteristics	
564-574	R	roman serif		e.g. **566** Belwe
575-576	R	,,	stencil or stencil effect	e.g. **575** Stencil Bold
577-579	SL	slab serif		e.g. **579** Profil
580-601	W	wedge serif		e.g. **585** Charleston
602-603	W	,,	sloping backwards	e.g. **602** Alfereta

NB. Typefaces in each group are arranged in alphabetical order.

roman serif

564 Abbott Old Style

ABCDEFGHIJKLMNOPQRSTUVWXYZ&

565 Antikva Margaret

ABCDEFGHIJKLMNOPQRSTUVWXYZ&

566 Belwe

ABCDEFGHIJKLMNOPQRSTUVWXYZ&

567 Bernhard Antique

ABCDEFGHIJKLMNOPQRSTUVWXYZ&

568 Greco Bold

ABCDEFGHIJKLMNOPQRSTUVWXYZ&

569 Koch Antiqua

ABCDEFGHIJKLMNOPQRSTUVWXYZ&

570 Milton

ABCDEFGHIJKLMNOPQRSTUVWXYZ&

571 Packhard

ABCDEFGHIJKLMNOPQRSTUVWXYZ&

572 Richmond

ABCDEFGHIJKLMNOPQRSTUUVWXYZ&

573 Skyjald

ABCDEFGHIJKLMNOPQRSTUWXYZ&

MODIFIED SERIF

Abbott Old Style
Antikva Margaret
Belwe
Bernhard Antique
Greco Bold
Koch Antiqua
Milton
Packhard
Richmond
Skyjald

Abbott Old Style **564**

abcdefghijklmnopqrstuvwxyz1234567890

Antikva Margaret **565**

abcdefghijklmnopqrstuvwxyz1234567890

Belwe **566**

abcdefghijklmnopqrstuvwxyz1234567890

Bernhard Antique **567**

abcdefghijklmnopqrstuvwxyz1234567890

Greco Bold **568**

abcdefghijklmnopqrstuvwxyz1234567890

Koch Antiqua **569**

abcdefghijklmnopqrstuvwxyz1234567890

Milton **570**

abcdefghijklmnopqrstuvwxyz1234567890

Packhard **571**

abcdefghijklmnopqrstuvwxyz1234567890

Richmond **572**

abcdefghijklmnopqrstuvwxyz1234567890

Skyjald **573**

abcdefghijklmnopqrstuvwxyz1234567890

MODIFIED
SERIF

MS

Abbott Old Style
Antikva Margaret
Belwe
Bernhard Antique
Greco Bold
Koch Antiqua
Milton
Packhard
Richmond
Skyjald

roman serif

stencil or stencil effect

slab serif

wedge serif

574 University Roman

ABCDEFGHIJKLMNOPQRSTUVWXYZ&

575 Stencil Bold

ABCDEFGHIJKLMNOPQRSTUVWXYZ&

576 Teachest

ABCDEFGHIJKLMNOPQRSTUVWXYZ&

577 Antiqua Pointed

ABCDEFGHIJKLMNOPQRSTUVWXYZ

578 Nubian

ABCDEFGHIJKLMNOPQRSTUVWXYZ&

579 Profil

ABCDEFGHIJKLMNOPQRSTUVWXYZ&

580 Algerian

ABCDEFGHIJKLMNOPQRSTUVWXYZ&

581 Blackfriars Roman

ABCDEFGHIJKLMNOPQRSTUVWXYZ&

582 Brutus

ABCDEFGHIJKLMNOPQRSTUVWXYZ&

583 Bullfinch

ABCDEFGHIJKLMNOPQRSTUVWXYZ&

MODIFIED SERIF

University Roman
Stencil Bold
Teachest
Antiqua Pointed
Nubian
Profil
Algerian
Blackfriars Roman
Brutus
Bullfinch

University Roman **574**

abcdefghijklmnopqrstuvwxyz1234567890

Stencil Bold **575**

abcdefghijklmnopqrstuvwxyz1234567890

Teachest **576**

1234567890 *no lower case*

Antiqua Pointed **577**

1234567890 *no lower case*

Nubian **578**

abcdefghijklmnopqrstuvwxyz1234567890

Profil **579**

1234567890 *no lower case*

Algerian **580**

1234567890 *no lower case*

Blackfriars Roman **581**

abcdefghijklmnopqrstuvwxyz1234567890

Brutus **582**

abcdefghijklmnopqrstuvwxyz1234567890

Bullfinch **583**

abcdefghijklmnopqrstuvwxyz1234567890

MODIFIED SERIF

MS

University Roman
Stencil Bold
Teachest
Antiqua Pointed
Nubian
Profil
Algerian
Blackfriars Roman
Brutus
Bullfinch

584 Chantrey

ABCDEFGHIJKLMNOPQRSTUVWXYZ&

585 Charleston

ABCDEFGHIJKLMNOPQRSTUVWXYZ&

586 Columbus

ABCDEFGHIJKLMNOPQRSTUVWXYZ&

587 Croydon

ABCDEFGHIJKLMNOPQRSTUVWXYZ&

588 Desdemona

ABCDEFGHIJKLMNOPQRSTUVWXYZ&

589 Eckmann

ABCDEFGHIJKLMNOPQRSTUVWXYZ&

590 Edda

ABCDEFGHIJKLMNOPQRSTUVWXYZ&

591 Fantail

ABCDEFGHIJKLMNOPQRSTUVWXYZ&

592 Hermosa

ABCDEFGHIJKLMNOPQRSTUVWXYZ

593 Hobo

ABCDEFGHIJKLMNOPQRSTUVWXYZ&

MODIFIED
SERIF

Chantrey
Charleston
Columbus
Croydon
Desdemona
Eckmann
Edda
Fantail
Hermosa
Hobo

Chantrey **584**

abcdefghijklmnopqrstuvwxyz1234567890

Charleston **585**

abcdefghijklmnopqrstuvwxyz1234567890

Columbus **586**

abcdefghijklmnopqrstuvwxyz1234567890

Croydon **587**

1234567890 *no lower case*

Desdemona **588**

1234567890 *no lower case*

Eckmann **589**

abcdefghijklmnopqrstuvwxyz1234567890

Edda **590**

1234567890 *no lower case*

Fantail **591**

abcdefghijklmnopqrstuvwxyz1234567890

Hermosa **592**

abcdefghijklmnopqrstuvwxyz1234567890

Hobo **593**

abcdefghijklmnopqrstuvwxyz1234567890

MODIFIED SERIF

MS

Chantrey
Charleston
Columbus
Croydon
Desdemona
Eckmann
Edda
Fantail
Hermosa
Hobo

594 Hogarth

ABCDEFGHIJKLMNOPQRSTUVWXYZ&

595 Lafayette

ABCDEFGHIJKLMNOPQRSTUVWXYZ&

596 Mikado Black

ABCDEFGHIJKLMNOPQRSTUVWXYZ&

597 Neptune

ABCDEFGHIJKLMNOPQRSTUVWXYZ&

598 Pretorian

ABCDEFGHIJKLMNOPQRSTUVWXYZ&

599 Tango

ABCDEFGHIJKLMNOPQRSTUVWXYZ&

600 Thalia

ABCDEFGHIJKLMNOPQRSTUVWXYZ&

601 Tip Top

ABCDEFGHIJKLMNOPQRSTUVWXYZ&

602 Alfereta

ABCDEFGHIJKLMNOPQRSTUVWXYZ&

603 Blanchard

ABCDEFGHIJKLMNOPQRSTUVWXYZ&

MODIFIED
SERIF

Hogarth
Lafayette
Mikado Black
Neptune
Pretorian
Tango
Thalia
Tip Top
Alfereta
Blanchard

wedge serif
sloping
backwards

Hogarth **594**

abcdefghijklmnopqrstuvwxyz1234567890

Lafayette **595**

abcdefghijklmnopqrstuvwxyz1234567890

Mikado Black **596**

abcdefghijklmnopqrstuvwxyz1234567890

Neptune **597**

abcdefghijklmnopqrstuvwxyz1234567890

Pretorian **598**

abcdefghijklmnopqrstuvwxyz1234567890

Tango **599**

abcdefghijklmnopqrstuvwxyz1234567890

Thalia **600**

abcdefghijklmnopqrstuvwxyz1234567890

Tip Top **601**

abcdefghijklmnopqrstuvwxyz1234567890

Alfereta **602**

abcdefghijklmnopqrstuvwxyz1234567890

Blanchard **603**

abcdefghijklmnopqrstuvwxyz1234567890

MODIFIED
SERIF

MS

Hogarth
Lafayette
Mikado Black
Neptune
Pretorian
Tango
Thalia
Tip Top
Alfereta
Blanchard

7. MODIFIED SANS SERIF

Specimen nos		Basic characteristics	
604-609	TH	thick and thin stress (vertical)	e.g. **608** Peignot
610	TH	thick and thin stress (horizontal)	e.g. **610** Sintex I
611-612	B	heavy bow-shaped	e.g. **611** Becket
613-614	SQ	square-shaped	e.g. **613** Tamil
615	SL	sloping	e.g. **615** Condensa
616-623	RO	rounded shape	e.g. **619** Frankfurter Medium
624	RO	rounded shape outline	e.g. **624** Helvetica Rounded Outline
625-629	EL	electronic	e.g. **626** Countdown
630-633	CU	cut	e.g. **632** Neuland
634-642	ST	stencil or stencil effect	e.g. **636** Futura Black

NB. Typefaces in each group are arranged in alphabetical order.

continued on next page

MODIFIED SANS SERIF

MSS

continued from previous page

643-654	INL	*inline or striped*	e.g. **646** Neon
655-662	SH	*shaded or 3D*	e.g. **659** Superstar Shadow
663-665	SH	*shaded or 3D inline or patterned*	e.g. **663** Baby Arbuckle

NB. *Typefaces in each group are arranged in alphabetical order.*

MODIFIED
SANS SERIF

MSS

*thick and
thin stress
(vertical)*

604 Britannic

ABCDEFGHIJKLMNOPQRSTUVWXYZ&

605 Florentine

ABCDEFGHIJKLMNOPQRSTUVWXYZ&

606 Inga

ABCDEFGHIJKLMNOPQRSTUVWXYZ&

607 Parisian

ABCDEFGHIJKLMNOPQRSTUVWXYZ&

608 Peignot

ABCDEFGHIJKLMNOPQRSTUVWXYZ&

609 Radiant

ABCDEFGHIJKLMNOPQRSTUVWXYZ&

*thick and
thin stress
(horizontal)*

610 Sintex I

ABCDEFGHIJKLMNOPQRSTUVWXYZ&

*heavy
bow-shaped*

611 Becket

ABCDEFGHIJKLMNOPQRSTUVWXYZ&

612 Revue

ABCDEFGHIIJKLMNOPQRSTUVWXYZ&

*square-
shaped*

613 Tamil

ABCDEFGHIJKLMNOPQRSTUVWXYZ&

Britannic
Florentine
Inga
Parisian
Peignot
Radiant
Sintex I
Becket
Revue
Tamil

**MODIFIED
SANS SERIF**

Britannic **604**

abcdefghijklmnopqrstuvwxyz1234567890

Florentine **605**

abcdefghijklmnopqrstuvwxyz1234567890

Inga **606**

abcdefghijklmnopqrstuvwxyz1234567890

Parisian **607**

abcdefghijklmnopqrstuvwxyz1234567890

Peignot **608**

AbcdEfGHijklMNOPQRstUVWXYZ1234567890

Radiant **609**

abcdefghijklmnopqrstuvwxyz1234567890

Sintex I **610**

abcdefghijklmnopqrstuvwxyz1234567890

Becket **611**

abcdefghijklmnopqrstuvwxyz1234567890

Revue **612**

abcdefghijklmnopqrstuvwxyz1234567890

Tamil **613**

abcdefghijklmnopqrstuvwxyz1234567890

Britannic
Florentine
Inga
Parisian
Peignot
Radiant
Sintex I
Becket
Revue
Tamil

MODIFIED
SANS SERIF

MSS

614 Topic

ABCDEFGHIJKLMNOPQRSTUVWXYZ&

sloping

615 Condensa

ABCDEFGHIJKLMNOPQRSTUVWXYZ&

rounded shape

616 Capone

ABCDEFGHIJKLMNOPQRSTUVWXYZ&

617 Dempsey Medium

ABCDEFGHIJKLMNOPQRSTUVWXYZ&

618 Formula I

ABCDEFGHIJKLMNOPQRSTUVWXYZ&

619 Frankfurter Medium

ABCDEFGHIJKLMNOPQRSTUVWXYZ&

620 Helvetica Rounded

ABCDEFGHIJKLMNOPQRSTUVWXYZ&

621 Horatio Medium

ABCDEFGHIJKLMNOPQRSTUVWXYZ&

622 Octopuss

ABCDEFGHIJKLMNOPQRSTUVWXYZ&

623 Pump

ABCDEFGHIJKLMNOPQRSTUVWXYZ&

Topic
Condensa
Capone
Dempsey Medium
Formula I
Frankfurter Medium
Helvetica Rounded
Horatio Medium
Octopuss
Pump

**MODIFIED
SANS SERIF**

MSS

Topic **614**

abcdefghijklmnopqrstuvwxyz1234567890

Condensa **615**

abcdefghijklmnopqrstuvwxyz1234567890

Capone **616**

abcdefghijklmnopqrstuvwxyz1234567890

Dempsey Medium **617**

abcdefghijklmnopqrstuvwxyz1234567890

Formula I **618**

abcdefghijklmnopqrstuvwxyz1234567890

Frankfurter Medium **619**

abcdefghijklmnopqrstuvwxyz1234567890

Helvetica Rounded **620**

abcdefghijklmnopqrstuvwxyz1234567890

Horatio Medium **621**

abcdefghijklmnopqrstuvwxyz1234567890

Octopuss **622**

abcdefghijklmnopqrstuvwxyz1234567890

Pump **623**

abcdefghijklmnopqrstuvwxyz1234567890

Topic
Condensa
Capone
Dempsey Medium
Formula I
Frankfurter Medium
Helvetica Rounded
Horatio Medium
Octopuss
Pump

MODIFIED
SANS SERIF

*rounded
shape
outline*

624 Helvetica Rounded Outline

ABCDEFGHIJKLMNOPQRSTUVWXYZ&

electronic

625 Amelia

ABCDEFGHIJKLMNOPQRSTUVWXYZ&

626 Countdown

ABCDEFGHIJKLMNOPQRSTUVWXYZ&

627 Data 70

ABCDEFGHIJKLMNOPQRSTUVWXYZ&

628 Digital

ABCDEFGHIJKLMNOPQRSTUVWXYZ

629 Russell Square

ABCDEFGHIJKLMNOPQRSTUVWXYZ&

cut

630 Ad Lib

ABCDEFGHIJKLMNOPQRSTUVWXYZ&

631 Kino

ABCDEFGHIJKLMNOPQRSTUVWXYZ

632 Neuland

ABCDEFGHIJKLMNOPQRSTUVWXYZ&

633 Othello

ABCDEFGHIJKLMNOPQRSTUVWXYZ&

Helvetica Rounded
Outline
Amelia
Countdown
Data 70
Digital
Russell Square
Ad Lib
Kino
Neuland
Othello

MODIFIED
SANS SERIF

Helvetica Rounded Outline **624**

abcdefghijklmnopqrstuvwxyz1234567890

Amelia **625**

abcdefghijklmnopqrstuvwxyz1234567890

Countdown **626**

abcdefghijklmnopqrstuvwxyz1234567890

Data 70 **627**

abcdefghijklmnopqrstuvwxyz1234567890

Digital **628**

1234567890 *no lower case*

Russell Square **629**

abcdefghijklmnopqrstuvwxyz1234567890

Ad Lib **630**

abcdefghijklmnopqrstuvwxyz1234567890

Kino **631**

abcdefghijklmnopqrstuvwxyz1234567890

Neuland **632**

1234567890 *no lower case*

Othello **633**

1234567890 *no lower case*

Helvetica Rounded
Outline
Amelia
Countdown
Data 70
Digital
Russell Square
Ad Lib
Kino
Neuland
Othello

MODIFIED
SANS SERIF

MSS

stencil or stencil effect

634 Braggadocio

ABCDEFGHIJKLMNOPQRSTUVWXYZ&

635 Folio Stencil

ABCDEFGHIJKLMNOPQRSTUVWXYZ&

636 Futura Black

ABCDEFGHIJKLMNOPQRSTUVWXYZ&

637 Glaser Stencil Bold

ABCDEFGHIJKLMNOPQRSTUVWXYZ&

638 Glyphic

ABCDEFGHIJKLMNOPQRSTUVWXYZ

639 Motter Tektura

ABCDEFGHIJKLMNOPQRSTUVWXYZ&

640 Stop

ABCDEFGHIJKLMNOPQRSTUVWXYZ&

641 Tabasco

ABCDEFGHIJKLMNOPQRSTUVWXYZ&

642 Traffic

no capital letters

inline or striped

643 Fatima

ABCDEFGHIJKLMNOPQRSTUVWXYZ&

Braggadocio
Folio Stencil
Futura Black
Glaser Stencil Bold
Glyphic
Motter Tektura
Stop
Tabasco
Traffic
Fatima

**MODIFIED
SANS SERIF**

MSS

248

Braggadocio **634**

abcdefghijklmnopqrstuvwxyz1234567890

Folio Stencil **635**

1234567890 *no lower case*

Futura Black **636**

abcdefghijklmnopqrstuvwxyz1234567890

Glaser Stencil Bold **637**

123-4567890 *no lower case*

Glyphic **638**

1234567890 *no lower case*

Motter Tektura **639**

abcdefghijklmnopqrstuvwxyz1234567890

Stop **640**

1234567890 *no lower case*

Tabasco **641**

abcdefghijklmnopqrstuvwxyz1234567890

Traffic **642**

abcdefghijklmnopqrstuvwxyz1234567890

Fatima **643**

1234567890 *no lower case*

Braggadocio
Folio Stencil
Futura Black
Glaser Stencil Bold
Glyphic
Motter Tektura
Stop
Tabasco
Traffic
Fatima

MODIFIED
SANS SERIF

644 French Flash

ABCDEFGHIJKLMNOPQRSTUVWXYZ

645 Michel

ABCDEFGHIJKLMNOPQRSTUVWXYZ&

646 Neon

ABCDEFGHIJKLMNOPQRSTUVWXYZ&

647 Optex

ABCDEFGHIJKLMNOPQRSTUVWXYZ&

648 Oxford

no capital letters

649 Piccadilly

ABCDEFGHIJKLMNOPQRSTUVWXYZ&

650 Pluto

ABCDEFGHIJKLMNOPQRSTUVWXYZ&

651 Prisma

ABCDEFGHIJKLMNOPQRSTUVWXYZ&

652 Pump Triline

ABCDEFGHIJKLMNOPQRSTUVWXYZ&

653 ITC Uptight Neon

ABCDEFGHIJKLMNOPQRSTUVWXYZ&

French Flash
Michel
Neon
Optex
Oxford
Piccadilly
Pluto
Prisma
Pump Triline
ITC Uptight Neon

**MODIFIED
SANS SERIF**

MSS

French Flash **644**

1234567890 *no lower case*

Michel **645**

abcdefghijklmnopqrstuvwxyz1234567890

Neon **646**

1234567890 *no lower case*

Optex **647**

abcdefghijklmnopqrstuvwxyz1234567890

Oxford **648**

abcdefghijklmnopqrstuvwxyz1234567890

Piccadilly **649**

1234567890 *no lower case*

Pluto **650**

abcdefghijklmnopqrstuvwxyz1234567890

Prisma **651**

1234567890 *no lower case*

Pump Triline **652**

abcdefghijklmnopqrstuvwxyz1234567890

ITC Uptight Neon **653**

abcdefghijklmnopqrstuvwxyz1234567890

French Flash
Michel
Neon
Optex
Oxford
Piccadilly
Pluto
Prisma
Pump Triline
ITC Uptight Neon

MODIFIED SANS SERIF

MSS

251

654 Zeppelin

ABCDEFGHIJKLMNOPQRSTUVWXYZ&

shaded or 3D

655 Bullion Shadow

ABCDEFGHIJKLMNOPQRSTUVWXYZ&

656 Old Bowery

ABCDEFGHIJKLMNOPQRSTUVWXYZ&

657 Pioneer Shadow

ABCDEFGHIJKLMNOPQRSTUVWXYZ &

658 Premier Shaded

ABCDEFGHIJKLMNOPQRSTUVWXYZ&

659 Superstar Shadow

ABCDEFGHIJKLMNOPQRSTUVWXYZ &

660 Tintoretto

ABCDEFGHIJKLMNOPQRSTUVWXYZ &

661 Umbra

ABCDEFGHIJKLMNOPQRSTUVWXYZ &

662 Uncle Bill

ABCDEFGHIJKLMNOPQRSTUVWXYZ&

shaded or 3D
inline or
patterned

663 Baby Arbuckle

ABCDEFGIHJKLMNOPQRSTUVXWYZ&

Zeppelin
Bullion Shadow
Old Bowery
Pioneer Shadow
Premier Shaded
Superstar Shadow
Tintoretto
Umbra
Uncle Bill
Baby Arbuckle

MODIFIED
SANS SERIF

MSS

Zeppelin **654**

abcdefghijklmnopqrstuvwxyz1234567890

Bullion Shadow **655**

1234567890 *no lower case*

Old Bowery **656**

no lower case or figures

Pioneer Shadow **657**

1234567890 *no lower case*

Premier Shaded **658**

1234567890 *no lower case*

Superstar Shadow **659**

1234567890 *no lower case*

Tintoretto **660**

abcdefghijklmnopqrstuvwxyz 1234567890

Umbra **661**

1234567890 *no lower case*

Uncle Bill **662**

1234567890 *no lower case*

Baby Arbuckle **663**

1234567890 *no lower case*

**MODIFIED
SANS SERIF**

MSS

664 Jim Crow

ABCDEFGHIJKLMNOPQRSTUWVXYZ

665 Quicksilver

ABCDEFGHIJKLMNOPQRSTUVWXYZ &

Jim Crow
Quicksilver

MODIFIED
SANS SERIF

MSS

Jim Crow **664**

1234567890 *no lower case*

Quicksilver **665**

1234567890 *no lower case*

Jim Crow
Quicksilver

**MODIFIED
SANS SERIF**

8. MODIFIED OUTRAGEOUS

Specimen nos		Basic characteristics	
666-671	**HE**	*heavy / distorted*	e.g. **668** Litzenburg
672-678	**INL**	*inline or striped*	e.g. **672** ITC Aki Lines
679	**BR**	*broken-surfaced and distorted*	e.g. **679** Shatter
680-684	**DOT**	*dot-formed*	e.g. **682** Pinball
685-694	**SH**	*shaded or 3D*	e.g. **688** Calypso
695-698	**B**	*with backgrounds*	e.g. **697** Process
699-700	**Z**	*pictorial*	e.g. **700** Zip

NB. *Typefaces in each group are arranged in alphabetical order.*

MODIFIED
OUTRAGEOUS

heavy/ distorted

666 Bottleneck

ABCDEFGHIJKLMNOPQRSTUVWXYZ &

667 Florist

ABCDEFGHIJKLMNOPQRSTUVWXYZ&

668 Litzenburg

ABCDEFGHIJKLMNOPQRSTUVWXYZ&

669 Pierrot

ABCDEFGHIJKLMNOPQRSTUVWXYZ&

670 Starvation

ABCDEFGHIJKLMNOPQRSTUVWXYZ&

671 Talbot

ABCDEFGHIJKLMNOPQRSTUVWXYZB

inline or striped

672 ITC Aki Lines

ABCDEFGHIJKLMNOPQRSTUVWXYZ&

673 Groove

674 Horseman Sidesaddle

ABCDEFGHIJKLMNOPQRSTUVWXYZ&

675 Matra

ABCDEFGHIJKLMNOPQRSTUVWXYZ

Bottleneck
Florist
Litzenburg
Pierrot
Starvation
Talbot
ITC Aki Lines
Groove
Horseman Sidesaddle
Matra

MODIFIED OUTRAGEOUS

Bottleneck **666**

abcdefghijklmnopqrstuvwxyz 1234567890

Florist **667**

1234567890 *no lower case*

Litzenburg **668**

1234567890 *no lower case*

Pierrot **669**

abcdefghijklmnopqrstuvwxyz1234567890

Starvation **670**

1234567890 *no lower case*

Talbot **671**

1234567890 *no lower case*

ITC Aki Lines **672**

1234567890 *no lower case*

Groove **673**

1234567890 *no lower case*

Horseman Sidesaddle **674**

1234567890 *no lower case*

Matra **675**

1234567890 *no lower case*

MODIFIED OUTRAGEOUS

676 Old Glory

ABCDEFGHIJKLMNOPQRSTUVWXYZ&

677 Sinaloa

ABCDEFGHIJKLMNOPQRSTUVWXYZ &

678 Stripes

ABCDEFGHIJKLMNOPQRSTUVWXYZ&

broken surfaced and distorted

679 Shatter

ABCDEFGHIJKLMNOPQRSTUVWXYZ &

dot-formed

680 Astra

ABCDEFGHIJKLMNOPQRSTUVWXYZ &

681 Chequered

ABCDEFGHIJKLMNOPQRSTUVWXYZ&

682 Pinball

ABCDEFGHIJKLMNOPQRSTUVWXYZ&

683 Spangle

ABCDEFGHIJKLMNOPQRSTUVWXYZ

684 Spotty Face

ABCDEFGHIJKLMNOPQRSTUVWXYZ&

shaded or 3D

685 Block up

ABCDEFGHIJKLMNOPQRSTUVWXYZ &

Old Glory
Sinaloa
Stripes
Shatter
Astra
Chequered
Pinball
Spangle
Spotty Face
Block up

MODIFIED OUTRAGEOUS

Old Glory **676**

1234567890 *no lower case*

Sinaloa **677**

1234567890 *no lower case*

Stripes **678**

1234567890 *no lower case*

Shatter **679**

abcdefghijklmnopqrstuvwxyz 1234567890

Astra **680**

1234567890 *no lower case*

Chequered **681**

1234567890 *no lower case*

Pinball **682**

abcdefghijklmnopqrstuvwxyz1234567090

Spangle **683**

1234567890 *no lower case*

Spotty Face **684**

1234567890 *no lower case*

Block up **685**

1234567890 *no lower case*

Old Glory
Sinaloa
Stripes
Shatter
Astra
Chequered
Pinball
Spangle
Spotty Face
Block up

MODIFIED OUTRAGEOUS

686 Bombere

ABCDEFGHIJKLMNOPQRSTUVWXYZ&

687 Buster

ABCDEFGHIJKLMNOPQRSTUVWXYZ&

688 Calypso

ABCDEFGHIJKLMNOPQRSTUVWXYZ

689 Italiennes Ombrees

ABCDEFGHIJKLMNOPQRSTUVWXYZ&

690 Perspective Italic

ABCDEFGHIJKLMNOPQRSTUVWXYZ

691 Speed Caps

ABCDEFGHIJKLMNOPQRSTUVWXYZ&

692 Stack

ABCDEFGHIJKLMNOPQRSTUVWXYZ&

693 Sunshine

no capitals

694 Talbot's Rocky Mountain

ABCDEFGHIJKLMNOPQRSTUVWXYZ&

with backgrounds

695 Good Vibrations

ABCDEFGHIJKLMNOPQRSTUVWXYZ&

Bombere
Buster
Calypso
Italiennes Ombrees
Perspective Italic
Speed Caps
Stack
Sunshine
Talbot's
Rocky Mountain
Good Vibrations

MODIFIED OUTRAGEOUS

Bombere **686**

no lower case

Buster **687**

1234567890 *no lower case*

Calypso **688**

no lower case or figures

Italiennes Ombrees **689**

1234567890 *no lower case*

Perspective Italic **690**

no lower case or figures

Speed Caps **691**

1234567890 *no lower case*

Stack **692**

1234567890 *no lower case*

Sunshine **693**

abcdefghijklmnopqrstuvwxyz1234567890

Talbot's Rocky Mountain **694**

1234567890 *no lower case*

Good Vibrations **695**

1234567890 *no lower case*

Bombere
Buster
Calypso
Italiennes Ombrees
Perspective Italic
Speed Caps
Stack
Sunshine
Talbot's
Rocky Mountain
Good Vibrations

MODIFIED
OUTRAGEOUS

696 Phase Two

697 Process

ABCDEFGHIJKLMNOPQRSTUVWXYZ&

698 Tonal

ABCDEFGHIJKLMNOPQRSTUVWXYZ&

pictorial

699 Via Face Don Black

ABCDZ7GHIJKLMNOPQRSTUVWXYZ

700 Zip

ABCDEFGHIJKLMNOPQRSTUVWXYZ&

Phase Two
Process
Tonal
Via Face Don Black
Zip

MODIFIED OUTRAGEOUS

Phase Two **696**

Process **697**

1234567890 *no lower case*

Tonal **698**

1234567890 *no lower case*

Via Face Don Black **699**

no lower case or figures

Zip **700**

1234567890 *no lower case*

Phase Two
Process
Tonal
Via Face Don Black
Zip

MODIFIED
OUTRAGEOUS

'TYPEFINDER' CLASSIFICATION SYSTEM

TEXT TYPEFACE CATEGORIES

1. Sloping e-Bar (Venetian Serif). *Nos 1-34*

Includes all roman, slab and wedge serif faces with a sloping bar on the lower case e, a traditional feature of 'Venetian' typefaces. The mixture of serif-style typefaces in this category means that other characteristics are mixed – for example, typefaces may have either vertical or angled stress and oblique or straight serifs.

e.g. Kennerley, Centaur, ITC Souvenir.

2. Angled Stress/Oblique Serifs (Old Style Serif). *Nos 35-53*

Includes 'Old Style' or 'Old Face' typefaces providing they have the above characteristics and do not possess a sloping bar on the lower case e.

e.g. Bembo, Plantin, Times New Roman.

3. Vertical Stress/Oblique Serifs (Transitional Serif). *Nos 54-110*

Includes 'Transitional' typefaces providing they have these characteristics and do not have a sloping bar on the lower case e. 'Transitional' typefaces with horizontal serifs or abrupt contrast will be found in either Categories 4 or 5.

e.g. Caslon Old Face, Baskerville 169 (Monotype), Garamond (Stempel).

4. Vertical Stress/Straight Serifs (New Transitional Serif). *Nos 111-150*

Contains 'Transitional' typefaces which have straight (horizontal) serifs or nearly so, as well as 'Twentieth Century Roman' typefaces with the same characteristics.

e.g. Joanna, Century Schoolbook, Cheltenham

5. Abrupt Contrast/Straight Serifs (Modern Serif). *Nos 151-187*

Contains 'Modern', 'Transitional' and 'Twentieth Century Romans' with good contrast and straight (horizontal) serifs.

e.g. Bauer Bodoni, Caledonia, Scotch Roman.

6. Slab Serif. *Nos 188-217*

Typefaces of a generally heavy appearance, either with square or bracketed slab serifs. Also includes rounded slab typefaces (typewriter designs).

e.g. Rockwell, Clarendon, ITC American Typewriter

7. Wedge Serif (Hybrid Serif). *Nos 218-240*

Includes some 'Glyphic' typefaces used for continuous text setting plus typefaces with wedge-ended, or wedge-shaped serifs. The category also includes 'hybrid' typefaces which are neither clearly serif nor sans serif in origin.

e.g. Albertus, Meridien, Copperplate Gothic

BRITISH STANDARDS CLASSIFICATION OF TYPEFACES (BS 2961: 1967)

Category		Description	Examples
No.	**Name**		
I	Humanist	Typefaces in which the cross stroke of the lower case e is oblique; the axis of the curves is inclined to the left; there is no great contrast between thin and thick strokes; the serifs are bracketed; the serifs of the ascenders in the lower case are oblique. NOTE. This was formerly known as 'Venetian', having been derived from the 15th century minuscule written with a varying stroke thickness by means of an obliquely-held broad pen.	Verona, Centaur, Kennerley
II	Garalde	Typefaces in which the axis of the curves is inclined to the left; there is generally a greater contrast in the relative thickness of the strokes than in Humanist designs; the serifs are bracketed; the bar of the lower case e is horizontal; the serifs of the ascenders in the lower case are oblique. NOTE. These are types in the Aldine and Garamond tradition and were formerly called 'Old Face' and 'Old Style'.	Bembo, Garamond, Caslon, Vendôme
III	Transitional	Typefaces in which the axis of the curves is vertical or inclined slightly to the left; the serifs are bracketed, and those of the ascenders in the lower case are oblique. NOTE. This typeface is influenced by the letter-forms of the copperplate engraver. It may be regarded as a transition from Garalde to Didone, and incorporates some characteristics of each.	Fournier, Baskerville, Bell, Caledonia, Columbia
IV	Didone	Typefaces having an abrupt contrast between thin and thick strokes; the axis of the curves is vertical; the serifs of the ascenders of the lower case are horizontal; there are often no brackets to the serifs. NOTE. These are typefaces as developed by Didot and Bodoni. Formerly called 'Modern'.	Bodoni, Corvinus, Modern Extended
V	Slab-serif	Typefaces with heavy, square-ended serifs, with or without brackets.	Rockwell, Clarendon, Playbill

Extracts from BS 2961:1967. Reproduced by permission of the British Standards Institutions, 2 Park Street, London W1A 2BS from whom complete copies of the Standard can be obtained.

BRITISH STANDARDS CLASSIFICATION OF TYPEFACES (BS 2961: 1967)

Category No.	Category Name	Description	Examples
VI	Lineale	Typefaces without serifs. NOTE. Formerly called 'Sans-serif'.	
	a Grotesque	Lineale typefaces with 19th century origins. There is some contrast in thickness of strokes. They have squareness of curve, and curling close-set jaws. The R usually has a curled leg and the G is spurred. The ends of the curved strokes are usually horizontal.	SB Grot. No. 6, Cond. Sans No. 7, Monotype Headline Bold
	b Neo-grotesque	Lineale typefaces derived from the grotesque. They have less stroke contrast and are more regular in design. The jaws are more open than in the true grotesque and the g is often open-tailed. The ends of the curved strokes are usually oblique.	Edel/Wotan, Univers, Helvetica
	c Geometric	Lineale typefaces constructed on simple geometric shapes, circle or rectangle. Usually monoline, and often with single-storey a.	Futura, Erbar, Eurostyle
	d Humanist	Lineale typefaces based on the proportions of inscriptional Roman capitals and Humanist or Garalde lower-case, rather than on early grotesques. They have some stroke contrast, with two-storey a and g.	Optima, Gill Sans, Pascal
VII	Glyphic	Typefaces which are chiselled rather than calligraphic in form.	Latin, Albertus, Augustea
VIII	Script	Typefaces that imitate cursive writing.	Palace Script, Legend, Mistral
IX	Graphic	Typefaces whose characters suggest that they have been drawn rather than written.	Libra, Cartoon, Old English (Monotype)

'TYPEFINDER' CLASSIFICATION SYSTEM

TEXT TYPEFACE CATEGORIES *continued*

8. Sans Serif. *Nos 245-304*

Includes 'Lineale' designs used for continuous text setting arranged according to the width of the capital G and whether or not it has a spur. There are additional groups for square, sloping, rounded and electronic designs.

e.g. Futura, Gill Sans, Unvers.

DECORATIVE (NON-CONTINUOUS TEXT) TYPEFACE CATEGORIES

3. Unmodified (Formal Text Shape). *Nos 382-428*

'Glyphic' typefaces not usually used for continuous text setting will be found here. The category contains serif or sans serif typefaces of a traditional letter shape normally used for titling or headings but not for continuous text setting.

e.g. Engravers Roman, Castellar, Latin Antique No. 9

1. Flowing Scripts *Nos 305-322* and
2. Non-Flowing Scripts *Nos 323-381*

'Script' and 'Graphic' typefaces are to be found in one of these two categories according to whether their letters are joined when typeset and therefore appear 'flowing' like handwriting. The Non-Flowing category includes blackletter and uncial typefaces as well as roman italic typefaces based on pen scripts.

e.g. **1.** Palace Script, Kaufmann, Mistral.
e.g. **2.** Bernhard Tango, Old English Text, Libra.

4. Fat & Thin Face (Modified & Unmodified). *Nos. 429-536*

Includes serif or sans serif typefaces of the extremes in weight – very bold or very light.

e.g. Falstaff, Cooper Black, Harry Thin.

5. Ornamental. *Nos 537-563*

Serif, sans serif or script typefaces of a very elaborately patterned or 'floriated' design.

e.g. Fry's Ornamented, Lettres Ornées, Ballé Initials.

6. Modified Serif. *Nos 564-603*

Serif typefaces of a 'non-formal/traditional' shape.

e.g. Belwe, Profil, Charleston.

7. Modified Sans Serif. *Nos 604-665*

Sans serif typefaces of a 'non-formal/traditional' shape.

e.g. Peignot, Frankfurter Medium, Countdown.

8. Modified Outrageous. *Nos 666-700*

Serif and sans serif typefaces of a highly unusual or 'way out' nature.

e.g. Shatter, Pinball, Calypso.

Bibliography

BIGGS, *An approach to type*. Blandford Press, 1949.

BRITISH STANDARDS INSTITUTION, *Typeface nomenclature and classification*. (BS 2961), 1967.

DOWDING, *An introduction to the history of printing types*. Wace & Company Limited, 1961.

GATES, *Type*. Watson-Guptill Publications, 1973.

HALEY, *A guide to in-house typography & design*. Robert Hale Limited, 1981.

JASPERT, BERRY & JOHNSON, *Encyclopaedia of typefaces*. Blandford Press, 1962 and 1970 editions.

KARCH, *How to recognise typefaces*. McKnight & McKnight, 1959.

LIEBERMAN, *Types of typefaces and how to recognise them*. Sterling Publishing Co. Inc., 1967.

McCLEAN, *Typography*. Thames & Hudson, 1980.

MERRIMAN, *Type comparison book*. The Advertising Typographers Association of America, Inc., 1965.

MONOTYPE CORPORATION, *Students type study leaflet*.

ROSEN, Type and typography. Van Nostrand Reinhold, 1976.

Catalogues & typeface information of the following companies were also referred to:

Alphatype Systems Limited

American Type Foundry

AM International Inc.,

Amsterdam Foundry

Association Typographique Internationale (A. Typ.I)

H. Berthold AG

Bobst SA (Bobstgraphic Division)

Compugraphic Corporation

Harris Communications

International Typeface Corporation (ITC)

ITEK Corporation

Linotype-Paul Limited

Letraset UK Limited

Mecanorma

Mergenthaler, Linotype, Stempel, Haas

The Monotype Corporation

Mouldtype Foundry Limited

Stephenson, Blake & Company Limited

Tetterode-Nederland ('*Lettertypen*')

Yendall & Company Limited (Riscatype)

INDEX OF TYPEFACES

'Bastard' names listed are cross-referenced to the appropriate typeface.

NB. *Bold figures refer to specimen numbers.*

NB. *Bold figures refer to specimen numbers.*